A Doctor on the Western Front

The Diary of Henry Owens 1914–1918

Edited by John Hutton

Pen & Sword
MILITARY

First published in Great Britain in 2013 by
Pen & Sword Military
an imprint of
Pen & Sword Books Ltd
47 Church Street
Barnsley
South Yorkshire
S70 2AS

ISBN: 978-1-78159-306-6

A CIP catalogue record for this book is available from the British Library.

Typeset in 11pt Ehrhardt by
Mac Style, Beverley, E. Yorkshire

Printed and bound in the UK by CPI Group (UK) Ltd, Croydon, CR0 4YY

Pen & Sword Books Ltd incorporates the Imprints of Pen & Sword Aviation,
Pen & Sword Family History, Pen & Sword Maritime, Pen & Sword Military, Pen
& Sword Discovery, Wharncliffe Local History, Wharncliffe True Crime,
Wharncliffe Transport, Pen & Sword Select, Pen & Sword Military Classics, Leo
Cooper, The Praetorian Press, Remember When, Seaforth Publishing
and Frontline Publishing.

For a complete list of Pen & Sword titles please contact
PEN & SWORD BOOKS LIMITED
47 Church Street, Barnsley, South Yorkshire, S70 2AS, England
E-mail: enquiries@pen-and-sword.co.uk
Website: www.pen-and-sword.co.uk

Contents

Illustrations

The
WESTERN
FRONT
1915-18
✠
Allied line, March 1915 ▬▬▬▬
"   "   April 1917 ▪▪▪▪▪▪▪▪
German line, July 1918 ▪—▪—▪—▪
Allied line, Nov. 11ᵗʰ 1918 ▬ ▬ ▬

Ostend
Nieuport
Dunkirk
Dixmude
Bruges
ANTWERP
Ghent
BRUSSELS
Iser
Ypres
Lys
Messines
Armentières
LILLE
Scheldt
N. Chapelle
La Bassée
Mons
Loos
Lens
Scarpe
Valenciennes
Vimy
Douai
Arras
Cambrai
Sambre
NOV. 11. 1918
Albert
SOMME BATTLE 1916
Bapaume
AMIENS
Somme
Péronne
1917
St Quentin
Roye
La Fère
Serre
Montdidier
1915
Oise
Laon
Sedan
1918
1917
Chemin d'Dames
Aisne
Longwy
Compiègne
1915
Soissons
Suippe
Ourcq
Vesle
REIMS
CHAMPAGNE
ARGONNE
Meuse
VERDUN
Chat.-Thierry
JULY, 1918
Marne
Chalons
St Mihiel
PARIS

BELGIUM
ARDENNES

0   25   50 Miles

J.F.H.

Introduction

A couple of years ago, while I was completing some research in the reading room at the Imperial War Museum in London, I stumbled across a remarkable document. It was the diary of a young British officer who served in the Great War with the Royal Army Medical Corps. This was not just a collection of fragmentary notes or observations. The diary spanned the entire duration of the conflict. It had been meticulously prepared. When I began to read it I was immediately enthralled. It provided a vivid and complete narrative, seen from the perspective of an army doctor, on what it was like to live and fight in the trenches of the western front. Something else was also immediately apparent – not only was the author a talented writer, he also had a keen eye as a painter. The diary was full of beautiful drawings and sketches.

This beguiling work was the product of Henry Barton Owens. Henry – Harry to his friends and family – was born into the comfortable security of middle-class English society in 1889. His father Charles was a country doctor who had, since the 1870s, been part of a successful medical practice in Long Stratton, Norfolk. Charles had joined the medical practice of Dr Barton (after whom Henry was named) as a junior partner. On Dr Barton's retirement, Charles took over the business and moved into a large Victorian house at 24 The Street. This became the Owens family home as well as the premises from which the practice was run. Charles had had an interesting early life. He was born in about 1846 in Montreal, Canada, and had come across the Atlantic as a young man in order to start his career as a doctor. He had trained initially in Dublin and, having qualified, moved to Dover where he took up his first medical appointment in the early 1870s.

Having established himself in Dr Barton's practice, Charles began to put down roots. He married Marion Hooley in 1881. Marion was the daughter of the vicar of Tharston, a small village near Long Stratton. The Owens household was a perfect example of professional Edwardian country society. They enjoyed many of the trappings of a comfortable life, although Charles had no family wealth behind him. He would have to earn a living for himself and his family and money was, at first, tight. But the family gradually prospered. Charles became a local magistrate. The Owens family took an active role in the affairs of the local hunt as well as in the Church of England. They were pillars of their local community, connected socially and professionally with all of the right people in south Norfolk society.

Their first son, John Herbert (Jack), had been born two years before Henry's arrival. Besides Henry, Charles and Marion also had another son and daughter together: Margaret Marion (known as Darcey) was born in 1891 and Charles Arthur (known as Pop) six years later. A life of comfort and privilege lay ahead for the Owens family. For Henry and his generation, all of this was to change dramatically on 4 August 1914, the day Britain declared war on Germany. On that day, their life of quiet serenity and calm security came to a shattering end. Henry's world, and that of his entire generation, would be altered irrevocably. Moved by an explosion of powerful patriotic emotion, both John and Henry would serve in the army medical services for the whole duration of the war. They both became officers in the Royal Army Medical Corps (RAMC). John had already signalled his interest in military matters well before war erupted that fateful August. He had joined the RAMC Territorial Reserve in 1912, just after he left medical school in London. John would serve initially in England in one of the newly mobilised general hospitals set up in the UK to treat wounded personnel before going out to France himself in 1916. The youngest of the three Owens brothers, Charles, known to his family as Arthur or Pop, took a different path and served in the infantry. He was commissioned as a lieutenant in the 8th Battalion, the Norfolk Regiment, joining his unit on the western front in April 1917. All of the Owen offspring contributed to the war effort in one way or another. Margaret, like many other young women, became a nurse and tended to the needs of the injured and wounded. Henry's mother also worked part time as a nurse caring for the wounded in hospitals in Norfolk.

Fortunately, all three Owens brothers would come through the war in one piece and would emerge physically unscathed. This was no small achievement given the very high rate of casualties amongst officers serving in the front lines.

The Owens children were all very close and, for Henry at least, the separation from his brothers and sister which was inevitably caused by active service was keenly felt. They saw each other at home from time to time while on leave, although Henry's diary did not cover these periods away from the front. But it seems that the Owens brothers' paths rarely crossed in France. Henry met Arthur several times for either a brief supper or a chat but there is no record of Jack and Henry ever meeting up while they were in France.

Henry went out to France almost immediately with the cavalry – allowing him to indulge his love of horses and riding – in the middle of August 1914. He would be amongst the first British soldiers to set foot in the European theatre of operations and, although neither a regular nor reserve officer, was therefore part of the original British Expeditionary Force (BEF) – the 'Old Contemptibles', entitled to wear the famous Mons Star. Henry spent the whole of the next four years on the western front: as a doctor and a diarist – an eye witness to some of the most bitter and violent struggles of the greatest conflict the world had ever seen.

Before war wrenched the Owens family apart, the children had enjoyed a happy childhood. Life in the country suited them well. John and Henry in particular became keen horsemen and hunters. Henry had an artistic temperament. He loved music and had a passion for sketching and painting – skills that would be evident in the diary he kept while he was on active service in France.

Like many other young boys at the time, the Boer War had left a powerful impression on young Henry. He became fascinated by the tales of heroism and battle on the Veldt. His drawings and sketches at this time reflected the reports of the campaign that filled the newspapers.

Like his older brother, Henry had begun his secondary education at a small private school in Suffolk, St Mary's in Beccles. During term time, Henry wrote home regularly to his parents. His letters reveal a home-sick young boy, trying hard to please his parents with his conscientious approach to school work. In 1905 Henry became a boarder at Epsom College in Surrey, where over the next two years he would finish his school education. He was a capable and diligent student. He did not stand out above the crowd, but he did well enough at science to gain entry to the medical school of the London Hospital, where he enrolled as a new student on 27 September 1907. He was just 18 years old.

Henry took up lodgings at 193 Winchester Road, Hale End. He would later move to Vincent Road in Higham's Park. Having spent all of his early years in the country, London was a big distraction to Henry and his initial studies suffered as a result. His attendance at lectures was poor. He only managed to attend two out of a total of thirty-six lectures on physiology and a paltry five out of thirty-nine lectures on anatomy. But he managed to complete all the academic stages of his studies without the need to resit any of the examinations. His clinical work in particular was highly regarded by his tutors, with the exception of post-mortems, where his efforts were judged to be 'indifferent'. Fortunately, these skills would not be required during his time in the RAMC. John obtained his medical qualifications in 1911 and Henry in 1913. The world was at their feet. Both could have looked forward to either joining their father in his practice in Norfolk, or setting out on their own independent paths.

Henry's first love was Constance Francis who, along with her family, lived at the Manor House at Long Stratton. Her father was a retired army officer. One of Henry's greatest pre-war friends was Constance's brother Basil. Basil was six years younger than Henry. They hunted and rode together. Basil joined the 2nd Battalion, The Highland Light Infantry as a lieutenant shortly after war was declared. He was killed in action with his regiment in France in February 1915. Henry wanted to marry Constance and proposed to her. She turned him down. Fortunately, Henry would find love elsewhere. In 1920, Henry married Winifred Mandeville. Winifred came from an aristocratic family with estates in Tipperary, in Ireland. Before the war, Winifred and her brothers and sisters had lived at Anner Castle with their father, Henry Mandeville, who had been an officer in the Royal Navy. They were almost certainly introduced to each other at some point towards the end of the war or shortly afterwards, while Winifred was on holiday in East Anglia, where she had some family friends. Like Henry, Winifred liked to ride and paint. Their friendship turned into a romance. They became an extremely close and devoted couple.

His studies at the London Hospital were successfully completed in October 1913. Henry became a Member of the Royal College of Surgeons of England and a licentiate of the Royal College of Physicians of London. He began his medical career as an assistant house surgeon at the Poplar Hospital in London's east end. The Poplar Hospital for Accidents was a good place for Henry to begin his professional life. In fact many of the newly qualified doctors from the London Hospital would take the first steps of their careers there. It had been opened in the 1850s by the East India Dock Company as a medical centre for its employees in the London docks. It had gradually expanded in the later decades on the nineteenth century and by the time Henry joined the medical staff, it had become a well-established general hospital treating large numbers of patients. The Poplar Hospital was a far cry from Long Stratton. By and large, Henry's patients were poor working-class people from some of London's roughest neighbourhoods. It would be a tough baptism of fire for the newly qualified doctor from rural Norfolk. But there was a lot of experience to be gained there as the hospital undertook a broad range of medical and surgical activities. In 1914 over 64,000 people were treated as outpatients and in the casualty ward. Over 1,500 patients were admitted to the 103 beds in the hospital. It would have provided an excellent grounding for Henry's future career.

One of Henry's best friends and colleagues at the time was another young doctor, Edward Phillips. Edward had qualified from the London Hospital at the same time as Henry and, like him, was also working at the Poplar Hospital. In the first few days of August 1914, as war became ever more likely, it was Edward who first made contact with the War Office to offer his and Henry's service to the RAMC. Edward's offer would be speedily accepted as the RAMC would rely heavily on those working in the civil hospitals to make up the large numbers of doctors, nurses and other specialist staff needed to support the army during wartime.

Britain's war mobilisation arrangements had been meticulously prepared and, when the moment came for them to be put into effect, things proceeded pretty well according to plan. It was a Herculean effort. The reservists were immediately telegrammed and given instructions to join their units as both the infantry and navy were rapidly brought up to wartime strength. Horses, equipment and vehicles were commandeered in huge numbers. Boats and trains were organised to move the various units from place to place according to a strict railway timetable. The signs of war were everywhere. The fear of invasion was real. Bridges, ports and railway lines were guarded by soldiers. Britain moved from peacetime to wartime conditions very rapidly. The medical mobilisation effort was also on a similar colossal scale. The corps that Henry joined was on the verge of an unprecedented expansion.

Britain entered the Great War with a clear strategy for meeting the extensive medical needs of an army deployed on expeditionary warfare in Europe. By August 1914 the RAMC had become a thoroughly professional medical service organised along efficient and effective lines. This had not always been the case. In previous campaigns, medical arrangements had been haphazard at best. The pre-war improvements to the RAMC were largely the product of failures in the provision of medical care to the troops fighting the South African War of 1899–1902. The war had exposed severe shortcomings in the organisation of the army's medical services. At the outbreak of the South African War, the army medical service was short of personnel, with barely enough even for peacetime requirements; it had no organisation in place to allow for expansion in times of emergency and failed to educate soldiers in even the basic elements of hygiene. It provided a rudimentary service at best, and during the campaign high levels of entirely avoidable casualties were sustained. These fundamental failures resulted in five times more soldiers dying from disease than from enemy bullets.

The army learned from this failure. In the aftermath of post-war royal commissions and War Office reports, the RAMC had gone through a major period of restructuring in the years leading up to the outbreak of war in August 1914. At the time of the Boer War, each brigade had its own medical teams, divided up into separate units, all under the command of different officers. The brigade units were comprised of a bearer company, who would gather and collect up the wounded soldiers from the battlefield, together with a field hospital designed to take up to 100 patients. Behind the front line, additional stationary and general hospitals would be set up to provide more permanent treatment. The fragmentation in command was a recipe for confusion, and so it proved.

In 1901, a War Office committee under Colonel Heath recommended that the bearer companies and the field hospitals should be joined together into one unit and in 1905 this was put into effect. The new unit was given the title of field ambulance. It also ceased to be a brigade unit. At the outbreak of war, three field ambulances were attached to each division. Others would be organised to provide support to the various lines of communication troops and other headquarters. A lighter, more mobile field ambulance was, however, specially organised for each cavalry brigade, again combining the previously separate bearer companies with field hospitals. Each field ambulance consisted of ten ambulance wagons. In the case of the cavalry field ambulances, the units in which Henry would initially serve, four of these horse-drawn vehicles were light ambulance wagons, which could take either two patients on stretchers or six sitting up, and six were heavy ambulance wagons for four lying or twelve sitting. The cavalry field ambulance would therefore be capable of accommodating 100 sick or wounded patients at a time. At the outbreak of war, all of these wagons were horse drawn. Motor ambulances were in extremely short supply, although their numbers began to rapidly increase as the inadequacies of horse-drawn vehicles became almost instantly apparent. Wounded men had to endure unnecessarily long and agonising journeys, adding considerably to their misery and suffering. A field ambulance was divided into three sections, a cavalry field ambulance into two. A cavalry field ambulance would have a complement of six medical officers and a staff of just under 120 other ranks. A field ambulance would have ten medical officers and a staff of over 200.

In addition to the field ambulances, each infantry battalion, cavalry regiment and artillery brigade had a medical officer attached to it and men from each of these units would also be designated as stretcher bearers. These medical officers and stretcher bearers would serve in the most forward areas of the front and would be frequently under direct fire from artillery, machine guns and rifles. Henry would also serve for a large part of the war as one of these regimental medical officers. This was medicine at the sharp end of things. Frequently under fire himself, Henry would have to face the same hardships and rigours as any other soldier in the firing line. He came close to death or serious injury on many occasions. In fact, Henry served in just about every medical role during the war. Serving in both the field ambulances and as a battalion and regimental medical officer, as well as in the base hospitals, gave Henry a unique vantage point from which to describe the reality of what it was like both to fight on the western front and care for the wounded and dying.

Together with the field ambulances, the battalion medical officers made up the totality of front-line medical organisation. Behind them, in the lines of communication, a network of stationary and general hospitals and convalescent depots would be established to provide more long-term care and treatment, pending the transfer of patients back to the UK. In the UK, the newly formed Territorial units of the RAMC would have the responsibility of staffing and operating the twenty-three general hospitals which were eventually planned, each with over 500 beds, forming part of this extensive network of care. As soon as war was declared, the capacity of these hospitals was greatly increased by appropriating additional buildings, often schools and poor law premises. Over the next three years the capacity in these hospitals would increase fourfold. The Territorial Army hospitals would work within a much wider network of civil hospitals, many run by the British Red Cross and the St John's Ambulance Brigade, to provide the permanent care and treatment of the wounded.

The work of re-organising the army's medical services did not rest here. The Russo-Japanese war had thrown an additional spotlight on the need for the army's medical services to be able to handle much larger numbers of casualties than had previously been anticipated. In particular, the prospect of full-scale conflict with another European army led to a fear that the resources of the field ambulances would very quickly become overwhelmed. To deal with this possibility, a new intermediate unit was created, to sit between the field ambulances and the larger hospitals behind them – the casualty clearing hospital. Like the field ambulances, this unit would also be mobile (although less so than the field ambulances, given the amount of extra equipment it carried) and be able to handle at least 200 casualties. It would prove to be an absolutely crucial innovation. The casualty clearing hospitals would be renamed casualty clearing stations (CCS) during the early part of the war and their role was gradually expanded to allow more surgical work to be undertaken. The size of the stationary and general hospitals was also doubled to match the size of the casualty clearing hospitals. Despite all of this careful work prior to 1914, the scale and intensity of the fighting on the western front meant that even this expansion in capacity and capability would prove insufficient. At the beginning of the war, there were about 7,000 beds in military hospitals in the UK. By the time the Armistice was signed in November 1918, this had risen to over 364,000.

Medical and surgical supplies are to the army's medical services what ammunition is to the fighting troops. Meeting the wartime requirements in this area would also be a huge undertaking. On the outbreak of war, contractors were put on alert to meet very large demands for medical and surgical stores. Special arrangements were made for the supply of vaccines and sera for the prevention of disease, including enormous quantities of anti-typhoid vaccine, tetanus anti-toxin, and anti-sepsis and cholera vaccines. Lists of requirements for the next twelve months were drawn up and emergency laws passed to prohibit the export of required drugs and surgical dressings. The scale of this build-up can be appreciated by comparing the amounts expended in the months preceding the war with those in later years. In the three years before August 1914, the average annual expenditure on medical stores was £28,500. In the financial year 1914–15, this sum had increased to £475,962. By 1918 this would rise to over £3 million. This represented an enormous exercise in logistics and procurement. The Home Front had become a vital part of Britain's war effort.

Finally, the RAMC put in hand a major effort to improve sanitation and hygiene, in order to prevent the kind of raging outbreaks of enteric fever and other diseases which had so debilitated the campaign in South Africa. Special sanitation sections were established, for example, to ensure the supply of pure water. The use of anti-typhoid inoculation amongst soldiers became widespread after August 1914, although the Army Council had, in 1912, declined to accept a recommendation that would have made its use compulsory at that point. These arrangements would also prove to be highly efficient and successful in preventing the spread of disease that had always accompanied previous expeditionary campaigns.

By 1914, therefore, a huge amount of additional planning had gone into preparing the RAMC for a large-scale conflict. Under Lord Haldane's reforms at the War Office, begun several years earlier, the army had been organised to fight as an expeditionary force of six divisions of infantry – each division having four brigades of artillery and a variety of engineers and divisional troops – and a cavalry division. This alone required the provision of a vast array of medical equipment and personnel. Medical personnel were needed for: twenty-one units of cavalry, seventy-two infantry battalions, and seventy-two units of divisional troops such as artillery, engineers and signallers, together with their divisional headquarters; a general headquarters and the headquarters of II Army Corps; twenty-four units of army troops; and four squadrons of the newly established Royal Flying Corps. Medical staff were also required for the five cavalry field ambulances and twenty field ambulances for the infantry, six casualty clearing hospitals, twelve stationary hospitals, twelve general hospitals, one convalescent depot, six ambulance trains to move injured personnel between the various hospitals, and three hospital ships.

In total, this required about 800 medical officers, fifty-six medical quartermasters and 9,000 other ranks, together with about 500 specialist nurses. The rapid growth in the size of the army during the war resulted in a similar expansion in the size of the RAMC. By the end of the war there were over 144,000 men serving in the RAMC, compared to just fewer than 10,000 in August 1914. The eventual scale of the military medical services during the war can only be described as remarkable. During the next four years of fighting, a total of 235 field and cavalry ambulances were mobilised, along with seventy-eight casualty clearing stations, forty-eight motor ambulance convoys, sixty-three ambulance trains, thirty-eight mobile bacteriological and hygiene laboratories, fifteen mobile X-ray units, 126 sanitary sections, forty-one stationary hospitals, and eighty general hospitals.

At the time hostilities began, the actual number of officers, nurses and men on the active list of the RAMC was always likely to be well below the numbers required to staff all of these units. In fact, only just over 406 RAMC medical officers were available to join the BEF when war was declared on 4 August 1914. Even relying on the available reserves, the RAMC needed several hundred more doctors in order to make up the full strength of the required medical complement. As a result, plans for a major European war had always involved recruiting a large number of doctors and nurses from the civil hospitals. Step forward Henry Barton Owens.

However, despite all of these enormous advances, the RAMC enjoyed a mixed reputation with the rest of the medical profession. Ernest Jones, a future psychoanalyst of great renown, and who in the immediate pre-war period had coached army doctors for their examinations, thought they were a 'jolly lot, recruited from that part of the medical profession who put adventure or an easy life before interests in their scientific activities'. The famous RAMC motto of 'NBR' – No Bloody Research – only served to reinforce this prejudice. The truth was altogether more complicated. The RAMC did possess some pockets of excellence. The Indian Medical Service had, for example, pioneered advances in tropical medicine. And for some doctors, especially those from more modest backgrounds, the RAMC offered a way to develop a career without waiting for whatever crumbs might come their way from the more well-established consultants, where social rather than medical connections were often more important.

On the day before war was declared, Henry was at home with his family at Long Stratton. He had spent what was a beautiful, warm last day of peace at a horse show at Harleston, a few miles from Long Stratton on the Suffolk border, riding a friend's horse. He later rode home, full of foreboding about what lay ahead. With war imminent, he had received a telegram that day from Edward Phillips in London telling him that he had wired both their names to the War Office, offering their services as doctors in the RAMC. Advertisements had already begun appearing in the national newspapers asking for medical volunteers. Up to that point in their lives, neither Edward nor Henry had shown any overt interest in military matters. Neither had offered to join the Territorial Reserve, even though all the medical schools were regularly visited by RAMC recruiting staff in the years leading up to war. Final-year students in particular were all being encouraged to join up as reserves. When war was declared, however, along with hundreds of thousands of others caught up in those extraordinary times, Henry did not hesitate. Now that war was almost upon him, he was clear about what he should do. The next day he caught the early train down to London and went over to the Poplar Hospital, where he met up with Phillips. Together they went straight to the War Office in Whitehall to offer their services and they were immediately signed up. Henry Owens became a lieutenant in the RAMC. His contract with the War Office was for twelve months' service or until their services were no longer required. Henry would be paid twenty-four shillings a day; he was given an outfit allowance of £30 and would be entitled to a gratuity of £60 on termination. In the next few days he would be sent over to Ireland to join the 3rd Cavalry Field Ambulance which was mobilising at the Curragh. Shortly after that, he would be in France. In less than two weeks, Henry would complete the transition from being a civilian to becoming a soldier at war. Through his diary we are fortunate to have a complete picture of this remarkable transformation in Henry's life.

Henry was demobilised in January 1919 and returned to the UK. Jack went into practice with his father. He would spend the rest of his long life at 24 The Street. Pop struggled to find any semblance of a career path. For him, the war had completely interrupted his education and he would drift from one business venture to another. Henry spent some time in Norfolk, indulging his love of field sports before he married Winifred in Tipperary in the summer of 1920 and settled down to a new life in Paulesbury, near Towcester in Northamptonshire. Henry had joined the local medical practice as a GP in October 1920. Their married life together would be painfully short. Henry died tragically from acute septicaemia. He was ill for only a few days before he died suddenly on 15 January 1921, aged only 31. The cause of this illness is unclear. It may have been connected with his exposure to poisonous gas towards the end of the war. A brief obituary appeared in the *British Medical Journal* a few weeks after Henry's death. It contained an intriguing but unattributed comment from someone who had served with Henry in the trenches, which contained more than a hint of troubled relationships between Henry and his senior officers in the RAMC: 'Many a time have I been cheered by his company and courage in France, where his gallantry and devotion to duty were so inadequately rewarded, though fully appreciated by his real friends.' Henry's diary contains no suggestion of any such problems and no trace of any bitterness towards any superior officer. Judged by his diary entries, it is reasonable to draw the conclusion that Henry was in fact quite indifferent to questions of rank or recognition. For example, his diary makes no reference at all to his promotion to captain in the spring of 1915 or to the two occasions he was mentioned in despatches.

Henry was buried in the churchyard at Long Stratton and today his grave lies with those of other members of his family. Henry and Winifred had no children together. Winifred never remarried and found it difficult even to talk of her life with Henry. Deeply traumatised by her husband's death, she went back to Tipperary and lived at Suir Lodge on the Anner Castle estate for most of the rest of her life. Fortunately the diary survived the fire that destroyed her home in the 1970s. Almost every other record of Henry and Winifred's life and times together was lost in the flames.

When Winifred Owens died in 1980, the diary came into the possession of the Imperial War Museum, where it has laid largely undisturbed ever since. The diary was almost certainly assembled by Henry soon after the war ended, using contemporaneous notes written during his years of active service. It is a meticulous account of Henry's life over those four momentous years. Over the course of that time, Henry would be involved in virtually all of the great battles of the war, caring for the wounded soldiers of all three armies – French, British as well as German. On occasions he would also treat injured civilians. He would, quite literally, be in the thick of things. His descriptions of the fighting on the Aisne and at Ypres in 1914, the diary entry for the first day of the Battle of the Somme, his account of the fighting at Messines and Ypres and the final advance to victory provide a moving and poignant portrait of what it was like to live and die in the mud and squalor of the trenches. The diary also recounts the other side of military life on active service – the quieter days when he was free to ride the French countryside with his fellow officers and enjoy the close friendships that developed with those he worked with.

Despite his own modesty and understatement, the diary leaves no doubt whatsoever that Henry Owens was a brave and committed officer who never hesitated to put himself in harm's way in order to care for those who needed his help the most – friend or foe alike. As the diary makes clear, like many doctors working as a battalion medical officer, Henry frequently came under fire during his service in the trenches. The random violence of life in the front line was indiscriminate. There was no respect or immunity granted to those whose only mission was to save life and tend to the wounded. Shell fragments and bullets whistled over his head, grazed his body and killed his friends and colleagues. Perhaps it was not surprising in these circumstances that Henry wanted to fight back. At times he became a combatant himself – a largely ineffective one – contrary to the provisions of the Geneva Convention. But he led a charmed life and, unlike many in the RAMC, he somehow managed to escape any serious injury.

As the diary progresses we are able to see the change in his character and personality. His love of country pursuits remained absolutely unshakable and provided him with an outlet by which he was able to escape occasionally the horrors of war. But he could never truly escape. The reality of death and destruction was all around him and it was his job to deal with its human effects. The true horror of the sights and sounds he must have witnessed can only be imagined. His relaxed, matter-of-fact style disguised many truly horrific scenes of death and destruction.

The diary therefore provides us today with a valuable insight into what it was like to be a doctor tending to the needs of Britain's fighting troops in France and Belgium during the Great War. It also paints a vivid portrait of daily life for the soldiers themselves. We can never repay the debt of gratitude owed to this brave and heroic generation of Britons, who endured so much pain and suffering in conditions we can barely imagine today, for a cause they believed to be right and honourable. And whatever view we might take now of the conflict itself, many would argue with considerable justification that the years 1914–1918 were perhaps the most defining years of the twentieth century. This diary gives us another perspective on those extraordinary years.

The very least this generation of Britons owe those who fought in those titanic struggles is not to forget their service and sacrifice on behalf of others. Henry's diary can help us do this.

Chapter 1

Baptism of Fire

August–December 1914

The first units of the British Expeditionary Force (BEF) began their deployments to France on 9 August, five days after the declaration of war. These were the so-called 'line of communication' troops who had responsibility for the railways, the supply and signalling services and other administrative headquarters. The field army – the fighting troops – consisting initially of four infantry divisions, split into two corps, and the cavalry division (along with the 5th Cavalry Brigade), did not begin to embark for France until 14 August. On that day, Field Marshal Sir John French, the commander of the BEF, landed in France, where he proceeded to Amiens to set up his first operational headquarters. The ports of Le Havre, Boulogne and Rouen were all used to disembark British forces. Le Havre was the principal port. The two remaining infantry divisions of the army in the UK – the 4th and 6th divisions – would be sent out to France within a few weeks, once the threat of invasion had passed.

The first units of the RAMC to leave for France were the sanitary sections and the stationary hospitals. No. 1 Sanitary Section arrived at Havre on 14 August. No. 2 Stationary Hospital arrived the same day at Boulogne. The first of the field ambulances arrived on the 16th. The medical services along the lines of communication were quickly established. The hospitals for all six regular infantry divisions stationed in the UK in August 1914 were all sent to France. The medical units which were directly supporting the field army took longer to move up and get into position. None of the cavalry field ambulances would reach the area of concentration before 19 August – the time when the BEF would begin its move forward to push into Belgium. Only one of the field ambulances in each infantry division was in a position to move with the infantry when they started to move forward to engage the enemy.

The plans that had been so carefully drawn up in peacetime came under immediate strain as soon as the army began to deploy in wartime conditions. The problem was one of logistics. The French railway system was under enormous pressure and the fighting troops had priority over everything else. The roads were equally heavily congested. The sanitary sections were also late in getting forward, with the result that the camp sites presented something of a health hazard to the troops. In short, the troops would have insufficient medical resources with them as they went into battle for the first time in the campaign.

As soon as the field army arrived in France, it began to move up to its pre-designated concentration area, which was close to the Belgian border along the River Sambre from Maubeuge to the neighbourhood of Wassigny. The cavalry division concentrated at Jeumont, Damousies, Cousolre, Wattignies and Hautmont. The II Corps concentrated to the south west of the cavalry, around the Forêt de Mormal. The I Corps was gathering further to the south. Staff plans drawn up in the pre-war period envisaged the BEF operating on the left flank of the French armies. Once hostilities had started, the strategy was for the British and French forces to meet and engage the German Army, which was expected to advance through neutral Belgium. The Germans were attempting to encircle the Allied forces by executing a giant wheeling movement at a point of perceived weakness in the Allied defences. The purpose of this manoeuvre was simple – to seize the channel ports and capture Paris, outflank the Allied armies and bring the fighting in the west to a rapid conclusion within weeks. Once victory in the west had been achieved, sufficient resources could then be transferred to engaging France's ally, Russia, and her enormous army on the eastern front.

The Belgian army offered heroic but largely ineffective resistance to the Germans. They were chronically under-equipped to fight a modern war and were hopelessly outgunned and outnumbered. Very quickly, the Germans fought their way to the French border areas. The British Army began its advance into Belgium on 21 August. The first contact with the German invaders took place the following day, when a squadron of the 4th Dragoon Guards (with whom Henry would serve as a regimental medical officer) opened fire on a patrol of German cavalry just to the north of Mons, a quiet industrial town near the French border. The next day the British and German armies would come into direct and substantial contact with each other for the first time. The patriotic euphoria which marked the outbreak of the war would now collide with the grim reality of modern industrial warfare. The BEF had taken up position along the banks of the Mons–Conde canal – a poor defensive position with only limited fields of fire due to the heavily industrialised nature of the area. The British position also included *an exposed salient looping round the town itself, making defence more difficult as its defenders would come under fire from three sides.*

There was one other problem for the British at Mons. They would have to defend a total of sixteen bridges across the canal if they were to stop the enemy's advance. This would spread the resources of the defenders very thinly. By the time the BEF arrived at Mons they were already feeling the effects of several days' marching in hot conditions on the rough pavé roads. Many of the reservists had fallen out along the way and had to be brought along in ambulance wagons. The prospects for a successful defence did not look encouraging.

Late on the evening of 22 August, the cavalry division, together with its field ambulances, was moved to take up a position on the left flank of the British line. Henry Owens and the 3rd Cavalry Field Ambulance followed the mounted troops to their new station. No one in Henry's unit had any idea of what was about to happen.

By the time serious fighting began on 23 August, the army's medical services at the front line were very thin on the ground. Many of the wounded would simply be left on the battlefield. Henry and his colleagues in the cavalry field ambulances were able to do very little to help. They had virtually no equipment to hand. Most of the hospital beds which were available near to the fighting came courtesy of either the French municipal authorities or convents and monasteries. It would prove to be a veritable baptism of fire for Henry and the cavalry field ambulance to which he was attached.

All of this lay in the future. In early August, Henry was spending the last few days of peace with his family and friends in Norfolk.

3rd August. War expected at any moment. Got a wire from Phillips saying civil surgeons were wanted for the RAMC and he had wired my name to the War Office; advised me to go and see them at the War Office as soon as possible. Beautiful day – motored over to the horse show at Harleston and rode Phyllis's mare 'Colleen' in the riding class. [*Phyllis was Constance's younger sister.*] A beautiful evening. Hacked back on 'Colleen'. Basil [Francis] rode up to Norwich on his motor cycle for news.

4th August. Caught the 7 o'clock train to London. Went to the hospital and found Phillips, then went to the War Office and signed on as a civil surgeon. Lunched at the Grand Hotel Grill. Went by evening train to Blaby (Leicestershire) to do a locum for Dr Couper.

5th August. Did some work in the morning. After tea a wire came from the War Office telling me to report there immediately. Dr Couper had not yet gone and said he would get another locum if he could, but 'war is war'. He kindly motored me into Leicester. Caught the last train and taxied to War Office. See Colonel Burtchaell[1] who told me to come back tomorrow at 10.30am.

6th August. Reported to the War Office at 10.30. Did not have to wait long. Saw Colonel Burtchaell and Major Blackwell[2] and was posted to the 3rd Cavalry Field Ambulance (which was mobilising at The Curragh in Ireland) with temporary commission as Lieutenant. I told them I wanted to see something of the war, if possible as soon as possible and wanted some job with a horse to ride in it.

Caught train at Euston in the evening. Got the boat at Holyhead. Great rumour about that there had been a great naval battle and that a lot of our best ships had been sunk and Admiral Jellicoe had gone down but the German Navy had been annihilated.

7th August. Smooth crossing – nice morning. Got a bath in Dublin and spent the morning ordering uniform etc. Dublin was full of officers trying to buy kit. Frightfully hard to get anything and things very expensive. Beautiful afternoon ... strolled in Phoenix Park.

8th August. My orders were to mobilise with the 3rd Cavalry Field Ambulance on the 8th at The Curragh. Went down by train in the morning and arrived at The Curragh about 12. Found my lot getting harness etc into order – Major [W A] Irwin, Captain Lathbury (RAMC), T O Graham (Togo) and J H Ward (Special Reserve). Our CO had not yet arrived. Very wet afternoon. My commission dates from today.

10th August. Went into Dublin. Beautiful day. Tried on uniform and brought a lot of kit of various sorts.

11th August. Rode over the camp to the training gallop. A lot of nice horses out. Have got a nice horse, a long tailed bay – well bred, nice mouth and manners and nice paces – 4 years old.

---

1. Colonel Burtchaell was in charge of the branch of the Army Medical Services at the War Office dealing with personnel and training issues. Later in October he would accompany Sir Arthur Sloggett, the director general of the Army Medical Services, to France as his staff officer.
2. Major Blackwell was in charge of the war mobilisation and organisation of the RAMC. He had himself only taken up this appointment in April 1914.

12th August. Rode to Curragh with the Major. 2000 remount horses there. Picked out 4 for the ambulance (light section).

13th August. Beautiful day again. Rode out on the Curragh and watched the training and race horses. Topping place and topping sporting country.

14th August. Very hot. Our CO arrived. Major J West. Dickens of a thunder storm all afternoon and evening. Deluges of rain. Messing with a few other stray officers in the Golf Clubhouse. Inoculated for typhoid yesterday and feel rather uncomfortable.

15th August. The whole ambulance paraded and marched out about 6am. Nice fine morning after the rain. Entrained at about 9 and arrived at Queenstown about 5pm. Rather a bad headache as the result of the inoculation. Got tea at Queenstown which cured it. Had dinner there with Major Irwin and his wife who had come down to meet him. Got on board the SS *Olive*, a cow boat, rather small and stank a bit, but we each had a cabin to ourselves. Queenstown harbour in the twilight looked very pretty. By this time all our transport and 80 odd horses were on board and we sailed about 10pm. Slept well. Destination unknown.

16th August. Beautiful day. Sea smooth. Passed Land's End. Captain Guiness (our padre) took service on deck. In the evening saw 5 warships and saw a destroyer hold up a sailing ship. After dark, saw the lights of (what we supposed was) the French coast.

The padre, who rather fancied himself as a signaller, began practising Morse Code with a flashlight on deck with the result that we were held up by a destroyer. She came up close, within shouting distance and turned her search lights on to us, but allowed us to go on. Lathbury very fed up.

17th August. Up early and found ourselves entering a large port. Arrived at the quay-side and saw soldiers in blue coats and red trousers. Found it was Havre. Got our horse and wagons off without any damage. Several big transports full of troops coming in. Marched through the town, people all cheering, into rest camp just above the town. Lathbury still fed up. Says the men are all 'know alls' and can't stand them. No letters from home. No news from the front. Guiness running [the mess] in great style. Still beautiful weather. Have got all my kit bar a pair of field service boots which I have paid for and which have been sent off and a pair of field glasses. Got a very nice Woolsey valise.

18th August. Havre full of our soldiers. Went into the town with Guiness in the morning. The 12th Lancers close by us.

19th August. Orders to entrain this evening. Left Le Havre at 9pm in very comfortable train via Rouen and Amiens. Slept off and on during the night.

20th August. Rouen 1am, Amiens 7am. St Quentin 10am. Busigny 11am. A good many troops here. The cavalry division have all gone on. No news from the front. Disentrained at Maubeuge, about 5 miles from the Belgian frontier … at about 2pm. Two or three aeroplanes were sailing around overhead.

Marched around 12 miles through a nice country … rather like Hampshire. Passed French troops in red trousers preparing fortifications – elaborate trenches and breastworks – trees cut away in front to give a field of fire.

Arrived at Cousolre about 5.30pm and parked the wagons in the square. Several officers of the 16th Lancers were sitting on the bridge smoking and talking when we arrived.

(I always remember that still August evening – the march through the quiet peaceful country, the dusty roads, the village in the cool of the evening, the excitement of an entirely new experience and the feeling of great events impending.)

21st August. Reveille at 5am. 3rd Cavalry Brigade, (16th Lancers, 4th Hussars, and 5th Lancers) under General Gough here. The rest of the division close by. Town full of cavalrymen. Was up at 4.45am. Washed all over. Had a beautiful big bowl of café au lait with Ward. Got the ambulance underway with some trouble and marched to a cross roads one and a half miles east of Colleret. Arrived 7.30am. Soft misty morning. There was an estaminet here called 'aux Quartre Bras' – the spot promptly noted down in the Major's diary as the scene of the great victory over Napoleon.

Two brigades of cavalry passed us here – the 2nd and 4th. Saw Frank Crossley (MO of the 9th Hussars) quite fit and well and very bucked up. Moved off after the cavalry at 9.30am.

Germans reported about 10 miles away on our right flank. Here I was sent with a light ambulance round by a different route where our Brigade had gone to pick up any casualties. Went by Marapent, Vieux Reny and Villers Sur Nicole. Passed some of the 4th Brigade. Arrived at Givry at 4.30pm. Rest of the ambulance apparently not arrived. Germans reported within 8 miles. General French just been through the town. At 8.45pm found the 3rd Cavalry Field Ambulance just outside Givry. Firing heard ahead. The people at Jeumont when we passed through were awfully hospitable; simply showered everybody with drinks, cigars, tobacco, buns, fruit, bottles of wine etc. All cheering and very excited. Bivouacked in a grass field. Orders to move at 4.30am.

22nd August. Up at 3am. Did not get any orders to move. About 8.30 had breakfast. Sun began to get hot. Heard artillery gunfire during the morning. During the morning moved into Givry where we had a long stop. Three German prisoners taken, two of them slightly wounded, in one of our ambulances. Great excitement amongst the civilians. Three o'clock still waiting for orders at Givry. One of our light ambulances went out to pick up someone at Bray could not get there – was turned back by a staff officer. Germans at Bray about 4 miles off and a village near Bray burning. An officer of the Scots Greys brought in (Lord Leven) with bullet wound in the thigh with fractured femur. Major West took him into a convent or monastery and put his leg up but had to leave him there as we at last got orders to move.

Most of our cavalry reported engaged. Moved off about 6pm and marched about 25 miles to Quievrain, very dark and pave slippery roads. Arrived there about 1am.

23rd August. *As the church bells tolled early on this Sunday morning the battle at Mons began when British outposts came into contact with German cavalry patrols. Heavy artillery fire on the salient began just after 9am and was followed by attacks from massed ranks of German infantry. The fighting quickly escalated along the whole line held by II Corps. 5th Division was attacked by two and a half German divisions and the 3rd Division by over three divisions. For several hours the British troops put up a heroic resistance but they were gradually overwhelmed by the sheer force of numbers, as well as by superior German firepower.*

None of the four cavalry field ambulances at Quievrain were opened for work during the battle. Only two field ambulances were available to support the whole of II Corps at Mons. II Corps sustained 1,600 casualties. Late in the evening of 23 August, with the Germans in control of the canal crossings, and with the BEF in danger of being encircled and overwhelmed by much larger German forces, Sir John French sensibly ordered the BEF to pull back. French's plan was to bring about a closer alignment with the French Army on his flanks, which was also retiring, and the taking up of better defensive positions. Retreat was in fact the only course of action open to him. The retirement would last a fortnight and take the British Army back nearly 170 miles, almost to the gates of Paris itself.

Billeted with officers of the 1st Cavalry Field Ambulance. Great supper, bed about 3.30am. Some of us had beds. Slept like a top until about 9am.

Breakfast at 11am. Had a bath. Slept soundly from about 1.30 till 5pm. Firing hard close by all the afternoon. Aeroplanes manoeuvring about. Sent a postcard home.

9pm, suddenly got orders to move off. Today, two light ambulances from each field ambulance detailed to march with its brigade. Arrived at Baisieux about midnight, tied the horses to the wagons and lay down in the street and tried to sleep. A lot of transport and ammunition columns passing.

24th August. Got up as soon as it was light and walked about. Two or three regiments of cavalry, some Lancers, came into a field close by and began cutting the wire fences in their line of retreat. Heavy firing close by on our left. Moved off about 7am rather in a hurry. Marched about 8 miles to Jenlain, arrived about 10am. Guns going hard all the time. Sat in a cornfield and watched shrapnel bursting in the distance, also cavalry etc. Moved on about 4.30pm. Our troops gradually retiring and fighting a good rear guard action. Few casualties on our side. [*On 24 August, II Corps lost another 2,000 men.*] Passed a batch of slightly wounded Tommies. Scores of poor people, women and children clearing off down the road – mostly walking. Germans burning everything behind them and said to be shooting women and children. Bivouacked for the night in a meadow at four crossroads 2 miles south of Jenlain.

Some 9th Lancers passed … said they were badly cut up. Charged and got mixed up with wire. Were looking for their regiment. Turned in about 10pm.

25th August. [*1st, 2nd, 3rd and 4th cavalry field ambulances form one column and begin their retirement.*] Up at 3am. Beautiful sky. Moved off about 6am to Vertain into France. Road crowded with refugees all the way, all walking with a bundle or two of belongings – pathetic sight. Arrived at Vertain about 11am. Gun fire going on. French infantry passed, retreating. Germans pressing on fast. German aeroplane passed over. Everybody blazed at it with rifles. Firing in the direction of Valenciennes louder.

Marched on to Solesmes. Stopped in Solesmes several hours waiting. Heavy thunderstorm and rain. Saw [Lieutenant] R A Preston [*a colleague of Henry's at the London Hospital serving with the 19th Field Ambulance, one of only two field ambulances supporting II Corps*] trudging along on foot with another officer; was looking for his field ambulance. Several infantry regiments came through – Argyle and Sutherland Highlanders, Manchesters etc. Moved off from Solesmes about 5pm in a deuce of a crush of transport, guns and ammunition columns.

Saw shrapnel bursting behind Solesmes. Passed through lines of our infantry [*almost certainly the newly arrived 4th Division*] lying in readiness in shallow scraped trenches both sides of the road. None had packs and greatcoats. Some had ground sheets. Some of our guns on hills to the right firing. Kept going on. Road frightfully crowded. Major Langstaff commanding 1st Cavalry Field Ambulance was behind me. Some guns cut into our column. The rest of the ambulance had turned off somewhere. [*They had in fact gone on into Le Cateau with some of the infantry.*] No destination had been told me or Major Langstaff. Found the village of Reumont about a mile ahead. Decided to stop for the night. Found the 4th Cavalry Field Ambulance there had lost their CO. Found myself alone with 3 General Service wagons, cook's cart, farrier's cart, a medical store cart, a water cart and a mattress cart with all the officer's kits. Orders from Major Langstaff to be ready to move with my wagons at 5am.

Fine night. Lay down in a straw shed but slept very little as there was too much row from transport etc passing and I had a sort of feeling we might be left behind and ordered to go on at any minute.

26th August. *The Battle of Le Cateau took place from around 6am until the late afternoon. General Smith-Dorrien, recently appointed to the command of II Corps after the sudden death of Lieutenant General Sir James Grierson, ignored his orders to continue the retreat that day. His rearguard was not in a position to protect his forces from the advancing Germans and many of his units were simply not ready to resume the retreat at the appointed hour. Instead, Smith-Dorrien decided to stand his ground and attempted to deliver a stopping blow to the advancing Germans. It was an unconventional plan of action conducted against all pre-war training and doctrine. He hoped this would allow his scattered corps a better chance of continuing their retreat unmolested. It was a huge gamble. Both flanks of the British position at Le Cateau were in the air and he faced far superior enemy numbers. Smith-Dorrien's gamble, surely one of the most important decisions made by any British general during the whole course of the war, paid off. Although another 4,000 British soldiers became casualties on the 26th, the retreat from Mons suffered no further serious interference from the Germans until the Allies began to turn the tide of the war at the Battle of the Marne in early September. To all intents and purposes, the men of II Corps had saved the BEF from probable defeat.*

Up at 4am. Moved off at 5am. Went about a mile west to Bertry [*II Corps' HQ*] and about 7.30am heard very heavy firing, guns, rifles and machine gun fire about a mile away towards Beaumont, Solesmes and Le Cateau. The 1st and 4th Cavalry Field Ambulances carried on a dressing station in the village of Bertry. A good many wounded and stretcher cases coming in. I did nothing as I had no medical equipment.

Tremendous artillery fire went on till about 4pm then we had to get off in a hurry. Shrapnel beginning to burst nearby. Germans broke through simply through force of numbers. Began to retreat about 4pm. Roads full of batteries and ammunition trains, infantry marching anyhow, transport, ambulances etc. Villages burning in the distance each side of us.

Frequent stops and a drizzling rain. Sat down on a doorstep and went to sleep at once and nearly got left behind. An agitated staff officer said we had had a great disaster and told me to do all I could to keep the column on the move.

27th August. *Many of the injured from the fighting at Le Cateau had been moved to St Quentin for hospital treatment. No. 6 Casualty Clearing Hospital had been set up in the town. All of its equipment and most of the wounded were left behind as the BEF continued its retreat during 27 August.*
Infantry chaps lying about all along the road absolutely dead beat. Got into St Quentin about 6am. Staff officers at the roads entering the square sorting out parties of infantry and directing them to their units. During the night I had completely lost the other two Field Ambulances so was now quite on my own with the 5 wagons.

Arrived at Ham about 4pm. Found Cavalry Division HQ here. Had to see a staff officer, a Major, who had shot himself in the head with a revolver in a motor car. He was still living.

Was told the 3rd Cavalry Field Ambulance was at Grand Seraucourt, back towards St Quentin and advised to go back and join up. Started off again with the wagons about 9 or 10pm. Arrived about 1am. Found two brigades of cavalry but no field ambulance. Lay down in the street and slept for one and a half hours.

28th August. Up at 3.30am. Intending to go back to Ham. Passed groups of infantry along the roadside cooking little meals over fires. Brought them on. Went through St Simon. Saw a staff officer who said we couldn't go to Ham so joined the retreating column. You could see it stretching away miles long. Passed General French at the side of the road. Sun very hot. Feel very sleepy. Can hardly keep my eyes open.

Arrived at Noyon at about 2pm. Crowds of troops came in. Parked the wagons in a square with a lot of big chestnut trees. Horses very beat. Been on the go for 48 hours.

Asked a French civilian where I could get lodgings and he very kindly offered to put me up. Had a bath – the first for a week – and a shave and got my hair cut. Turned in at 9.30pm. Slept like a top.

29th August. Madame and Monsieur came in and said I must get up quick as they had been told to go away by the first train. Said 'goodbye' and thanked them very much half in French and half in English. Got orders to attach myself to 1st Cavalry Field Ambulance. My lot still not found. A hell of a lot of stragglers everywhere looking for their units. I hear our army has suffered awful losses.

Hear some artillery fire. By now inhabitants have nearly all left this town. Had lunch and white wine with two men of the 4th Cavalry Field Ambulance. Sat under the chestnut trees for half an hour with one of them and came to the conclusion that we were, on the whole, enjoying ourselves thoroughly.

Moved off with 1st and 4th Cavalry Field Ambulances at 3pm and marched south west. The 4th Cavalry Field Ambulance came under a very heavy fire at Le Cateau. Am rather jealous. Have not been under fire yet.

Got into Lassigny about 7.30pm. Bivouacked in a field. Slept soundly from 11.30 until 3.30am.

30th August. Moved off about 5.15am. No troops coming by this road. Parked ambulances outside Compiegne with the Cavalry Division. Received first letters from home, Phyllis and Thompson. Left about 4.30, then through the forest of Compiegne. Beautiful old beeches and oaks. Halted about 7pm. Slept in my valise on the side of the road. Transport, guns etc passing all night within 6 feet of my head but slept like a top.

31st August. Reveille about 5am. Moved off about 10am. Very hot. Halted at about 1.30pm. A damned fool let off his rifle by mistake and shot 2 French soldiers – through the arm and the leg. Another chap did the same thing this morning, only through his own foot. Some French cuirassiers passed with steel breast plates on. Looked like people at a pantomime. Left for St Gervais about 6pm. Bivouacked [there] for the night.

1st September. Lots of troops began to crowd up. Artillery fire not far off. Big scrap imminent. Saw lots of French cavalry, Hussars, Dragoons, Lancers, Cuirassiers. Arrived at Senlis about 3pm. A German aeroplane came over. Expected shrapnel soon after so the column went on at sunset. Camped for the night in a beautiful big park with a big chateau. [I think it] was Cavalry Division HQ.

2nd September. Up at 3am. Went through beautiful big pine woods. A lot of cavalry and artillery passing us. Got into Villaneuve about 4pm. Got orders from HQ to move off at 11.30pm.

3rd September. Marched all night. Moved off about 12.15am. Felt very sleepy. Had the usual difficulty in keeping people awake. Men were going along lying on the horses' necks fast asleep. Arrived about 8am at Gournay, about 6 miles east of Paris. Passed the Chantilly racecourse on the way. Huge concentration camp. Prepared to move off about 5pm. Another long night march south east.

Getting fed up with this perpetual trekking. Might as well be a travelling circus. Wish I could find my own unit. No news of them yet. About 6.30pm, orders to stop the night. Thank God.

Went to find Divisional HQ. A fellow motored me in a beautiful big Rolls Royce to a beautiful Chateau. Beautiful Italian gardens and terraces. Found Colonel Hickson [*the divisional director of medical services*] inside and got orders, also found the field cashier and got £5 off him. Had a ripping sleep – 10.30 till 5.30am.

4th September. Went to Divisional HQ to draw pay for the men. Came back and had a bathe in the river at the edge of the camp (The Marne). Very deep and cool and wet. A lot of French cavalry came into camp – a Division I think. Turned in about 10pm. A little rain in the night but I had rigged up a canvas shelter overhead.

The German Second Army, in an effort to close a gap in their line of advance, had begun to turn away from Paris and towards the south east, exposing an inviting flank to the Allies. Dramatically reinforced by a newly formed French Sixth Army under General Gallieni, the military governor of Paris, the French and British armies ended their long retreat and began to counter-attack. Late in the afternoon of 5 September, Field Marshal Sir John French ordered the BEF to advance the following day towards the north east and the Grand Morin. The French Sixth Army would advance on the British left, threatening the right flank of the German Second Army. The French Fifth Army would attack on the British right. The advance of these three Allied armies unnerved von Kluck and the German High Command and they began a retreat to the high ground along the banks of the River Aisne to the north. The Battle of the Marne halted the seemingly relentless German progress through France and ended any German hopes of a quick victory. The Allies would eventually push the Germans back over sixty miles. On the heights above the Aisne, the Germans managed to halt the newly invigorated

French and British forces. The fighting was fierce and bloody. The scene was now set for a different phase of the campaign – the war of movement of the first few weeks of fighting would soon be replaced by static trench warfare.

5th September. Reveille at 3am. Came to Mormant and remained there overnight. About 40 kilometres today. The padre went into Paris yesterday – whole place empty, shops all shut, everybody gone, only 2 hotels open, streets barricaded. Parked the wagons and slept in a stubble field.

6th September. Ready to move off at 8am. Heard heavy artillery fire in easterly direction. Moved off about 11am and marched about 8 miles. Arrived at Castins about 1pm. In the middle of a mid-day meal Ward turned up with three or four light ambulances. Astounded! Says Major West and Irwin are coming on just behind. All quite fit bar Graham who went sick with pleurisy. The 3rd Cavalry Field Ambulance got left behind in Le Cateau and only just got out in time. Major West actually saw the German infantry coming up the street. Bivouacked under an apple tree with West, Irwin, Ward and the padre. Turned in about 9.30pm and had a good night's rest.

7th September. Up at 5.30am. Heard gunfire to the east. We now seem to be advancing north east. Paris left behind. Orders arrived at 9.15am to advance. Our army successful all along the line. Enemy retreating. Marched about 10 miles to crossroads a mile east of Le Corbier. Arrived about 12. Found 4 Germans with lance wounds sitting under a stack and dressed them, also 2 or 3 British. Marched on about 4.30pm and arrived at La Haute about 7pm.

8th September. Off at 6am. Saw holes where shells had burst, also fragments. Passed long train about 2 miles long of French motor busses. Passed through La Ferte Gaucher. Germans here yesterday. Whole place upside down. Full of French infantry this morning. Artillery fire on our left. Saw a few shrapnel burst in the far distance. Halted a mile or two beyond Ferte and had some food. Dressed about a dozen wounded, chiefly bad shrapnel wounds. One was an RAMC officer. [*This was almost certainly a Captain Painton who had sustained a serious gunshot fracture of the thigh.*] Moved on about 4pm. Heavy gun fire from 4 until dark in the east. Heavy thunder-storm broke, torrents of rain.

Dead horses about all over the place. Halted beyond Bellot. Place looted. Ward took wounded back to railhead in motor transport. Marched again at

9.30. Passed a German limber with live shells lying about. The men tried to bring them along as souvenirs. Arrived at La Noue about midnight.

9th September. Heavy gunfire to the north. We advanced all along the line yesterday. The Cavalry Division to seize some bridges in the rear of the Germans (I think over the Petit Morin).

Buried a private of the Coldstreams – abdominal wound – we picked up yesterday. Marched at 12.30pm through to La Chapelle. Here we passed a lot of Algerian cavalry, with khaki coloured turbans, big baggy blue trousers, red tunics and red cloaks … mostly blind drunk. Very picturesque. Came down into a beautiful valley to Chezy. A very long pull up the far side and came to Divisional HQ and camped.

10th September. Still raining. Marched about 8.30am. Roads very greasy. Horse slipped down with me and pulled two shoes off. Major Irwin did likewise, also 2 or 3 others. Arrived in camp at 2pm. Had a wash and hair cut (by Major Irwin). Bivouacked for the night at Courchamps.

11th September. Moved off at 4.30am to Grisolles. Our padre managed to get 11 loaves of good crisp French bread. Gave 9 to the men, kept 2 for our mess. Terrible afternoon. Cold wind, sheets of rain. [Billeted] at Saponay.

12th September. *The Battle of the Aisne began on this day and would come to an end three days later. French and British forces would cross the River Aisne and begin an attack on the high ground to the north. The objective was to dislodge the Germans from the plateau which ran between the valleys of the Aisne and the Ailette. The fighting was heavy and often conducted at close quarters with the bayonet. Fighting continued on the Aisne front on and off throughout the remaining days of September.*

Heavy firing in front. Smoke all along the sky line. Halted about 8.30am at Loupeigne. Major Irwin got a painful septic hand. A lot of infantry and artillery passed. Infantry looked pretty dirty and war stained. Officers nearly all growing beards. 10am – firing still pretty hot. Shifted on a little way then a very long halt. Very heavy firing on our left all the time.

Moved off about 5pm [*to Bazoches*] – roads ankle deep in mud and water. Camp found to be a howling wilderness of mud … some French soldiers had left some fires smouldering. Made them up and got warm … Found an empty room in the village and slept warm and sound till 6am.

13th September. Found we had lost Divisional HQ. No orders. Graham turned up unexpectedly after breakfast. Was sent with three light ambulances to Braisne. Road full of troops and transport. Ran foul of an irate staff officer at a crossroads. Got to Courcelles and found road blocked by artillery. Got on to Braisne about 11.15. Found a large military hospital there with nursing staff. There were some French nurses working here, also some German prisoners and a German doctor. Not worth taking any [patients] away so came back. Guns firing quite close.

Couldn't get my ambulance on because of road block. Went on alone and found the others at about 2pm in a cornfield. Crowds of troops (British) of all kinds coming through. Infantry piling arms and having dinners in the cornfields. Watched across a wide valley our batteries firing and our shells bursting along the German lines in crowds. Very pretty to watch. Shifted on about 5 miles down to the valley of the Aisne to Villers. Gunfire continued till after dark.

14th September. *Having succeeded in getting most of their troops across the Aisne, the British launched their main assault on the high ground in front of them. On the right of the attack, I Corps made good progress up the slopes and managed to capture and hold on to some sections of German trenches on the plateau. In the centre and left of the attack little progress was made against strongly defended positions. Overall, the results of the day's fighting were disappointing. German fire superiority was too great for the British infantry to overcome. Despite this, the British made repeated efforts to break through, sustaining heavy casualties in the process. At 11pm, Field Marshal French ordered his army to entrench on the positions they occupied, but to be ready to resume offensive operations when the moment presented itself. To all intents and purposes, trench warfare had begun.*

Thin driving rain. Trekked a mile or two on across a pontoon bridge over a canal which the Germans had crossed yesterday and parked the wagons. Tremendous artillery fire going on almost continuously – quite close. Sat in ambulance wagon, wrote letters and read some papers and magazines. Big guns, guns of all sorts going off. Very big fight going on. Shifted back across the canal and cleared a house for a dressing station.

6.30pm – wounded coming in fast. About a score of cases came in and one or two anaesthetics. Ward and Major Irwin helped. Got the rooms of a house opposite cleared out – in an awful state of confusion.

15th September. *The Germans launched a series of counter-attacks against the ground won by the British the day before. These were all repulsed.*

We are now attached to the 2nd Cavalry Brigade. 4am – crossed the canal and The Aisne. Had to cross by pontoon bridges. Arrived at Verneuil at 5am. Full of troops. Heard HQ were at Soupir. Got across country about 2 miles and found Brigade HQ. Told to [get my ambulance] joined up. Lot of gun fire and machine gun fire began about 6.30am close in front. Went back and found ambulance below Verneuil. Came along to Brigade HQ with Major West for orders. Brought up the wagons under the wall of the Chateau Caluette. Shrapnel was bursting along the hill close by – a huge row. Our own guns firing shells over our heads. The air seemed alive with whistling shells. Machine guns going hard close by.

Just as our ambulance arrived, two shells (high explosive) burst just ahead of us, about 100 yards, just after Major West had passed, and killed two men, several horses and wounded about 10 others (gunners I think), including an officer. Three died within a few minutes. These wounded men were evacuated in motor lorries within half an hour, luckily. Ward went off with 3 light ambulances to pick up wounded.

Watched German shells bursting in Verneuil. [They] then began searching a wood just beyond and just stopped short of a lot of cavalry who were just behind it. They then swung round and began dropping one after another in a wood just to our right – a long whistle then a biff bang and black smoke. They then came nearer into the same field within a couple of hundred yards and Major West thought it time to shift and we cleared off at the run. A very exciting morning. Moved back about a mile to the river where there was a pontoon bridge.

4pm – dressed a batch of wounded. After a bit, [the Germans] began dropping shells after us again so had to shift off. Went over the pontoon bridge and through the village. Had just got over the Pont d'Arcy over the canal when a shell dropped just behind us. Whole show, wagons and all went off at the gallop. Next shell dropped just alongside and mud and dirt dropped on our heads and all around. Got to the last house when Major Irwin said 'Don't go down the road, get behind the house.' Dodged behind the house with him. Next moment heard a loud screech coming right at us. Ducked low. It went over our heads and dropped in the road about 50 yards in front of us. Just missed our last wagon, knocked Sergeant O'Rorke and Driver Hobbs over but didn't hurt them. Unfortunately, during the general bolt Corporal McSweenie fell under a wagon and was killed.

Halted just beyond Ville Arcy till about 6pm. Dressed several wounded and buried Corporal McSweenie then moved back to Oeuilly, just north of the Aisne. Found a billet for the night where we were snug and warm.

16th September. Had a good breakfast at 5.30am. Whole unit moved off at 6.30am to Soupir. Got shelled out of there by shrapnel. Moved back to the Chateau. Got under fire of the beastly siege guns (5.9s) again. Was sent up to the Chateau with some dressings for Lathbury who was working there. About 200 wounded there and a Field Ambulance.

Lathbury was amputating a Guard's officer's arm in a beautiful state room on a table. Priceless table cloths torn up for swab, priceless carpets covered with mud and blood. Helped to dress a few cases. Came back about 4pm. Major West was amputating a man's hand in the ditch under the Chateau's wall. Some more shells burst near us. Knocked Ward over, killed 3 or 4 and badly wounded several men. Was ordered to take the heavy transport back to Bourg. Went on ahead with the leading wagon and was nearly up to the bridge, when round a bend in the road came a most appalling sight – heavy wagons, water carts, cavalrymen, spare horses, rider less horses, cavalry limbers all coming hell for leather and went past like mad. Most extraordinary sight!

Major West came in [to Bourg] with about 100 wounded from the Chateau. Formed a hospital in a church. Dressed a few. Turned in about 2am and slept till 4.

17th September. Took 3 light ambulances to act as Advanced Dressing Station at 2nd Cavalry Brigade HQ at Soupir. Sent back one wagon with 5 cases. Stopped just behind an RFA battery in action. Hell of a row. Had to send back 4 of my men blind drunk. Had got hold of some rum. Several shrapnel bursts round us. About 11am, rifle fire close in front. (The cavalry were now in the line in trenches as infantry and carried bayonets.)

About 1pm another little lot of shrapnel, one man wounded near us, but bar that, very little shelling near us. Stopped till 5pm and then got leave to go back to Oeuilly. Got simply soaked going back.

18th September. Had a slack day. Saw a few cases in our hospital in the church. Evacuated 5 cases over the canal to Villers at 5pm. Got a good pair of ammunition boots from the Quarter Masters Store. Turned in at 11pm. Woke up at 1am. Very heavy firing – gun and rifle fire. Night attack I suppose.

19th September. Had another slack day. Heavy artillery firing close by, also sound of big shells bursting. Made myself very comfortable outside on a chair with some magazines and some Pera cigarettes which came from home about a week ago. Very nice in the sun. About 2pm the Cameronians came in after 6 days in the trenches. I believe only 400 of them left. The Scots Guards also came in for a rest.

Moved back over the canal to the sugar factory at Villers and got there about 4pm. Got into a little building at a station there. Got it cleared out. Cement floor but had some straw put down and made a nice room. Major Irwin very groggy. Lost about two stone and feels very rotten. Probably going back to base. Heavy firing till about 6.30pm. Ward still out at Soupir. Had some rum punch and felt very warm and comfy.

20th September. *The 3rd Cavalry Field ambulance established two advanced dressing stations – one at Paissy (the western ADS) and the other at Pargnan (eastern ADS).*

Had to shift off at 4.30am with 2 light and 2 heavy wagons and a forage cart. Major West came with me. Heavy rifle fire in front. Formed dressing station in a field near the road one an half miles short of Paissy. Went out with stretchers but found nothing in front but a signalling staff and some French batteries so came back.

An artillery sergeant came and said there were several badly wounded about a mile and half in front and no medical officer to attend to them. Took a light ambulance; halted them out of sight. Went on a half a mile under shrapnel and shell fire, past the Tour de Paissy Farm. Found some French artillery and our artillery and the 18th Hussars in Paissy. Shrapnel bursting around and 2 or 3 of the big black brutes. 'coal boxes' (5.9 howitzers) burst close by, and sent mud and stones all over us. Found there was a medical officer there in his aid post so came away and was glad to be out of the place. Sent off 2 wagons with 12 cases – none very serious – back to Villers.

When I went out with the stretchers this morning, had a good view of the position. Saw our guns along the edge of the hills of a big valley. Had the dressing station just below the hills where our guns were.

Seems to be simply an artillery duel going on. Guns all around us, English and French kicking up the devil's own row. Dressed 2 French artillery men who were wounded.

Beautiful evening. Low September sunshine. Little village on the hillside and the hills looked very pretty.

About dusk, Graham turned up with 2 more light ambulances. Left the heavy wagons by the roadside and walked on foot with the light ones to Paissy. Passed the Tour de Paissy Farm in flames. Shell fire along this road had been tremendous. Damned great holes all along the actual road, anything up to 6 feet across and up to 4 feet deep. Got into Paissy ... Found the MO all alone with some wounded in caves behind a house. Two dead artillery men there. Took over 6 bad cases – also about a dozen black chaps. Walked with them back to the sugar factory. Place looked most clean and cosy. Fires in the ward rooms and the operating room very nice with a bright glowing fire, table, panniers, and acetylene light. Major West and Ward attended to the cases and Graham and I got some supper.

21st September. Had a day off. Heavy gun fire all day. Very few casualties.

22nd September. Took over the hospital for the day. Heavy artillery fire again. Graham and Ward came in about 12 with about 20 cases from Paissy.

23rd September. 3rd Cavalry Field Ambulance in reserve today. Watched 'black marias' bursting along the ridge at Pargnan. Make an awful crash and an enormous column of black smoke. After tea walked to Serval with Graham. Trees just starting to turn brown. Found a woman gathering apples in an orchard and bought some off her. Got back at 6pm.

24th September. Went with 2 light ambulances up the hill to just below Pargnan with distinguishing flags etc. forming an advanced dressing station. 10.30am – no shells this way, so far no casualties turned up. No excitement. Went back at 7pm with 2 sick.

25th September. Some bad shell wound cases came in during the evening. Ward out at the Eastern Advanced Dressing Station [at Pargnan]. The 9th Lancers were shelled at long range in their billets at Longueval. Major West amputated a thigh. I gave the anaesthetic. Turned in about 11pm.

26th September. Heavy artillery fire going on. Had a bath in the Major's rubber bath. Had orders to shift back about a mile for some reason. The whole unit marched out and parked in a stubble field. Had just got some good bivouacs prepared when we got orders to go back again. Got back at 5.30pm and found our nice little shanty pinched by some Army Service Corps people. Had to go into a stuffy little room at the top of the sugar factory.

27th September. Shrapnel bursting occasionally. Graham on the Western Advanced Dressing Station [at Paissy]. Not called out.

28th September. After lunch went and relieved Graham. Walked with him towards the Tour de Paissy and on to Geny. Whole country pitted all over with shell holes. Counted about 8 in 30 yards. While we were on the road they were bursting in the valley below us in groups of 5. No troops nearby at all and heard of no casualties.

30th September. Some Frenchmen digging some trenches behind us and apparently drew fire. Several shrapnel and some Melanite shells came over and burst in the field behind us about 2pm. Thought we were out of range!

Orders to move. Moved off about 3pm back about 8 miles to Paars. Hilly road. Billeted with 1st and 4th Cavalry Field Ambulances in a nice country house, Chateau de Paars, belonging to the Viscomte Dauger. The Germans had been in the place and had broken into all the cabinets, drawers etc and taken all the valuables.

1st October. During the morning got several rooms ready as a hospital. Sat in the garden in the sun in the afternoon. Funny contrast – tonight in a very comfy chair, in front of a nice bright wood fire with magazines etc, in a Viscomtesse's boudoir. In a couple of nights very likely shall be in the middle of a ploughed field.

2nd October. Inoculated half the men against typhoid.

3rd October. Took horses into Courcelles morning and afternoon and also bought some bread at the boulangerie there. Padre Bates went out with a gun today and got 2 hares. Living in comfort and luxury now.

The gradual withdrawal of the BEF from the Aisne front began in early October. As soon as it was clear that the Germans were no longer retreating and were firmly entrenched on the Aisne, the Allies resumed their efforts to try and envelop the German right flank. The Germans naturally wanted to outflank the Allied left. The line to the south now stretched all the way to the Swiss border and so neither side could be outflanked from that direction. The result was the so-called 'race to the sea'. The BEF would eventually move north to take up positions around Ypres in Belgium and Bethune and Armentières in France, simplifying their supply lines through the Channel ports. Their place on the hills above the Aisne would be taken over by French units.

4th October. Hardly anyone coming into hospital. Orders to move off at 5pm. Had a meal. Moved off about 8pm. Walked on foot nearly all the way. Arrived at Plessier Huleu at 4am. Got into a farm house and slept till 8.30am.

5th October. Marched to Vaumoise – about 18 miles. Got stopped at 11pm by some motor transport sticking in the mud. About 100 French motor busses full of troops. The other 2 Field Ambulances just got through – we had to hang about for 5 solid hours in the road before we could get on. Arrived at billets at 9am.

6th October. Moved off again at 12 o'clock. Marched about 25 miles to Arsy. We have two very nice motor ambulances, Wolseys, with us now. Very useful ... Arrived at Arsy about 1.30am.

7th October. Absolutely perfect autumn day. Blue sky and bright sunshine. Did about another 20 miles northwards. Carry a sweater in my haversack and put it on after sunset. Very chilly. Got into billets at Villers at 11.30pm. The people gave us some bread and butter and some excellent coffee. Turned in at 1am.

8th October. Off at 10.30am. Had my horse led on and walked on foot. Another beautiful cool day with bright sunshine. Can hear firing in the distant north east. Passed through Amiens about 9 or 10pm. Quite a big town. Shops all open, everything as usual. Got into billets at Longpre, 4 miles further on. About a 25 mile march. Most of these marches [we] have the whole road to ourselves and take our own time.

9th October. Did another good march of 22 miles. Came through Doullens about 7pm. Arrived at Bouquemaison about 9. Comfortable billets at a farm house. Slept well from 10.30 till 7am.

10th October. Short march; only about 15 miles. Horses pretty fit on the whole after 6 days marching, but a lot of them badly rubbed and galled. Half the men ride part of the time on the wagons while the other half march and they change about. Heard firing on our right. Got into billets by 6pm at Monchy-Breton. Nice farm house. People very nice.

11th October. Went in motor ambulance to 1st Brigade HQ. Found Lathbury. Took over a few sick. Back at 8.30 just as ambulance was moving off. Billeted at Berguette.

12th October. Off at 7am. Halted nearly all day at St. Venant. Then through a big wood to Roussel Farm. Divisional HQ here. Sharp rifle and machine gun fire just ahead. Heard a few bullets whistling over. Few shrapnel bursting as we came out of the wood about a mile ahead. Billeted at La Motte – small farmhouse.

13th October. Up at 6am. Stood by for further orders till about 11.30. Moved off at 12 about 4 miles to Pradelles and halted about 3 hours. Heavy artillery, machine gun and rifle fire on our right. Moved on about 3 miles to Caestre about 6pm and got into very snug billets for the night. Excellent coffee and cream going. Hear our troops have done good work, gaining ground.

14th October. Up at 5am. Wet morning. No orders to move. People here talk Flemish, only the daughter understood French. Moved off about 3pm to St Jans Cappel. Not very fit today so rode in a light ambulance. Road badly blocked and didn't get in till about 11pm. Only around 8 miles. Billeted in a farm with 1st Cavalry Field Ambulance.

15th October. Motored 6 cases over to Hazebrouk. Pave road all the way. Bailleul, Meteren choke full of infantry and artillery. Big fight at Meteren a few days ago when we took it. Hazebrouk not much disturbed. Lots of troops there, but shops open.

16th October. Foggy morning. Up at 5.30. Moved off at 7 about 4 miles. Stopped in the road all day near Neuve Eglise (Belgium). Sat in the ambulance and the Major told us funny stories. Did nil all day and got orders to return to same billets at St Jan Cappel. Major Irwin came back from hospital.

17th October. At St Jan Cappell, about 20 miles east of St Omer. Moved out to a point about half a mile west of Neuve Eglise and halted. In afternoon, went on with Major Langstaff in motor ambulance to Ploegsteert – 1st Cavalry Division HQ. No wounded. A shell burst about 200 yards from the road as we arrived. Watched one of our aeroplanes signalling result of fire of one of our batteries close by. He kept sailing round and round over the battery and dropped different coloured stars after shots were fired. Inhabitants still in the town but show signs of clearing off. Came back at 6pm. Roads full of artillery and cavalry to Neuve Eglise. Got into billets at Locre by 9pm. Several letters and parcels from home.

18th October. Moved off about 4.30 and billeted in a farm house about a mile west of Neuve Eglise on the Dranoutre Road.

19th October. About 11.30 motored up to Divisional HQ at the Chateau on the hill above Ploegsteert. Waited there with another ambulance to clear any wounded. Nothing much doing. Some staff officers went out to shoot pheasants. Took the motor ambulance into St Yves and fetched a wounded civilian from a farm near there. The 5th Dragoon Guards were digging trenches there. The cavalry all acting as infantry now. The 1st Cavalry Division in front of Ploegsteert and holding a line somewhere along the river down by Warneton. Some of our heavy guns just behind the Chateau, firing overhead. Make a deuce of a row (60 pounders). Can't hear any German guns; apparently are only 1–2 miles ahead. Very little about here to show there is a war going on at all.

4pm. Some village people going away with bundles. Occasionally some Maxim fire near St Yves. No more casualties.

20th October. Hear they shelled the Chateau at Ploegsteert and HQ had to shift. Several servants hurt and horses killed. Occasional machine gun fire heard and pretty continuous gun fire during the morning. Pretty heavy artillery and machine gun fire between 2 and 3pm.

From 21 October until 19 November, British troops around Ypres and down to Armentières were attacked and counter-attacked continuously by vastly superior numbers of the enemy in the heaviest fighting of the war so far. The Germans were desperate to break through the British lines, get behind the British and French armies, and seize the Channel ports, cutting off the British forces from their main line of supply. Ground was lost, re-captured and then lost again on many occasions. The British line held, although by the end of the fighting the front line had been pushed back in several places. For much of the time, French and British troops fought alongside each other. Henry's diary, for example, is full of references to treating wounded French soldiers. At the end of November, after the fighting had largely died down, the British concentrated on a line which extended from Festubert just to the north of the Bethune–La Bassee canal up to Hollebeke, just to the south of Ypres.

21st October. Out at 1st Cavalry Division HQ at La Hutte at a small chateau there. Had 2 light ambulances and a cottage near by as a dressing station but had only 5 or 6 slight cases in. Chateau surrounded by RFA guns – 30 or 40 at least, stuck in innocent looking root fields. Watched 4 60 pounders firing near the Chateau. About 60 German prisoners were marched up – pretty shabby looking lot. Seemed very pleased to be captured. Yells from the Tommies of 'Waiter!' Watched 'coal boxes' bursting around the Chateau where HQ were [yesterday]. Met Somerville from the London Hospital. Very fit. With the 32nd Brigade RFA. Out here as a 'civil surgeon'. Very nice billet at Neuve Eglise. All slept on the floor of the front room. Hospital fixed up in a very nice big sort of school room, part of a convent. Several bad cases in.

22nd October. Heavy firing quite continuous all night and all day towards Armentieres till about 4pm. Took 12 cases in 2 wagons to the Clearing Hospital in Bailleul in the afternoon. [*This was probably No. 2 Clearing Hospital and was based in a seminary about a mile from the railway station.*] The Lahore Division of Indian troops there. Look very business-like. They were moving them up to the front in motor busses when we came back and we got hung up for 3 hours.

23rd October. Hacked over with Irwin and Ward to the dressing station at Wulverghem. Took over from Major Cowie and Captain Crean, VC. Brought our kits with us. Rest of unit still at Neuve Eglise. No casualties in yet. Only 5 or 6 slight cases. Slept at Wulverghem.

24th October. Crean took over at 9am. Walked back to Neuve Eglise. Heavy gunfire to the south this evening.

25th October. With Graham and Ward at the Dressing Station at Wulverghem. Quiet day. People all went to mass as usual. Heavy rifle and machine gun fire from 11 till 11.30pm. Heavy rain after dark.

26th October. Windy day after the rain. Walked back to Neuve Eglise. Soon after got orders to follow the 2nd Cavalry Brigade about 25 miles south to Bethune. Saw Frank Crossley. Quite well, but wants to get home to the hunting. Lost touch with the Brigade after a bit. The CO found out from some signals officer where Brigade HQ was to be formed and found our way somehow and arrived about 10.30pm.

Billeted at the Chateau de l'Abbaye near Choques. Brigade HQ in the same place.

27th October. About 3pm heard the Brigade were to go into the trenches at Neuve Chappele. Marched a few miles north and billeted at Zelobe and opened up a dressing station. Graham went out and formed a dressing station at Lacoutour.

28th October. Went out to Lacoutour and relieved Graham. Very nice little white house nearly opposite the church. Ward came out about midday. About 5pm a lot of casualties reported. Graham and Ward went forward and took a lot back to the Ambulance. They had about 46 casualties – chiefly 9th Lancers and 4th Dragoon Guards. I dressed 3 officers of the 9th Lancers. Several wounded Indian troops also. Ward and I got to bed about 1am.

29th October. Brigade ordered back. Ambulance moved off about 1pm. Got a drink in Estaires.

30th October. Big mail last night. Several letters and parcels. Up at 7am. Very heavy firing indeed towards the east; big guns, little guns, machine guns and some rifle fire all day till 5pm. Heaviest I have heard so far – especially machine gun fire to east and south east. No news of any heavy casualties. Slack day for us.

31st October. Very busy day. Heavy firing. Had a great crowd of wounded in. In the afternoon and evening went into Bailleul three times with wounded. Had about 500 cases through in 24 hours. Got back about 11pm.

About 12 went out to the Advanced Dressing Station at Wulverghem. Sent on a good many Indian troops.

1st November. The Germans broke through in the night at Messines. Cleared off at once. Kept the ambulance just outside Wulverghem and went back to Neuve Eglise to get some dressings. Saw the Dorset's coming up to do a counterattack. Graham went back with Tommy Crean towards Messines to pick up some wounded and got under a hot rifle fire but came along alright. Began shelling Wulverghem just as they were coming through. Our men holding a line about half a mile beyond Wulverghem.

Told by Major Davison [*deputy divisional director of medical services*] to take the ambulance to cross roads at Lindenhoek and wait there. Waited [there] all day. Watched our guns shelling Messines, saw the shells bursting on the hillside opposite and in the village on the ridge.

In the evening, formed a dressing station in a pub at Lindenhoek with Ward and Lewis. Had several cases in; some London Scottish wounded who told us their part of it. Two or three said it was quite alright but were surprised that volunteer troops were sent actually into the fighting line – they hadn't actually expected it. [*The London Scottish lost heavily during the fighting at Messines. They were the first Territorial unit to go into battle in the Great War.*]

Had an awfully hard day's fighting. The [infantry] came up and did splendid work. But lost awfully heavily.

2nd November. Guns began about 8am. Very heavy firing again. [Saw] some French 75s firing at a tremendous rate. Tommy Crean got shelled out of his dressing station about midday, just this side of Wulverghem.

20 batteries in position around Lindenhoek and defence pretty secure today but the 1st Cavalry Division must be awfully tired. At Crean's dressing station this morning I heard General de Lisle [*commanding 2nd Cavalry Brigade*] say that the French were going to counter attack on a large scale. Apparently this didn't come off. Some big shrapnel bursting down by Wulverghem. Went in motor ambulance into Kemmel and picked up some wounded French who had just been hit there and an old woman who had been hit. Waited all the afternoon in a cottage just south of Lindenhoek. Some shells came over and Ward and Lewis had some pretty close to them down the Dranoutre road. Got back into the same pub again in the evening at Lindenhoek. The 12th Lancers came past going out. Relieved about 9pm by Wagstaff and Arnott. Came back to the ambulance at Dranoutre. Lathbury back with us. Had a rotten time in Messines. Was in a cellar with 'coal boxes' dropping all about and houses knocked to bits.

3rd November. Slack day. Ward, Graham and I went out about 6pm to Lindenhoek. Crowds of French cavalry on the road. The 1st Division relieved tonight by the 2nd Division. Five of us stopped out there for the night and dressed one Frenchman.

4th November. We expect to attack today. Slack day. Heavy firing. Formed advanced dressing stations in the evening.

6th November. On duty. Only a few cases in – chiefly French. The French attacked Messines today. Relieved Lewis and Murphy at the dressing station at the usual pub at 9 o'clock with Graham. Had one or two wounded through.

7th November. Tremendous fusillade (rifle fire) about 12 for about 15 minutes. Then all quiet for the night. Had very few wounded in. French attacked again in the afternoon. Came into Dranoutre about 9 o'clock and brought in about 10 French wounded.

10th November. Shifted in the afternoon to a very nice little farm house near Croix de Poperinghe. Very heavy firing towards Ypres.

11th November. 1st Cavalry Division coming out of the line for 48 hours rest, so nothing doing. Went into Bailleul about midday with a few sick. In the afternoon strolled towards St Jans Cappel. Cloudy day, very rough wind blowing. Living in luxury at present. Cold bath every morning.

12th November. Moved off at 7.45am about 300 yards to the corner of the Locre–Bailleul road and waited for orders. Ward, who has Lathbury's old job attached to the 2nd Brigade with light ambulances, came past looking blue with cold and rather miserable. On his way up to Ypres. Heard news of the repulse of a great attack by the Prussian Guard at Ypres. Said to have fired shrapnel with fuses set at zero at them and mowed them down in hundreds. At 2pm got orders to return to billets – apparently we are not wanted. Bob Bannerman joined the unit.

13th November. Major Irwin left sick.

17th November. Went into Bailleul in the morning and got 5 remount horses. In the afternoon, walked to Locre with Graham. A lot of howitzers in the church yard. Went into the church – service going on, rather nice and impressive. Heavy firing again towards Messines.

21st November. Walked into Bailleul with Bannerman and Arnott. Saw where a bomb had dropped into the Clearing Hospital. One ward blown up. One patient and 12 orderlies killed or hurt. All the windows of the place smashed. At 1.30pm moved off through St Jans Cappel to a farm near the 'Mont des Cats'. Got in about 4pm. Got the men into the barns. Very small bedroom for the CO, all the rest of us slept in one room on the stone floor in our valises. We mess in the same room. Heavy firing again Messines way.

22nd November. [Major Steel], the ADMS [*assistant director of medical services*] came in and told us to form a dressing station at La Clytte beyond Locre. West, Graham and Bannerman went off. Stopped behind with Lathbury.

23rd November. Major Steel severely wounded by a shell at the dressing station at La Clytte. Arrived at La Clytte about 8pm. Major Steele was taken straight in to Bailleul but died in about an hour.

24th November. Great news! Whole of the 1st Cavalry Division out for a rest – a fortnight! Officers to have 72 hours leave in England. To go home in turn.

25th November. Major West and Ward left at 6am for leave in England. Went in with Lathbury and Arnott and 40 men from the two ambulances and attended Major Steele's funeral at the cemetery at Bailleul.

We began to settle down for our winter quarters. The 2nd [Cavalry] Brigade, to which we are now affiliated, were billeted in farms between Berthen and Meteren. The regiments were distributed roughly a squadron to a farm. We settled in to our little farm below the Mont des Cats. We had our fair sized room in which we messed. Our room had the usual Flemish iron stove. It wasn't luxurious but it was warm and dry and we appreciated any kind of a fixed home after being continually on the move for four months. 1st Cavalry Field Ambulance (Major Langstaff) were in the farm next door.

We all began building stables for the horses out of hop-poles and thatched them with brushwood, hops and straws and floored them with faggots. We had all our horses under cover in about a week.

Our men were served out with fur coats to wear over their khaki. They were wonderful things made of different kinds of fur from China and Siberia, patchworks of white, black and brown. The Cavalry were served out with 'British Warms', cut just to cover the knee.

We had an easy time. The sick were evacuated direct to the CCs in Bailleul. Later, a sort of Divisional Hospital was formed at Meteren and run by Lathbury.

3rd December. A very cold showery day. In the afternoon we marched with a party to the road between Fletre and Meteren. The whole Division lining both sides of the road to be inspected by the King. Waited from 3 till 3.30 in the wind – very cold. Then the King came along with the Prince of Wales. General Allenby [*commanding the Cavalry Corps*] on foot and as he passed each regiment every man waved his sword and cheered. As soon as he had passed – home to tea.

5th December. Up at 4.30am. Left in motor ambulances at 6.15 for La Motte where motor busses started for Boulogne. A very cold slow journey to Hazebrouck. Here we got a lift in a beautiful Daimler going down to fetch a General. Snowing now. Buzzed down to Boulogne in no time and caught the morning boat. Very rough [crossing]. Rather ill. Had a private cabin to myself. Folkestone in one and a half hours and arrived in London about 3.30pm and met my people.

Everything and everybody looked so clean and civilised and ordinary that I felt that I had never been away at all and there had been no war. Slept on a snowy bed that felt like a cloud.

7th December. Got a day's hunting with the Dunstan with Jack. The Springfield's [*family friends*] and a few people out, also 4 or 5 officers of the Cheshire Yeomanry and the Adjutant, Captain Lockett the polo player. It did one good to see hounds again. Had some galloping and jumping on a very full day.

9th December. Left Folkestone by the morning boat. A motor ambulance waiting for us at Boulogne. Back to billets with Griffon (4th Dragoons), Hall (5th Dragoons), and Captain 'Rattle' Barrett (15th Hussars), the polo international. Arrived at my billets near Mont des Cats about 8.30pm with a large sack containing, amongst other things, plum puddings, a brace of pheasants and a turkey.

25th December. Had a quiet Xmas dinner with Lathbury, Marshall and Freeland, the new Roman Catholic padre. The rest were on leave or elsewhere. Graham had his Christmas dinner at home as he said he would, only he didn't think it would be on leave. We had chickens, plum pudding and champagne.

31st December. Went temporarily to the 9th Lancers for about a week at Fontainhoek. Comfortable billet in a farm house with a bed. This meant seeing the morning sick and inspecting the squadron billets each morning.

From there I went to the 4th Dragoon Guards while Griffon was on leave till about 20th January.

For the next few weeks of winter, as the fighting was now a largely localised affair and not particularly frenetic, Henry indulged his passion for hunting with his friends in the cavalry. Officers in the 4th Dragoons had sent out to Flanders an entire pack of beagles and they hunted most afternoons.

Altogether we had great fun. It's the only time I have ever hunted 7 days a week! It kept our minds off the war and kept us fit. On January 20th an order came out prohibiting all shooting and hunting.

Chapter 2

Trench Warfare

Ypres 1915

The heavy casualties of the August–December fighting meant that the BEF needed urgent reinforcements. From the outbreak of war to the end of 1914, the British Army sustained a total of over 177,000 casualties. Over 2,000 officers were either dead, missing or had become prisoners of war. The equivalent figure for the other ranks was 41,000. Nearly 4,000 officers and 130,000 other ranks had either been wounded or suffered from illnesses of one sort or another. The 'Old Contemptibles' had, by the end of the year, virtually all disappeared.

Indian troops began arriving towards the end of 1914. The 27th and 28th divisions, made up of regular troops drawn from garrisons across the Empire, arrived in late December 1914 and in January 1915 respectively. The Territorials began arriving in larger numbers from February, the 46th and 47th divisions being the first to deploy. The 1st Canadian Division arrived at the same time. The New Armies, raised at the outbreak of the war, would start landing in France from May onwards. There were similar increases to the artillery and other branches of the army, including the RAMC, where large numbers of new field ambulances and casualty clearing stations were mobilised and sent to France.

7th February. Posted to the 4th Dragoon Guards [*an Irish cavalry regiment*] as MO. Took my little horse with me. The regiment was about a mile away towards St Jans Cappel, Colonel Solly-Hood commanding, Major Sewell second in command and 'Fox' Aylmer adjutant, Gallagher ('Golliwog') signalling officer, a French interpreter, Count de Lentillhac. I had a comfortable billet with the vet, Weir, the Quarter Master, Dunham, and the interpreter in a little farm next door and a bed with nice clean white sheets. Very obliging people in the house. The squadrons were all within a mile – A

Squadron, Captain Ogilby, B Squadron, Captain Macgillicuddy and C, Major Pilcher.

The usual routine went on. No more hunting. Graham, attached to Brigade HQ and collecting and evacuating the sick, was close by. The Field Ambulances were within a mile.

23rd February. The [1st Cavalry] Division going into the trenches near Ypres for about 10 days. Went in motor busses through Poperinghe to Ypres. Arrived in Ypres square about 10pm. Fine night and the moon nearly full. The town looked rather fine; the Cloth Hall and the tall Cathedral tower half ruined by shell fire standing up in the moonlight. Billeted in a huge redbrick reformatory ('Ecole de Bienfaisance') just outside Ypres on the Menin Road. Regimental HQ in one of the small houses in the garden. Quite a nice little house only knocked about by shells and draughty. The chef soon had a jolly good dinner ready. [*During the fighting at Ypres in October and November, the Ecole de Bienfaisance had been one of the main centre for treating wounded soldiers and was operated by the medical staff of 3 Field Ambulance. Over 5,000 soldiers were treated there until the hospital was evacuated on 6 November 1914.*]

24th February. About an inch of snow on the ground. One of our batteries in front of the reformatory was shelled rather badly with some big shells. One gun was knocked out and several people killed. A gunner Major came in wounded. Went down to Brigade HQ in the Square at Ypres to get some whale oil to rub the men's feet in to avoid frost bite.

Regiment ordered up into the reserve trenches for one night. Marched about 6pm. Clear moonlight. Got shelled a bit on the road to Zillebeke but they didn't seem to explode properly – didn't hit the road. Zillebeke absolutely in ruins – never saw such a desolate looking place. Church tower standing. Holes made by 'Jack Johnson's' as big as small duck ponds all along the road. A few stray bullets whistled over beyond the village. Stopped at 'Lord Cavan's dugout' where there was a sort of rough dressing station. Went on to our place in some larch woods. One squadron just in front of us and the other two away some distance on each side. I think they were digging a support trench.

Regimental HQ in a perfectly beautiful dugout made of pine logs; sort of redoubt place all round with pine logs and sand bags and a splinter proof roof. Plenty of room inside for 5 of us and 4 or 5 servants. Not high enough to stand up. Very cold night – freezing. Had no blanket. Quiet night – a little firing.

25th February. Beautiful morning, sun shining, birds singing. Looked like the sort of place you read about in books about red Indians and log cabins. Ground white. Strolled about. The advanced trenches hidden by the trees and hill. In the afternoon was sitting inside the dugout. The Huns suddenly burst 3 or 4 shrapnel just over us. Wild scramble for the dugout! You couldn't hear them coming. Apparently fired at close range. After dark the 9th Lancers took over. Back to billets. Men all given a hot bath and soup.

26th February. Moved into better billets in Ypres – Rue St Jacques. Had a sitting room with a nice bright open fire burning. Most of the tower and walls still standing; roof gone. Cathedral ditto. Quite a lot of shops open and going strong. Several quite good restaurants; lots of civilians, although the place gets shelled almost every day. Lentillhac got a frost bitten foot and went back to billets at Meteren.

28th February. In the evening went up to the trenches, about a mile north east of Zillebeke. We were on the right of the Brigade, the French on our left. A French battery working with us. Got into my dugout and had some supper. A fair amount of rifle fire going on. 'Star shells' going up most of the time making it as light as day. Rifle fire making a funny sort of echoing sound in the trees and hills. Sounds like the sea at low tide – not a bit like rifles. Slept like a top.

1st March. Regimental HQ in dugouts on the lee side of a hill so quite out of sight of the German trenches. There was straw on the floor and earth thrown on top making it splinter proof. [My dugout] was about 7 feet long and about 4 feet broad and about 3 feet high. I rigged up a ground sheet under the ceiling to catch the drips and lay on the straw and read novels and had my meals handed in to me. There were dugouts just below under a bank, enough to hold 2 reserve squadrons. Quite safe. Could hardly be hit by anything except howitzers. Communication trench started just by my dugout straight up to the fire trenches about 100 yards in front.

Quite a fine view behind to Ypres. Could just see the Mont des Cats on our right in the distance. 'Lord Cavan's dugout' about a quarter of a mile behind us on the road on the next hill. During the morning the Huns shelled it hard with small high explosive shells over our heads for about 10 minutes. Strolled up into the trenches. Quite good trenches, quite wide, plenty of room. Most of them had plenty of dugouts all along.

The right hand trenches were rather wet – about a foot and a half of water up one end and a corpse half buried in the mud. The rest of the trenches pretty dry – in some places floored with pine and quite dry. Plenty of sandbags piled up on the parapet. All the men using periscopes and looking through. Could see the German sandbags about 100 to 200 yards away, in some places, smoke from cooking fires. In between a lot – 100 or so – dead Germans and a few French soldiers. Had been there since November. Also the remains of a cottage all smashed up. Trees all splintered up by shell fire. A little sniping going on. I watched a loophole in a steel plate and saw a blighter pot through it. At dusk, took one or two sick and one or two slightly wounded to 'Cavan's dugout' where they were met by light ambulance wagons from Ypres. Rifle fire started again as soon as it got dark.

2nd March. Went round the trenches. Letters and parcels come up every morning with the rations.

4th March. Germans got into our trenches with some high explosive shrapnel. Some men hit. Went up with Corporal West, my orderly, to see what was the matter. They had got the range absolutely plumb. Sandbags knocked in and a gap made in the parapet; the machine gun there smashed. One man, Chilton, dead, another had a bad splinter wound in the head. Still shelling hard. Some more men hit further to the left. Dressed these men and then lay low in a dugout. [Shells] kept bursting all around, knocked some more sandbags in. Another man got killed just by us. When they stopped, went back to my dugout. At dusk got the wounded men to Cavan's dugout. Awful job getting one man down the communication trenches, very narrow and crooked. Had to be carried in a blanket.

Rather exciting this evening. On the left of the Brigade our miners had mined right up to the German trenches and were to blow them up this evening. Was on my way to Cavan's dugout. Terrific fusillade going on – bullets whizzing about our head like gnats. A lot of shelling going on, one or two very near our dugouts. Didn't notice when the mine went off, but I believe about 20 Germans went up, legs and arms flying about. A troop of the Queen's Bays got into the hole but had to come back as the French mine hadn't gone off or something.

Got relieved by the French about 8pm. Got away about 10 and back to billets about 11.

5th March. Left by motor busses about 7pm, back to Meteren by 11pm. Glad to get into a nice comfortable bed again. The men all in the afternoon in Ypres. In the morning quite a lot of shells came into the town. I saw one shrapnel burst over the square when I was there.

6th March–22nd April. Billet life again for a few weeks. Saw the sick each morning and rode around the billets. The squadrons did training each morning. During March Captain Carton de Wiart came out and took command of B Squadron. He was away from the regiment at the beginning of the war fighting in Somaliland, where he lost an eye. He was very popular with the regiment.

[On 14 March] we suddenly heard a tremendous bombardment a little to the south of Ypres. It started suddenly and was quite continuous and I think was the heaviest bombardment I had heard up to then. I walked up the Mont des Cats and watched the shrapnel burst in the distance. This was the German attack on St Eloi when they took 'The Mound' [*a bank of high ground formed when the nearby railway line was constructed and which gave good observation over the surrounding area*]. Phillips was in our counter attack which I think was only partly successful. [*The German attack began at 5pm. Several hours later, troops of the 82nd and 80th brigades of 28th Division finally launched a counter-attack after midnight which succeeded in recapturing the village and some of the surrounding trenches. The Mound, however, could not be retaken. The Germans had strongly consolidated their hold on the position during the lull in the initial fighting. A further German offensive was successfully repulsed on 17 March.*]

Next morning [15 March] the whole Brigade was turned out and saddled up and rendezvoused at Berthen and waited for orders. The 1st Cavalry Division was I think in Army Reserve. Lentillhac, Golliwog and I sat in a barn where Lenti taught us French songs. Later we drifted into an estaminet and had coffee and omelettes. Finally, I suppose we were not wanted and we got orders to return to billets, but to be ready to move off at 2 hours notice.

For the next few weeks we were 'standing to' most of the time and once or twice were turned out, but these turned out to be false alarms.

During April and May 1915 a series of heavy battles were fought in and around the Ypres salient which collectively become known as the Second Battle of Ypres. It was an enormously significant engagement. The Germans used gas for the first time in the war on 22 April against the allied line at Poelcapelle and Langemark.

The German tactics employed during the battle would also come to typify the attritional nature of trench warfare on the western front. Tactics were methodical but largely predictable. An attempt would first be made to destroy the enemy's defensive positions by concentrated artillery fire, with the occasional use of gas and mines. The infantry would then launch their own attack. The element of surprise would usually be the first casualty. Whenever a position was captured by the infantry it would be immediately consolidated for defence against counter-attack prior to any subsequent advance.

The Germans took full advantage during the Second Battle of Ypres of their superiority over the Allies in artillery and took a heavy toll in British lives – over 2,000 officers and 57,000 men were killed, missing or wounded. After inflicting these huge losses on the British Army and gaining some strategically important ground, the Germans eventually gave up the struggle at Ypres in May for want of men and ammunition. Their resources were needed elsewhere – on the Russian front and to hold off the Franco–British attacks further south. By the end of May the British too were down to just a few thousand rounds of high-explosive ammunition for their guns. All that was left was a little shrapnel. Large-scale British offensive operations would be effectively suspended until the autumn, once ammunition stocks had been replenished.

23rd April. Woken up at 4am. Orders to be ready to turn out at once. The regiment paraded and marched to Berthen and halted. Heard that the Germans had attacked north of Ypres using poisonous gas, the effects of which were felt as far as two miles behind the front line. Enemy said to have advanced about 3 miles taking the Pilkem heights which threaten Ypres.

Marched past Poperinghe to some reserve trenches about a mile short of Elverdinghe. Arrived about 4pm. After several false starts we had all finally come away without any kit, thinking this was another false alarm. Wind very cold. Waited about here for two hours. Sent back for my kit and my 'British Warm'. About 6pm went back to a farm and bivouacked for the night. We all slept in a shed – one of the coldest nights I have ever spent.

24th April. Reveille about 4am. Saw a lot of aeroplane shelling. About 9am walked up to Elverdinghe to hold some reserve trenches just beyond the village. Halted in the village to draw ammunition, spades, picks etc. All at once they began to shell the village with 'coalboxes'. The squadrons were withdrawn just behind the village into some meadows by the brook. One man had been hit near the brook. Was dressing his arm when some more shells came and one landed right in the middle of B Squadron in the soft earth at the edge of a dyke. Unfortunately 3 men were killed and poor Brown also. The bodies were blown right up in the air and fell about 50–80 yards from the place. One came down just behind me. Only one other seriously wounded. Captain de Wiart was talking to Brown and was knocked clean over but was quite undisturbed – didn't even lose his stick. Shows the local effect of these kind of shells in soft ground. Went on shelling hard, but most of them over towards the chateau and no one else hit. The regiment went on to dig trenches just beyond the village. Expected the Germans to come through but they did not attack. Got some mattresses on the floor and slept well. Was talking and ragging with Brown only an hour before he was killed. Seems awfully sudden.

25th April. Relieved. Marched to a wood near Eykhook with the 9th Lancers to remain here in reserve. Bivouacked outside in the wood around a beautiful fire.

26th April. At 2pm a tremendous bombardment began. For an hour, the biggest artillery row I've ever heard – French and our counter attack. Continuous roar of guns till about 7pm. Cold night. Still in the wood.

27th April. Wet flannel masks being made and served out, to protect from asphyxiating gases. Bivouacked in the same place in the wood again.

28th April. About 7am, orders to saddle up. Watched a lot of aeroplanes coming over and the guns potting at them. Seem more German than allied aeroplanes. Left our wood about 9 and marched to another wood behind the chateau at Proven, about 3 miles north west of Poperinghe. Very hot. Sun shone all day. Marched off again in the afternoon and got into billets late at night about a mile south of Wormhoudt [*about 5 miles to the west*]. On the way we passed one of the Indian cavalry divisions which included the 7th Dragoons, sister regiment of the 4th and the men met a good many of their pals.

29th April–5th May. Quite a nice billet for HQ – a farm and grocer's shop and estaminet combined, on the main road to Wormhoudt. Major Sewell took over command. We spent three or four very peaceful days here and then moved to very bad billets just west of Wallon Cappel, between Hazebrouck and Cassel. My new gramophone had just come out.

6th May. About 4 in the afternoon got sudden orders to saddle up and ride up to Ypres to dig reserve trenches. Got there just after dark. Left our horses in a field somewhere near Brielen and went on on foot. Crossed the canal. A big fire was burning with a red glow in Ypres about a mile up the canal to the right. Walking along the canal bank I fell into a deep trench which I mistook for the path. Got a horrible shock but didn't hurt myself much. The squadrons were put on to dig a little in front of the canal bank. Sat on the ground with Lentillhac and watched the fire in Ypres.

Quiet night. A few spent bullets dropping. About every 15 minutes a shrapnel swished over our heads with a bright kind of streak of flame and burst a few hundred yards behind – just about the road we should have to go back along. One had gone just over our head as we came up. We knocked off just about dawn and went back. I heard one shell go over as we crossed the canal and wondered if we should get clear before the next one came. We were almost past the place and just coming to a house at the corner when there was a sudden whiz and a flash just behind, calls for 'medical officer' and I found a lot of men had been hit.

I dressed them behind the shelter of the house, where I found Griffin with his 3 light ambulances and he took them away. Butler [*a subaltern in the 4th Dragoons*] was slightly wounded. Altogether 25 men were killed or wounded by that shell, also an officer of the 18th Hussars (abdominal) and 2 or 3 others.

7th May. It was now quite light and I rejoined the regiment in the meadow with the horses. We spent the day lying about on the grass. In the evening went up and dug again at the same place – this time by a cross country track. The fire in Ypres was still burning. Quiet night. Came back to the horses at dawn, got mounted and rode right back to our old billets at St Jans Cappel.

8th May. Nice fine day. Settled into our old billets and imagined we were out for a good rest. Had had no sleep for the last two nights and so was glad to get to bed in nice clean sheets tonight.

The 28th Division had suffered heavily during the last few days of fighting in the front line around Wieltje and Potijze as the fighting for the Frezenberg Ridge, a gently rising slope two miles to the north east of Ypres, began to develop. It was decided to send up the 1st Cavalry Division to support it. The main body of the 1st Cavalry Division was sent into a trench system known as the 'GHQ line'. Built by the French, it was a strongly constructed second line of defence around

Ypres, running from Zillebeke Lake, northwards to a point about half a mile east of Wieltje, from where it turned in a north-westerly direction, covering Boesinghe village and railway bridge. The real strength of the line was its wire defences, a continuous belt some twenty feet wide. Henry's regiment was sent to join the infantry of 85th Brigade in the forward positions around Potijze.

9th May. Was enjoying a jolly good sleep when I was woken up by an orderly in the room – at 2.30am. Orders to turn out at once! Crawled out of bed, got dressed, got mounted. Nice sunny morning. Regiment marched to Vlamertinghe, left our horses here and went on on foot. Went through Brielen. Heard coalboxes bursting in front. Had to walk down some meadows to the canal, shelled all the way with coalboxes (5.9 howitzers), some over us and some short. Near the canal, one had landed just in the track and half a dozen of the 18th Hussars were lying dead in a ring round the shell hole. Dressed one or two wounded under the canal bank then went on over the pontoon bridge. The canal looked beautifully cool and blue. Went on up the meadows beyond, shells still falling all about. One fell a little behind me. Shouts of 'medical officer!' Went back and saw 3 men hit. Began to dress them and heard a shell come right at us. It landed about 10 yards over us and only threw mud over us. Got these men into a battalion aid post in the village of St Jean. If they had shelled us with shrapnel we should have had a lot of casualties. These big things did very little damage in the soft ground.

Went on to catch up the regiment, through the village of Potijze. Houses knocked about, trees and branches lying about over the road, dead horses, unpleasant smells – unpleasant place. Found the regiment waiting at the far end of the village. Waited here rather a long time. Pretty quiet but some stray things flying about. Very thirsty. Got a drink out of O'Donnell's water bottle. Some infantry coming out of some dugouts and trenches about a couple of hundred yards away got badly shelled. Just after, another party of infantry coming along the road got a shell right in the middle of them – a lot of them badly wounded. Got some stretchers and went and found 6 or 8 badly hit and brought them back behind a house and dressed them. Went back into the village and found a dressing station where there was an old London Hospital man who took them in.

In the afternoon went into some reserve trenches just to the right of the White Chateau at Potijze. HQ in a good dugout behind a farm house. A good many shells came over but no one hit. Most of them trying for our batteries behind. Bursting in groups of four.

Lay down and was hoping that I would get some sleep during the night when I heard a message coming through the 'phone – the 4th Dragoons to take over front line trenches tonight. Had to dash about and get a lot of respirators, made of gauze and stuffed with cotton waste soaked in solution of hyposulphite of soda in a bucket and served out to the squadrons.

Had some food and about 11.30pm went up the road and halted at some broken down houses about a mile beyond the chateau. The guides who were supposed to show us our trenches hadn't turned up. Major Sewell, Captain de Wiart, Golliwog and a couple of orderlies went on up the road to investigate. We waited for some minutes when Golliwog dashed back very excited with a revolver in his hand, and just after Major Sewell came along helping De Wiart who was using awful language. He had been badly wounded in the left hand and wrist. I got him on a stretcher and dressed it as well as I could in the dark and gave him some morphia and sent him off down the road to the dressing station at the chateau. [*The injury was a serious one necessitating the amputation of de Wiart's hand.*]

What happened was that they had walked right into the German lines; they were challenged and a volley was blazed at them. Only de Wiart was hit and they were very lucky to get away as the Germans went on blazing away. Golliwog fought a tremendous rearguard action with his revolver and apparently they were very lucky to escape also.

Finally got the squadrons into their front line trenches and the relief complete, and just as it was beginning to get light the CO and HQ went off to find some HQ dugouts. Verey lights were still going up. The ground was a mass of shell holes – one or two dead men. It was nearly light when we found a row of dugouts near some tall trees and a cuckoo began singing close by. Just then a messenger came up and said we had some men hit in B Squadron trench. Major Sewell asked me to go and see them. Took Harding, my servant with the 'monkey box' [*containing emergency medical supplies*] and followed the guide down two or three fields to a barn. He pointed vaguely out of the open door at the back and said 'now you crawl'. He wasn't coming any further.

It wasn't light enough to see any trench, but I proceeded to crawl, followed by Harding with the 'monkey box' on his back. I had on a Tommie's greatcoat which I had picked up as I hadn't any coat with me, so didn't mind getting dirty. Crawled down a big hole where there was some straw and a dead horse, then up again and into another hole where there was a dead soldier. Began to hear bullets whistling over our backs. Made rather better going over an old stubble field for about a hundred yards and then saw heads in front sticking up out of the ground and some earth thrown up. Recognised Lillingstone [*a subaltern*] who told me to keep low and guided me a little to the right where the parapet was a little higher. Just then, 3 or 4 men who were also trying to get into the trench, got up and made a rush for it and one got hit through the stomach.

Slid into the trench and found the man I had come to see was dead. I dressed the man who had been hit in the stomach [*Staff Sergeant Warwick*] and gave him morphine. Dressed two or three others who were wounded. There was also an infantry man, hit in the head, who was dying. Quite out of the question now to go back, so settled down in the trench.

It was quite a fresh dug trench, no sandbags, no communication trench to get in by, no dugouts and I think stopped short of the road, where there was a gap between it and the next one of some breadth.

Had to sit cramped up in the narrow trench from about 4am, all day. We got hold of an entrenching tool and a spade and scooped out a small hole under the parapet which gave us a little more room. There was nothing to do and no rations had come up last night – altogether I was rather 'fed up'. Tried to sleep but people kept passing along the trench and they began shelling us with whiz bangs with a nasty metallic bang and some 4.2s which gave me a headache.

During the morning we heard a tremendous roar of rifle fire on our left and thought an attack was on, but found it was an ammunition dump near the road which had got on fire. It went blazing away for quite a long time. One or two men in the trench were hit as the enemy shot at everybody who showed his head over the parapet. Lillingstone had some bread with him and we dug up a tin of Maconochie ration out of the bottom of the trench which we ate cold with the bread.

Three shots hit the back of the trench where we were and made a definite sharp explosion with a distinct smell of burnt powder. Whether they were explosive bullets or whether they were bullets which hit some rounds buried in the earth in the parados, I never discovered.

It was a clear sunny day and about the slowest day I ever spent. About 8.15pm it was pretty dark and I crawled out and got back to HQ where I found my stick that I had carried all the war and was afraid I had lost. I also found we were to be relieved. Gibb (another young subaltern) was shot through both temples bringing up the ration party. They got fired on coming up and no rations got up that day. He lay unconscious all day in a shell hole. Two orderlies were sent to fetch him but both got killed. If I could have got to him, which is doubtful, of course I could have done nothing for him.

I went back to the trench and got two stretcher cases out, which was a rough business as the ground was all shell holes and the Germans were quite close by and star shells kept going up. We had about 5 men killed and 2 officers and about 10 wounded.

Walked back to a chateau between Vlamertinghe and Ypres. Got into a big room, me and the 9th Lancers and all had a jolly good supper. Slept like a top.

11th May. The whole Brigade in the chateau, the men bivouacking. The lilac all out in the garden. Went up and saw them at 1st Cavalry Field Ambulance.

12th May. Another beautiful day. Up to the trenches again at dusk. Just as we were starting, had to draw a big case of flannel smoke helmets with talc eye pieces. Hadn't time to issue them so took the case up to the trenches. Got into a rotten lot of trenches between Wieltje and Potijze. The 9th Lancers and 18th Hussars were on our left. We were in reserve but our trench was continuous with the trenches of the 9th. The 5th Dragoons came in somehow on our right flank. HQ was in the trench with a door overhead for a roof.

The Germans launched a massive attack against the British line on the Frezenberg Ridge, attacking the line held by the 1st Cavalry Division, the 27th Division and the 4th Division. The cavalry were holding about a mile and a half of the front line from Bellewarde Lake to Wieltje. The trenches were very poorly constructed, as they had been made in haste and under heavy fire. There were no communication trenches and there were practically no wire defences in front of the firing lines. The rain was also incessant, reducing the trenches to a quagmire. The Germans broke into the British line in places during the day, but were gradually driven out again in many places by counter-attacks. Unrelenting enemy artillery and machine-gun fire throughout the day made it impossible to remain in the old British front line and a new defensive position was occupied 1,000 yards to the rear, consisting largely of shell holes on the reverse slope of the ridge. The cavalry lost heavily in the severe fighting, although the 1st Cavalry Division escaped relatively lightly, with just under 500 either killed or injured.

13th May. At 4am they began to shell us and simply plastered the whole line with every kind of shell, chiefly high explosive, and never stopped until 4pm. Looking along the line there seemed to be a continuous wall of shell bursts, brown and yellow and black. In the middle of all the commotion, Barrie, the CO's servant, appeared with a cheerful grin and a steaming breakfast which he politely but firmly insisted on the CO and everyone eating. We were just sitting down to it when Golliwog was hit in the side of the head by a small splinter from somewhere and collapsed on the ground unconscious. He looked awfully bad at first and was unconscious for some hours. In the afternoon he recovered a good deal and could write but couldn't speak.

During the morning, Major Sewell was hit in the thigh and Major Pilcher took over command. We were very lucky. Most of the shells seemed just over or just short. The 9th got their trenches blown in and got very heavy casualties. In the afternoon, Graham came up from his dressing station in a cottage a few hundred yards behind us. While he was with us we watched 3 or 4 shells go bang into the roof of his cottage. Two or three wounded men in it came out and ran away across country.

A little later the shelling got heavier still and we thought they were going to attack. Every man was ordered to fix bayonets and man the fire step. Barrie dashed out with his rifle, greatly delighted. The 18th Hussars, who had been getting it awfully hot, left their trenches, all except two troops, and came back on our left. Some of the 5th Dragoons left their trenches and came back through us. Major Pilcher shouted to the 4th to stand fast. It was rather an exciting moment and I wondered what was going to happen. Some armoured motor cars dashed up the road on our right and I believe did very good work with machine gun fire and then dashed back (I didn't see them). At any rate, no Germans came over on our front.

Two of our squadrons were sent up to hold a line of shell holes in front. Barrie, who was making tea, went out over the parapet with another man and fetched in a wounded man of the 5th Dragoons. Just as they were getting him into the trench the other man was hit through the chest. I saw him, but he died soon after. Barrie wiped his hands and went on making the tea as if nothing had happened. He was really wonderful all day. He really kept people's spirits up wonderfully.

The shelling slacked off after 4pm and by night it was quite quiet. Our casualties were only about 20. Ward came up to Graham's dressing station with ambulance wagons and took them away. We also got Gallagher away all right.

Lunan, MO to the 9th Lancers, was killed and I went up to help them get their casualties away. Their trenches were badly blown in and a good many dead lying about. I believe the 18th Hussars lost about half the regiment.

Chapman, MO to the Queen's Bays, was killed. I believe the 3rd Cavalry Division lost heavily. [*They lost over 1,000 men.*]

Were relieved about 9.30pm and shifted to reserve trenches (GHQ Line) in front of Potijze Chateau. It had begun to rain during the morning and rained all day and it was horrible trying to get about in the mud. The box of respirators was left behind and so was never used. Four of us crawled into a low splinter proof shelter for the night. I got rained on a good deal but kept my feet warm against a brazier and burnt my boots.

14th May. In the GHQ line. A fairly quiet day but got a certain amount of shrapnel over which burst very accurately and killed one man and wounded about 8 others. Graham had his dressing station today in a stable block of the Chateau and again got a shell right into it, but no one hurt. Relieved at dark and walked back to Vlamertinghe. Parts of Ypres around the square were burning and it really looked rather fine. They were burning dead horses in the streets. Got into some quite good huts near Vlamertinghe.

The regiment spent two quiet days resting.

17th May. In the evening went up to the trenches again. Ypres still burning as we passed through, the red glare lighting up the Cloth Hall and the Cathedral tower. One burning house fell in just as we were passing. Went into front line trenches between Hooge and the railway to the left. We were I think just to the right of the railway. HQ in a good dugout in Railway Wood. Aylmer up with us again, his knee more or less recovered. Major Pilcher commanding.

18th May. Cold wet day. Only one or two casualties. Did not have to go into the trenches. The left hand trenches very wet – waist deep. Barrie 'found' a pig in a deserted farm and we had pork chops, kidneys etc.

19th May. Used a deserted farm just behind as an aid post with another MO. There were some pigs running about in the yard. Two or three times some shrapnel came over and burst over the yard and they all scuttled under cover behind things till it was quiet again. Relieved at dark by the 9th Lancers. Went back to the GHQ Line. Had a good many sick after the wet. The two squadrons who had had the worst time went back in the Reformatory where the dressing station was. Graham got their clothes dried and got them hot Bovril. C Squadron were 48 hours in the trenches up to the waist in water.

20th May. Went up and joined the regiment in the GHQ Line. Quiet day. Two squadrons joined up in the evening and went to a line of dugouts along the edge of the Bellewarde Lake. Had a good dugout with tables and chairs.

21st May. A little shelling just behind us, otherwise quiet. The Germans were on the other side of the Lake. Waited with a rifle for a long time to see if I could shoot one, but didn't see any. [*Under the Geneva Conventions, medical officers were recognised as non-combatants, thus facilitating the release of captured medics back to their own lines, a practice widely observed by both sides during the early stages of the war. Henry's actions on this day would seem to be in direct conflict with his status under the international laws of war. He was, however, certainly not alone amongst doctors in the front line who sought on occasions to look for the opportunity to join the fighting.*] A few of our howitzer shells fell short into the Lake sending up big fountains of white spray. Relieved by some infantry at night and went into front line trenches in the garden of the Hooge Chateau. HQ in the cellars of the Chateau about 40 yards behind. Fairly good trenches, deep and narrow – no dugouts. The Germans in the trees just off in front. Went up to look at some Vermorel Sprayers filled with solution to spray out trenches after a gas attack.

The cellars pretty comfortable, one of them roofed with some French arched corrugated steel and a lot of bricks piled on top – 3 or 4 feet. Colonel Solly-Hood re-joined us here from England where he had been in hospital.

22nd May. Beautiful day. Swallows flying about. The Chateau must have been a very pretty place. Now smashed almost flat, a pile of stone and rubbish. The outhouses and stables behind still standing. Sat in the courtyard most of the day and had tea out there. Fearful stink every now and then – corpses or something.

23rd May. Another beautiful clear sunny day. A little sniping about the garden at night and a few casualties. One or two of a draft just up tonight were hit and went back after only a few minutes at the front. Relieved at dark by the 18th Hussars. Ambulances came up the Menin Road to within about three quarters of a mile of the Chateau. The dressing station still in the Reformatory.

At the last minute we were ordered to stop in Ypres. The regiment went into some enormous casements or vaults in the canal ramparts not far from the Menin Gate. The vaults were big enough to hold a Brigade. We got to sleep around 2am.

24th May. At 3.30 was woken up and smelt a strong smell of chlorine gas. Everybody turned out and put on the gauze respirators. Immediately after, all our batteries opened fire. At the same time the Germans began to shell our batteries in front of the canal and shells kept crashing into the houses and the church just behind us. Went up to the Menin Gate. Lots of infantry coming down the road more or less gassed – some very bad. A lot were stopped and sent back. No one knew what had happened so our machine guns were got up onto the ramparts to command the road in case of accidents. General Mullens [*commanding 2nd Cavalry Brigade*] was here, a bit gassed but carrying on. I got several of the gassed cases into one of the casements. They looked awfully bad, as if they couldn't live long. Sal volatile seemed to relieve them a good deal. [*Ammonium carbonate used as a powerful smelling salt.*]

The regiment was ordered to carry ammunition up to the GHQ Line and we went up to the Lille Gate and waited. A gunner officer here very kindly brought us some hot cocoa and sandwiches which we were very glad of as we had no rations. Some big shells were coming in and one very big one – the biggest shell explosion I have ever seen – landed just the other side of the canal. The detonation was tremendous and it made you feel a bit shaken all that way off. Earth, debris were falling into the canal for quite a long time after.

10 of our men bringing up ammunition were wounded by a shell back near the casements. Went back and dressed them and left them with the gassed infantry men in the casement. Barrie was there making tea as usual. Went back to the Lille Gate and found the regiment going up. Went over the bridge and past the hole made by the big shell in a meadow, as big as half a tennis court. Perhaps it was one of the famous 17 inch howitzers. Advanced up the railway line with ammunition. A good deal of shrapnel about.

A and half of C squadrons went into the GHQ trenches, immediately north of the Menin Road. HQ and the rest stopped in the railway cutting behind the small bridge there, which they shelled hard all day with shrapnel and whiz bangs – most unpleasant. During the day, fresh clouds of gas came down the cutting which made us cough and got into eyes and nose and made them smart badly and run. Some of the shells said to give out gas but I am not certain about it. It was a hot day and I had very little water, most of which I had given to some wounded.

Spent the whole day dressing wounded, our own men and infantry – Cheshire's, Buffs, Durham's etc and sending them off, if they could walk down the railway. I got into a bit of a hole scraped out in the side of the cutting which gave some more protection.

In the afternoon, the 27th Brigade came up to make a counter attack. The Cheshire's came up the cutting to our bridge, climbed up the bank to the left of the railway and advanced across the open by platoons, I suppose to get into the GHQ Line. It was wonderful to watch them go up – no fuss or muddle. Each time a platoon went over a hail of shrapnel came over and wounded came streaming back.

The Cheshire's came back again after a bit, again under heavy shrapnel fire and then advanced again on the right of the railway. I had several badly wounded in my dugout and two of them died. A Cheshire officer was brought down the bank, shot through the chest and died in a few minutes.

During a lull I walked along the bank to see the colonel. A whiz bang shot under the arch and burst about a yard off my left foot but didn't hurt me.

Captain Wright and Captain Wylie were coming up the Menin Road to join the regiment. Captain Wright got hit in the leg, so left Wylie to go on and came back. I dressed his leg and he went off to the dressing station. Captain Wylie was never seen or heard of again. Must have got a direct hit from a shell. O'Donnel [*subaltern in C Squadron*] was wounded and poor Boosey [*an officer in A Squadron*] was killed. Aylmer crocked his knee again and had to go back.

No rations or water. After dark things quietened down and the regiment went back. I went across and got in about 5 of our stretcher cases from the GHQ Line with the help of Graham who met me there with some bearers. Found Boosey's body in a trench. Could see no wound. Brought him back with the wounded down the Menin Road and into the Reformatory. There were a lot of wounded here.

After that went after the regiment at the casements and found they had gone back to huts in Vlamertinghe. I had left what little kit I had in the casements. Plodded after them, passed Major West on the way, and arrived about 2.30am.

A rotten day. Our casualties were about 70 men and 5 officers and no good was done. Got some food off the mess cart and turned in.

25th May. Up about 8am. Bad headache after the gas. Had a jolly good bath in the stream and felt better. Sat in the sun and caught a large number of pediculi [*lice*]. All the dugouts are infected with them and almost everybody got them. Sent Harding down to the Field Ambulance at Vlamertinghe and Major West kindly sent me up some clean clothes.

Very little gunning heard. After lunch Phillips turned up on his pony – very fit. Very glad to see him. Captain Edwards and Captain Grenfell, VC of the 9th Lancers were both killed yesterday at Hooge. The 9th Lancers MO was gassed. [*He died the next day.*]

28th May. In the evening the Brigade went back to billets by motor bus. I think everyone was very glad to get away. I certainly was. I never enjoyed a bus ride so much in my life. We went right back to our same billets about a mile south of Wormhoudt.

29th May. We settled down to have a quiet peaceful time in our billets. It was rumoured that we should not be sent into the line again for some [time] at any rate. Colonel Solly-Hood was pretty bad after his dose of gas and had to be sent into hospital. [*The battalion war diary of the 4th Dragoon Guards recorded that Henry ordered the CO to receive hospital treatment.*]

We were in a nice bit of country about 5 miles north of Cassel. We were a long way back, away from any other troops. The country was nice and quiet, and at this time of year very pretty. I think everybody was jolly glad to have a slack time and enjoyed the fine sunny weather after our month at Ypres.

The BEF was being steadily reinforced over the summer, building up its strength again in order to resume the attack against the enemy. Not until the end of September would it be in a position to begin offensive operations. Henry took full advantage of this quiet time.

In 3 or 4 days I got home on 72 hours leave, and again another 72 hours leave at the end of June.

The Field Ambulance were in Wormhoudt, quite a nice little town and Brigade HQ at a chateau just outside. Graham still with his ambulance at Brigade HQ. We rode into Cassel sometimes, a rather picturesque town built on the top of quite a large solitary hill sticking up in the middle of the level Flanders plain. We used to lunch at the 'Sauvage'. You can sit out on a balcony here in the summer and drink coffee and you look right away over the country below to St Omer and Bethune.

General Foch's HQ were in Cassel. He stabled his horses in the stables under the 'Sauvage'. There were no British troops then at Cassel.

I rode round the squadron billets every morning. In the evening we often played polo. The difficulty was to get a level smooth field.

12th July. We moved further back to very nice billets at Bollezeele. A nice clean little town and we and the 3rd Cavalry Field Ambulance had the whole place to ourselves. Lentillhac and I had a very nice bedroom in a wine merchants' house opposite the church. These were very nice people. They were always asking me to drink liquors and Madeira and used to send me up a very nice cup of tea every morning.

We had beautiful weather every day.

17th July. The 3rd and 1st Cavalry Field Ambulances arranged a dinner at Bollezeele to commemorate our landing in France a year ago. It was a great success. All the original 3rd were there except Major Irwin and Lathbury.

September. During August I applied for a change of duties to a Base Hospital. Vickers and Griffin had both gone down to one. In the early part of September I got my orders. I was very sorry to leave the Regiment and the Division, especially my little bay horse that I had ridden for 13 months. I handed him over to the care of McArthur, the vet.

I was posted to No. 11 General Hospital at Boulogne, where I found Vickers (MO of the 1st Field Squadron). I found life here was a complete change in every way. I was able to refresh my memory in medicine and surgery. The Hospital was in the Imperial Hotel, on the sea front. We lived in luxury in a very nice house let to us fully furnished with bed rooms, bathroom, billiard room, dining room, smoking room, etc, on the sea front at the north end of the town. We bathed in the sea whenever we wanted to, played a good deal of tennis and altogether had a good time and were not too busy.

On 25 September, the British launched a major attack on the Germans around the mining town of Loos, as part of a joint offensive with the French. It was the largest British attack of the war to date. The attack was mounted on the direct orders of the Secretary of State for War, Lord Kitchener, against the preferences of both Field Marshal French and General Haig, the First Army commander. French and Haig believed that the growing infantry and artillery resources of the BEF should be harnessed until the spring of 1916, when they could be unleashed against the Germans with greater impact in a more decisive encounter that could herald the end of the war. Both of these senior commanders were concerned that the BEF still had insufficient numbers of heavy guns and artillery to mount such an attack. They also felt that the urban and industrial nature of the proposed battlefield at Loos was not conducive to a large-scale infantry assault. They were right on both counts. The Battle of Loos was essentially fought for political reasons, in order to demonstrate support for the French armies who were attacking in great strength, but with equally limited effect, in the Champagne region further to the south.

The British used gas as a weapon for the first time at Loos, partly to make up for their deficiency in heavy artillery. It proved largely ineffective. The prevailing wind blew some of the gas back into the British lines. Six infantry divisions were involved in the initial attack, which was preceded by a four-day artillery bombardment. The bombardment inflicted some damage on the front-line German positions, but failed to destroy the heavily defended redoubts and strongpoints. The British made some important gains on the first day of the battle, particularly at the southern end of the battlefield around the village of Loos itself. Over 8,000 yards of German trenches were captured during the battle as a whole. They failed, however, to make the comprehensive breach of the German lines that had been planned. These early breakthroughs at Loos could not be exploited at the crucial moment in the fighting as the British had inadequate reserves in place to push forward the attack. This lull in prosecuting the attack allowed strong enemy reinforcements to arrive on the scene to bolster the German defences. The Germans launched highly effective counter-attacks against those pockets of British troops now occupying their former trenches. The fighting was intense. Much of it was hand to hand.

In an effort to try and break through, subsequent attacks were made on 26 September by two New Army divisions just landed in France, the 21st and the 24th, who had never even been in the front line before, let alone taken part in combat. They were disastrous failures involving enormous loss of life amongst the men of Kitchener's newly raised volunteers. In total, thirteen divisions were eventually plunged into the fighting. Between 25 September and 16 October, when fighting subsided, over 61,000 officers and men had been killed, wounded or missing. On the first day of fighting alone, over 20,000 cases were admitted to the field ambulances and casualty clearing stations. Before the battle started, it was estimated that the total casualties would be fewer than 40,000.

The outcome of the battle was a bitter disappointment to the BEF. There appeared to be no end in sight to the war. The strength of the German Army in conducting defensive battles was once again shown to be formidable.

Just after the Loos fighting, myself and 2 or 3 others were sent off at about an hour's notice with a light kit by car to No. 1 Casualty Clearing Station at Chocques for temporary duty. This CCS was in the Chateau de l'Abbaye where we had billeted one night in October 1914. The rush of cases was just quietening down when we got there and as there was about 14 or 15 MOs there altogether, there wasn't much for us to do. [*No. 1 CCS was the biggest in operation during the Battle of Loos and had the capacity to admit over 1,600 patients.*]

After about 3 days there, Wordley and I were sent off to No. 23 Casualty Clearing Station at Lozinghem where we found Vickers, also on temporary duty, also Attlee on the same job. [*This small CCS was under canvas in the spacious park of the chateau at Lozinghem and was initially equipped to admit 200 men. Two large hangars were later acquired from a neighbouring aerodrome, as well as a large wooden structure belonging to a travelling theatrical company, and were erected temporarily in the grounds of the chateau, allowing a further 300 cases to be admitted.*]

There were about 6 extra MOs here and very few cases were coming in now, so there was nothing to do. We expected to be sent back in 2 or 3 days, but the weeks went past and we still stopped there. The weather was wet and cold and we lived in chilly damp tents. We were miles from anywhere, there was nothing to do, the mess was bad and altogether we had a very boring time.

Towards the end of November, Vickers and I got back to No. 11 General Hospital and I applied at once for 14 days' 'special' leave (having done 12 months service and having signed on for another 12 months). I got away in 3 or 4 days and got in three very jolly days with the harriers at home. People were very good about lending me mounts.

I got back to France about 13th December and about 2 days later was sent up to report to the [head] of medical services at 19th Division and was posted to 57th Field Ambulance which I found at Vielle Chapelle, where we had been in October 1914. It was a 'K' Division [*one of the New Army divisions made up of volunteers who enlisted at the outbreak of war*] commanded by Major General Bridges (4th Dragoon Guards, left them on The Aisne). Major Powell commanded the Field Ambulance, the others were Special Reserve or temporary – Kidd, Smalley, Wilkinson, Dew, an Australian and second in command and Mackenzie.

The 57th Field Ambulance had arrived in France in the middle of July. On 6 August, the field ambulance became attached to the 56th Infantry Brigade. It began receiving its first cases – sick rather than wounded – in the first few days of August. Most of the sick were influenza cases. There was a steady trickle of wounded cases, but these never amounted to more than around 20 per cent of the caseload at any one time. For surgeons like Henry, this meant that there would be little practical doctoring to do.

Soon settled down to my new job. Quite a comfortable billet at a small brasserie in Vielle Chapelle. The line was very quiet and except for a certain number of sick, things were pretty slack. The usual landscape is a dark, sad looking expanse of flat ploughed land dotted here and there with farm houses each in a clump of poplars, stretching away to a low straight horizon broken here and there with a tall church spire.

We were running an advanced dressing station at St Vaast – just east of Richbourg St Vaast. After a week or 10 days, Smalley and I went up and relieved Kidd and St. Johnston. Motor ambulances ran right up to the dressing station, which was about a mile behind our front line along the Rue du Bois. It consisted of a dressing room built of timber and sandbags, proof against a small shell and with room enough to dress two cases on stretchers comfortably; accommodation for 6 stretcher cases and a few 'sitters' [*lightly wounded*] also dugouts to hold 50 or so bearers. There was also a sandbag room for the MOs, 'pipsqueak' proof with a tiled floor. We both slept and messed in it. There was a stove made out of a 'cresol' drum, the walls were covered with pictures and we were comfortable there. A cat and several kittens also lived there.

Nesbitt (South Wales Borderers), who was OC Trench Tramways had a very palatial dugout a few yards off. He had a bedroom with a bed and a washing stand and looking glass salvaged from some house in Richbourg; a smoking room with a fire place, walls about 7 feet high, a table, several easy chairs and a roller-topped writing desk and muslin curtains. He also had a bathroom with a bath 6 feet long and a boiler for heating water. These dugouts were made by the Lahore Division several months ago.

We spent a very peaceful time here. One of us usually went round the battalion Aid Posts each day which was a pretty comfortable walk and we had afternoons off in turn when we could ride back to Vielle Chapelle or Bethune or wherever we liked. We had very few casualties in, on average not more than half a dozen in 24 hours. Two or three of our field batteries behind us made rather a noise sometimes. The Hun occasionally sent a little shrapnel over to these. He also shelled Richbourg once or twice with heavy stuff, but beyond that the place was extraordinarily quiet.

31st December. Another New Year's Eve in Flanders. Five of us had dinner at the Advanced Dressing Station at St Vaast. Drank to the New Year. Our batteries all round let off a few New Year rounds for luck and the Bosch sent a few back – nearly all duds. Nice warm starlight night. Just as we came out two falling stars fell. A few flares were going up along the line, an occasional rifle shot with a long echoing sound, a few bursts of machine gun fire – otherwise the night was quiet.

By the end of 1915, each of the field ambulances had been given a new establishment of ambulance transport, which included seven motor ambulances and three horsed wagons. In addition, twenty wheeled stretcher carriers had also been provided, or were being provided for each division. As the BEF continued its offensive operations, the New Year would bring an enormous escalation in the scale and intensity of the fighting. These extra medical resources, and more still, would be needed to cope with the remorseless flood of casualties that 1916 would bring.

Chapter 3

Calm Before the Storm?
January–June 1916

On the whole, there was very little to comfort the Allies on the western front as the New Year began. The British had repeatedly flung themselves against the German lines during the course of several searing battles at Neuve Chapelle, Festubert, Aubers Ridge and at Loos throughout the spring, summer and autumn of 1915, with practically no effect whatsoever. The line had hardly moved at all. The Germans remained in possession of large parts of northern France and virtually all of Belgium. Despite desperate losses, it had proved impossible for either the British or French forces to bring about a breach in the enemy's defences.

Effecting such a breach remained the purpose and objective of Allied military strategy and operations in 1916. There was no other alternative open to France and Britain. It was not possible to manoeuvre around the system of trenches that had become so firmly established after fifteen months of warfare. Only through forcing a breach in the line would there be any prospect of securing a significant advance. Making this happen would be no easy task as most of the advantage still lay with the enemy. The basic truth was that the Germans occupied a better set of defensive positions than the Allies. In particular, the ground they held was usually higher, had better fields of fire and was less vulnerable to flooding than the trenches held by the British. It was politically unacceptable to the French for the British to improve their line by retreating to better prepared positions in the rear as this would mean ceding even more French territory to the aggressor. Instead, the Allied cause itself could only be improved by an advance through the opposing German trenches. This obviously implied more, not less, fighting. In any case, the overriding goal was to break the stalemate and, notwithstanding all of the obstacles, this was the only way to do it as there was no prospect of a political settlement to the conflict in sight.

The Germans enjoyed one other major advantage over the British in the early part of 1916, other than their general superiority of position and defences. Despite all the advances made by the British over the last year or so, the Germans were still better equipped in every department of trench warfare. They had better hand grenades, rifle grenades and trench mortars, and more of them than the British.

The first six months of 1916 saw episodes of heavy but localised fighting between the German and British armies on the western front. The British attacks were themselves conducted partly as a precursor to the main effort that was planned for the Somme front in the summer, and partly in response to German attacks in and around Ypres in February. These German attacks were originally conceived as diversions to their main assault at Verdun. They were more than just demonstrations. They took a significant toll in human life. Between the end of December 1915 and the beginning of the Battle of the Somme in July 1916, this fighting generated another 125,000 casualties amongst the BEF alone.

Henry would avoid most of the early fighting of 1916. During the first few months of the year, he found himself in the line around Neuve Chapelle. This had been the scene of feverish fighting in the spring of 1915 when the British had launched their first major offensive operation of the war. By 1916, it had settled down into being a relatively quiet part of the front. The two front lines had a permanent air about them. Each side would engage in trench raids and patrols in 'no man's land' at night in order to dominate the ground and hopefully gain a flow of intelligence by capturing prisoners and seizing papers.

Artillery and trench mortar fire was usually sporadic but deadly nonetheless. Both sides continued to use gas against each other, released directly from cylinders. It was a risky delivery mechanism as it relied ultimately on the prevailing wind to carry it in the right direction. Frequently, the gas would inflict more harm on those who had released it than those it had been aimed at. At the end of 1915 the Germans had used phosgene gas – far deadlier than chlorine – for the first time in their attacks against the British. The British responded by ordering a huge expansion in their own capabilities.

The 57th Field Ambulance was not particularly busy during the first few months of 1916. Most of the patients they treated were suffering from influenza as opposed to being injured on the battlefield.

The more junior doctors working with the field ambulances would frequently find themselves detached from the ambulance and sent to work with the various battalions and units of the division in order to provide medical cover. Over the next few weeks Henry would find himself working as medical officer with an infantry battalion and an artillery brigade. His duties in this capacity were to take a daily sick parade, and attend to any wounded or injured men.

1st January. Hacked over to Estaires to the 62nd Field Ambulance at Nouveau Monde. Phillips second in command here. Had lunch with him, did a little shopping in Estaires and back to tea.

2nd January. Damp drizzly day. Had to go temporarily to the 4th King's Liverpool Regiment (Territorials) who were in the front line just to the right of Neuve Chapelle, a little to our left. Took over from their MO, Mr Munro, very obviously from Montreal, Canada, who I think had completed a year's service and was going back to Canada.

Found the HQ dugout and Mr Munro and was told to 'come right in'. Comfortable dugout (very different from our Ypres days) with plenty of room for 4 of us to feed and bunks for two at the other end. The CO and the Adjutant came in and we had lunch. Mr Munro 'guessed he'd get his grip and quit' and he did so. There were two Companies in the line and two back in billets. I had to stop here two nights until these two Companies came out. The HQ dugouts were just to the left of the La Bassee road. The ruins of Neuve Chapelle were about 200 yards further to the left. In daylight you walked up a duckboarded trench running along the side of the road, past a few knocked out farms. At night almost everybody went down the road, although they machine gunned it pretty often.

Our batteries are sending a few shells over almost every day now as we seem to have as many batteries parked in behind our lines as the space will hold. After lunch the Hun sent the usual few 'pipsqueeks' over and one or two 'crumps' on Neuve Chapelle. They put a pipsqueak right into one of our machine gun emplacements and killed one man and wounded 4 others today.

Every man now carries the 'tube gas helmet', a flannel helmet treated chemically, covering the head and neck, fitted with glass eye pieces and a valved metal tube for the outlet of expired air.

Quiet night, very dark. We had a bombing stunt on. The idea was to bomb a suspected listening post. The spot was bombed by a party about 80 yards in front of our front line trench. No one there apparently and the thing seemed to be rather a washout.

Quite a long time since I had been in the trenches. The usual Verey Lights going up and an occasional poop off of one or two of our heavy guns. A little rifle fire with the usual long rattling echo. Then our motor machine guns just behind somewhere would start crackling off doing indirect fire over our heads on some cross roads or something.

3rd January. Nothing doing. Rather a bore sitting around doing nothing. The Major had some quite good port and plenty of whiskey. It was just eating and drinking and waiting for the next meal. Just after dinner had to see a man hit through the abdomen just outside on the La Bassee Road – machine gun I think. Obvious internal haemorrhage. Very noisy and restless. Sent him down the road to the ADS at Greenbarns but he died when he got there.

4th January. Strolled round part of the trenches. Most of the line about here approached by breastwork communication trenches half a mile or more long. Just here they were not so long. Went up Oxford Street into the fire trench. Very bad trench – merely a breastwork. Very good parapet in front but no use against enfilade shrapnel fire. In other places a little better but very wide and shelving. The Hun here is about 500 yards away. The Bois de Biez lies just out in front. All this section of trench well boarded underfoot and quite dry. Coming back scampered over the top and got into Hun Street half way down up to where it is trench boarded. Above this it is thigh deep in water. In all these trenches the approaches and dugouts very much better than any at 'Wipers' [*Ypres*] last spring. Of course this is now an old permanent line.

Last week I strolled down to the Rue du Bois trenches to the right. There were approach trenches (chiefly breastwork trenches) well boarded and wired underfoot (trench boards laid on U frames which also support the revetment) for half a mile behind. Very good dugouts in the ruined houses along the Rue du Bois. Went up a communication trench, Plum Street, about knee deep, into the fire trench. Rather bad trenches – wide and wet, over the ankles. Saw the Hun sandbags about 80 yards in front. Saw our gas cylinders buried in the trench under the parapet in groups of 8 or 10.

The two Companies of the 4th King's relieved this evening. Some muddle – two platoons went the wrong way and we had to wait 3 hours. Returned to the ADS about 8.30pm.

22nd January–12th February. Smalley and I handed over our ADS at St Vaast and re-joined HQ at Vielle Chapelle. The Field Ambulance marched to new billets at Robecq. The roads were wet – flooded in places. Good billets; a comfortable mess and a bedroom in the village for everybody.

Nice little village on one of the Flanders canals. Further along the canal – about 5 miles – is Bethune. Often rode into Bethune for tea and shopping. Rather nice town, fine church, very nice old quaint looking roofs on a lot of the houses and good shops. A very good tea shop for officers. Met Aizlewood and Lillington (4th Dragoons) there one day. The 2nd Cavalry Brigade doing a tour in the trenches about the Hohenzollern Redoubt. Next day rode over to Sailly la Bourse and saw the 4th Dragoons. Nearly all the same officers there, Colonel Sewell, Captain Ogilivy, Chance, McNeil, Greenhill, Mason, Farley, Wickham etc. Also saw Corporal West and Harding – all very fit. Had tea with Graham and Ward.

Had a very quiet time at Robecq. Not busy. Still within sound of the guns. Used to spend a good deal of time chatting to Victoria, a charming damsel in a small estaminet next door. She used to make us coffee and very good omelettes au rhum. She talked excellent English and was very amusing.

12th February. Went for temporary duty with the 8th Gloucester's while their MO, Chambers, was on leave. They were out of the line in Divisional Reserve close by at Hamel. Colonel Moore commanding. Next evening went to a show of the Divisional Follies at St Venant.

19th February. Regiment marched to billets in La Gorgue. Got a very comfortable bedroom over the school in the schoolmistress's house.

22nd February. Cold morning, sharp frost. Rode up the La Bassee Road to Croix Rouge with the CO and had a look at our HQ dugouts and Aid Post in a ruined farm (Ebenezer Farm). Dugouts much more elaborate and better than anything I had seen up to May 1915.

24th February. Two inches of snow on the ground.

24th February. Freezing hard, still 2 inches of snow. Beautiful sunny afternoon. Did a couple of rough sketches of the town. Went up to the trenches about 4.30pm. Got into Ebenezer Farm about 7.30. Very cold as we had not yet got any kind of a fire. Chambers suddenly turned up about midnight so cleared off to the Greenbarns ADS and spent a night there in the farm house with Miller and Johnston [*two doctors working with the field ambulance*].

25th February. Had lunch in Estaires and then walked down the canal bank to Merville where the Field Ambulance were now running the Divisional Rest Station.

26th February–17th April. Life was not strenuous here. The hospital – some huts in a meadow about 300 yards up the road – didn't occupy very much of our time and the rest of the day we filled in as we liked. We had one pretty sharp spell of frost and snow for 3 or 4 days. We did a few fatigues unloading coal barges on the canal at Merville which gave the bearer section a little exercise.

On February 29th I saw Captain de Wiart passing through Merville in a car. Just out again from England. His left hand had been taken off above the wrist but he is very fit and as keen as ever. He is coming to the 19th Division as second in command of the 7th North Lancashire's.

We had some nice weather in April. I used to walk about and ride a good deal. Walked to Hazebrouck and back one day. The Forest of La Neippe was close by. There were a lot of fallow deer in it, the leaves were beginning to come out and the blackbirds and thrushes were singing beautifully in the evening.

18th April. The Ambulance marched to billets for the night at Busnes. Walked into Lillers and had dinner with Burton at No. 6 Casualty Clearing Station.

19th April. Marched to Cottes, about 4 miles south west of Lillers – out of the flat country. Pretty place – beautiful trees – in the edge of a nice hilly country, like the South Down country at home. The whole Division out of the line for training. [*The division was being prepared for its eventual deployment in the Somme battle.*]

20th April–6th May. Our Field Ambulance was open for sick otherwise we had nothing to do. The Brigades were kept busy training. We had some wet weather at first. At the beginning of May we had some glorious warm spring weather. Our billets at Cottes were on the slope of a hill with orchards above and below and all round were some tall elms, limes and beeches, oaks and especially poplars. The swallows were all back, the nightingales singing everywhere and the cuckoo. We sat and basked in the sun and revelled in the spring weather. After a winter spent in the cold, wet Flanders mud one appreciates the spring.

Went over two or three times to the North Lancs and saw Major de Wiart and Wibberley, their MO.

7th May. Up at 6am. Motored to Lillers. Train started at 8.21 to Longeau near Amiens with 56th Brigade HQ. Went by motor ambulance to La Chaussee, on the Somme, about 6 miles west of Amiens. Picquigny on the opposite side of the river where there is a very big ruined chateau.

8th May–5th June. Colonel Powell turned up with the motor ambulances, next day about midday, the rest of the Ambulance from Longeau station in the evening.

We had a very good time here. Beautiful weather. The valley of the Somme was very pretty – about half a mile of low marshy ground with lots of poplars growing, also alder. High green hills on each side of the valley. We bathed in the Somme which had rather a swift current, and in some big pools or ponds in the marshes behind the village. Leech, the Roman Catholic padre and Bennett the Quarter Master spent a lot of their time fishing; lots of perch and tench. We rode a good deal as it was pretty open country on the hills around.

We went into Amiens pretty frequently, either hacked in or walked in by road or went by train from Picquigny. There were some good restaurants here and we often lunched or dined at The Rhin or a little place called The Chevallier in the Rue des Corps Nuds Sans Tetes where the cooking was very good.

The cathedral was very fine. Very fine decorations all over the façade. The doorways were all sandbagged up for protection. Some beautiful stained glass windows but I think most of the glass had been taken down and stowed away.

At La Chaussee on the hill overlooking the river was an old Roman camp – very like the one at Caistor at home – a big grassy rampart enclosing a square of 20 or 30 acres and the steep sides of the hills sloping away on two sides.

On Sunday, 14th May, the South Lancs held some sports there. Everyone was invited to be there and we had a very amusing afternoon. Tug of war for officers, wrestling on mules, balaclava melee on mules, 'V C' race, jumping competition (horses) I got second in the V C Race.

In the middle of May the weather was very hot indeed. Smalley, Fry and I spent three or four days training the bearer squads in collecting [the] wounded and bivouacked out two nights in pine woods near St Pierre and practiced collecting wounded by night. It was beautifully warm at night.

On 5 June Henry sent a birthday greeting letter to Darcey:

Many happy returns on the anniversary of your birthday. How old are you? I think I'm getting on for 30. It seems absurd as I haven't even got a moustache yet. How is yours? I'm sorry I can't send you a birthday present. I can't find anything nice. Many thanks for your letters. Sorry there is no news. I don't know about leave. I might get home almost any time or I might not get away for months. Of course there is no hunting but I'd like to get home just for a change and to see everybody.

Should like to get a leave next winter anyhow. This is an awfully nice place where we are – pretty country and a nice river and a town not far off. I find Alec Ficklin is not far from here. I must try and get over to see him.

My very best love,
Harry

[The Ficklin family were neighbours of the Owens in Long Stratton.]

6th June. Had to go off to do temporary MO to the 88th Brigade, RFA while Rhodes went on leave. Went by train to Abbeville and on in a car to Caours about 3 miles off on the road to St Ricquier. 88th Brigade in a rather nice house at Caours. Colonel Tovey commands the Brigade. Looked after three 18 pounder batteries and one 4.5" howitzer battery. Very pretty country here; a valley full of trees with a little trout stream which runs down to the Somme at Abbeville. Some of the fellows went down almost every evening and caught several smallish trout – chiefly about ½ pound size. Went down several times with Tovey, the Colonel's brother who had a fly rod.

On June 7th, watched a Brigade field day. Troops advancing in artillery formation, then extending etc and then ending with the assault. Had a chat with Barry (4th Dragoons), now General Bridge's orderly. Heard of the death of Lord Kitchener.

June 10th was a cold drizzly day. The Brigade did some wire cutting tests with shrapnel and high explosive. Very interesting to watch. A very few rounds of shrapnel cut it very effectively at about 800 yards.

The 88th Brigade, attached to the 19th Division, was preparing for its role in the Battle of the Somme. Acting in support of the 19th Division it would take part in both the preliminary bombardment and in the fighting that followed.

11th June. Beautiful fresh sunshiny day. The Brigade marched to new billets. Went along the Somme valley. Lunch by the roadside. Got into billets at Belloy and stopped two nights there.

13th June. Cold, wet and stormy. Marched to Behencourt. HQ for two or three days at the chateau here then moved into a billet in the village where they had a big kitchen garden full of strawberries. We ate strawberries morning, noon and night.

We went out about 4am three or four mornings and the Batteries did practice with live rounds on the practice range. They galloped into action and opened fire from different ranges, on objects on a hillside – hedges, woods etc. The fire [was] directed by the observation officer – the Battery commander – from the top of the hill where I was. I learnt quite a lot about 18 pounders, how they are sighted, dial sights, and about fuses, correctors, ranges etc. Also how the range, angle of a target is found by the observation officer.

Chapter 4

The Battle of the Somme
July 1916

Planning for a major Anglo-French campaign of 1916 had begun in December 1915, shortly after Haig had succeeded French as Commander in Chief of the British Expeditionary Force. Despite the huge losses at Loos, the steady build up of the BEF continued throughout 1915 with more British and Canadian divisions arriving on the western front. The British would be in a position to resume offensive operations as soon as there were sufficient reserves of men and munitions – 1916 was set to be a year of major conflict along many parts of the front.

It was on the banks of the Somme River that the French and British armies joined up and where they could therefore attack alongside each other in a display of Allied unity. Haig would have preferred to have mounted his attack elsewhere than on the Somme. The politics of coalition warfare dictated otherwise.

The original plans for an attack in the Somme area involved a very large French offensive south of the river which would be supported by a subsidiary British attack to the north. The powerful German attack at Verdun in February 1916, however, quickly put paid to these plans. The attack planned for the Somme became less of a French and more of a British affair, as French manpower and resources were needed at Verdun. The planning mutated into an essentially British-led campaign to relieve pressure on the French army, who were grimly holding on at Verdun – now the symbol of French resistance against the invader. It was not an exaggeration to claim that the outcome of the war once again hung in the balance.

Field Marshal Sir Douglas Haig had ambitions to do more than just come to the aid of Britain's principal ally. Despite the more cautious attitude of his subordinate commanders, Haig planned a breakthrough battle. The massed ranks of Kitchener's New Army would be used to smash through the three lines of

German defences, allowing the cavalry to pour into the breach, threatening the enemy's lines of communication and endangering his entire frontal defensive system in France.

The five corps of General Rawlinson's Fourth Army, with eleven divisions in the line, would spearhead the assault on a sixteen-mile-long front stretching from Maricourt Wood, close to the Somme River in the south, to just below Hebuterne in the north. One corps of the Third Army would mount a diversionary attack to the north at Gommecourt. General Gough, commanding the Reserve Army, had three divisions of cavalry ready to exploit any success.

British planning for the battle went through several iterations before it was finally settled. Rawlinson himself was inherently much more cautious than Haig in his planning for the battle and envisaged a step by step advance through the German lines. Haig essentially overruled Rawlinson and by early June the stage was set for the greatest British campaign of the war. The newly raised divisions of the British Army would come up against some of the toughest troops in the world.

A campaign on this scale would require an unprecedented effort on the part of the RAMC. The RAMC had already learned a great deal since the early days of the war. The high numbers of casualties led to continuing changes to the way its services were organised. The experience so far was clear – unless casualties could be sent quickly to the main hospitals in the rear, there was only a small chance of being able to minimise death and serious injury. Regimental stretcher bearers were therefore doubled in size from sixteen to thirty-two. Relay bearer posts were set up at roughly 1,000-yard intervals. Special communication trenches were reserved for the wounded (although this inevitably broke down during the battle itself due to the enormous number of dead and wounded soldiers). Regimental aid posts – the units closest to the fighting – were made more elaborate with greater protection and accommodation.

By this time in the war, casualty clearing stations had become better equipped in both material and personnel as extensive operative surgery became much more common. Sites for the CCSs were selected near to the main railway lines, enabling the specially adapted ambulance trains to take their patients away to hospital for longer-term treatment as quickly as possible.

For the Somme campaign, sixteen casualty clearing stations were established in the battle area itself. Most of them were housed in tents, but some were in huts erected by the RAMC. The field ambulances organised nineteen main dressing stations – in houses, in the ruins of houses and in any other cover that could be found. Thirty-nine advanced dressing stations were also set up in or near the front line itself, usually in dugouts. All of these resources would be tested to the limit in the weeks and months ahead.

Haig had selected a very strongly held part of the German line to press home his attack. Many people saw it as the most strongly defended section on the entire western front. There were two completed lines of trenches and wire defences, with a third already under construction. The second line lay between 2,000 to 4,000 yards behind the front line and was largely hidden from direct observation from the British positions. This hidden line was well within the range of the British guns, but in practice proved to be beyond the range of the gunner's capabilities to destroy. A five-day bombardment had been planned to precede the infantry assault. This was extended by a further two days to compensate for poor weather and the difficulty experienced by the RFC in observing the accuracy and effects of the gun fire.

Even though the British had concentrated over 2,000 guns, few were of sufficiently heavy calibre to destroy the numerous strong German bunkers which had been dug deep into the chalk soil. In these shelters the enemy's machine guns and crews were hiding, ready to emerge with deadly effect as soon as the bombardment came to an end. Most of the British guns were 18-pounders – standard field artillery. On such a long front, even 2,000 guns were inadequate for the task in hand. Neither did the bombardment involve the proper mix of high-explosive and shrapnel shells. The British gunners attempted to clear away much of the wire defending the German lines using shrapnel shell. These efforts, not surprisingly, proved ineffective, seriously hampering the ability of the attacking infantry to move quickly across no man's land. To make matters worse, many of the shells were dud and failed to explode.

The British attack also lacked any element of surprise. It was not just the heavy bombardment that alerted the enemy to the prospect of an infantry assault. The British had made no secret of the build up of troops and guns and the mountains of supplies needed to support them. German reconnaissance aircraft had a ring-side seat to the whole project weeks before a single shot had been fired.

At 7.30am on the morning of Saturday 1 July 100,000 British soldiers began their attack on the German trenches. Row upon row of khaki figures stepped up the ladders out of the shelter of their trenches and walked headlong into a hailstorm of shells and bullets.

On the front of the XIII Corps in the south, the 30th and 18th divisions, aided by the heavy guns of the French artillery, made heroic progress and broke through the German lines up to a depth of two miles. Elsewhere, little progress was made. At the northern end of the front, around Serre and Beaumont Hamel, the British troops failed to get into the German front line at all. The same was largely true in the centre of the front being attacked around La Boisselle, Ovillers and Thiepval. Pockets of British troops managed to gain toeholds in the German lines in some places but most were driven out again by counter-attacks later in the day. The focus of the battle over the next few weeks would concentrate on the southern flank where British troops had enjoyed their greatest success.

The result of these failures was a catastrophic level of casualties. Nearly 20,000 officers and men were killed, most in the first couple of hours of fighting. A further 36,000 were wounded. In the first twenty-four hours of the battle, 26,675 wounded soldiers were collected by the field ambulances. It was the bloodiest day in the long history of Britain's armed forces.

On the opening day of the battle, Henry was with the 57th Field Ambulance, attached to the 56th Brigade of the 19th Division behind the British front line at La Boisselle. The division was in reserve, ready to deploy in order to carry forward the first wave of attacks. La Boisselle was a tiny hamlet astride the Albert–Bapaume road – the main axis of advance for the British in this sector of the front. The houses had all been destroyed during the fighting here in 1915 between the French and Germans. It occupied the apex of one of the most important German salients on the Somme battle front and with opposing trenches as little as ten metres apart in some places, had always been one of the hottest parts of the line.

21st June. The day of battle was approaching. Rode up through Dernancourt with two or three others to have a look at the line. Very hot. Crowds of horse lines, camps etc along all the valleys behind Albert. Any amount of big heavy howitzers dug in ready. Walked up a communication trench overlooking Fricourt. The ruined village (in the Hun lines) looked very quiet. The trenches dug in the chalk showed up very plain in long white lines. We could see up the hollow below us to Becourt Wood and into some of our reserve trenches, advanced gun positions etc. Any amount of people walking about.

Very little shooting. Went into Albert and had a very good tea at the café near the station there. The square and houses round the church pretty badly 'strafed'. The rest of the town, bar the railway station, was in pretty good repair.

23rd June. We moved up into camp at Dernancourt and slept the night in a tent. A big 'sausage' observation balloon tethered close by.

24th June. Rejoined the Ambulance, now at Lavieville. The village on a hill with a very good view over the valley at Albert to the trenches about La Boisselle and Fricourt. Walked into Albert in the afternoon. Town deserted.

Café shut up. Got tea with a Field Ambulance there. The bombardment began about 10 o'clock.

25th June. Went out and looked at the bombardment. Couldn't see very much – expect most of our stuff was bursting away behind the ridge. Very continuous fire from the heavies at night. Lots of flashes all along the valley by Albert, but very little noise. The house seemed to shake all the time.

26th June. Cloudy and hot and showers. Could see gas clouds blowing over to the Bosch from our front trenches. Very heavy bombardment after tea on our right. Wet evening.

27th June. Cloudy and cool. Pretty steady gunning.

28th June. Raining steadily. Zero hour postponed.

30th June. Fine afternoon and evening. Lots of infantry coming through. Cavalry all around. 1st Cavalry Division at Querieu. Very quiet over the line. Everyone very excited. Most exciting time since the war began. Zero hour tomorrow. The 19th Division go up into assembly trenches tonight. Smalley and I to be ready to go up with the bearers tomorrow. Again, as on the day we marched to Cousolre before Mons, I had the feeling of being on the eve of great events.

1st July. As long as I live I shall never forget the tense excitement of this first day of July. It was a beautiful summer morning, the sun shining and the birds singing. A tremendous bombardment began about 6am – not very much noise actually, but the house and the air seemed to be vibrating all the time with the gunfire. We got up and went out to look. 7 o'clock came and we knew they had gone over. It was hard to realise it. There was nothing much to see. Shells were bursting in Ovillers and La Boiselle with black, yellow and reddish clouds of smoke and dust and big dark smoke clouds were rising all the time along the Ovillers–Contalmaison ridge.

While we were watching, the Hun put several 'crumps' into Albert and we began making bets on how long the leaning statue would remain on the church tower. [*This is a reference to the golden Madonna and child statue on top of the church in Albert. It had assumed a special significance. Some were said to believe that when the statue fell, the war would end.*]

The 19th Division were already up in assembly trenches just behind the Usna–Tara Line, behind the 8th Division [*who made the initial attack at this point in the line*], ready to go on, I think when La Boiselle was taken. The 56th Brigade was in reserve just behind Albert. Smalley and I, with the bearer division, were standing to ready to go up. We had been given suggested sites for our dressing station that night and the night after which we should use if things went well in La Boiselle.

The 4th Dragoons came into the village to water. They were waiting just behind the village ready to go for the 'g' in the 'gap'. I recognised lots of the men and saw Corporal West and Harding and gave them a drink. After that we waited for news. Everybody was asking everybody else for news. Then the first of the wounded came in – light cases in wagons. They couldn't tell us much, except that they had crossed various numbers of Hun trenches before being hit.

Then rumours came in – we had taken Fricourt for certain. Someone said we had got La Boiselle, then this was contradicted. We seemed to have got most of the Hun front system including Fricourt but appeared to be getting hung up rather badly in places, especially on the left. I met General Solly-Hood (late CO of 4th Dragoon Guards) in the village. He was very fit but had no news. The sun was very hot and we waited around all day.

About 6.30 in the evening orders came for the bearers to move up to Crucifix Corner at Aveluy to assist the bearers of the [front-line] Division. Went up with Smalley and Doherty and the bearers to Albert. It was dark by now. We went over the railway, crossed the river and turned left-handed on the far side. Here the most infernal din was going on. All our guns were blazing away into our ears from just across the river. They seemed to be going at the rate rifle fire did at the beginning of the war. Others were on our side of the river just on our right and one battery of 18 pounders was firing salvoes which nearly deafened us.

We arrived at the dressing station at Crucifix Corner where they seemed to be working as hard as they could go. Sent off our bearers up to the advanced dressing station. I got a guide and went up what seemed to be an endless communication trench squeezing past infantry and working parties etc. After I think a couple of hours, we got to the Quarry Aid Post somewhere at the top of Aveluy Wood where I found two MOs. This had apparently been a regimental aid post. It was on the rear slope of a hill just at the edge of the wood and the whole place stank of lachrymatory gas shells mixed with the well-known smell of ordinary shell. The Hun seemed to be putting over very little now. Smalley arrived soon after with some more bearers.

Crowds of wounded were lying about, some on stretchers and some on the ground, waiting to be taken away. Two or three communication trenches were full of [the wounded] for a hundred yards or more. It was a pretty depressing situation. We dressed some of the cases and soon after it got light and we got the bearer squads to work.

A total of 462 cases were admitted to the 57th Field Ambulance during the first day of fighting on the Somme. A further 397 cases were evacuated by motor ambulance.

2nd July. Went up one of the communication trenches with a bag of shell dressings and some morphia from one case to another and tried to do something. They were nearly all bad cases and most of them so cold and so stiff that it was hard to move them. About 10am Colonel Powell came up and told us to go back as the 36th Field Ambulance had come up. Went back to Crucifix Corner where we had a wash and some breakfast and sat in the sun. Beautiful day again.

About 12.30 pm we moved to assembly trenches near the railway just to the right of Albert and sat in an oat field. The sun was very hot. I rigged up a shade with a ground sheet and dozed a bit in the afternoon. There was a big 15" howitzer close by but she didn't fire while we were there.

The South Lancs were close by and in the evening we went across and saw O'Flynn [*the regimental medical officer*] and Colonel Winser having dinner on the railway. The 56th Brigade was to go up at 3am next morning. We dossed down in the oat field and had a good night. Very heavy bombardment, especially about 2.30–3.30am.

3rd July. *During the morning on 3 July, 19th Division attacked the village of La Boisselle from the north and south. They succeeded in partly clearing the village itself but made no real progress on the flanks. Strong German counter-attacks were launched from the direction of Pozieres, which succeeded in re-capturing the eastern edge of the village. The surviving troops of 19th Division dug in for the night on a line running through the village, having gained only 100 yards in the attack. Fresh reinforcements arrived during the early hours of the following morning.*

Walked up the railway towards Dernancourt and watched the big 12" long gun firing from a truck on the line. It looked like a factory chimney on its side. Watched them shove in an enormous shell about 6 feet into the barrel then two or three big packets of cordite and then they knocked it up to an angle of 45 degrees. When it fired the whole thing seemed wrapped round in flame and a hot blast hit you with a bang which was quite painful. The whole truck slid about 15 yards up the line.

In the evening orders came to go up to the Bapaume Post (Advanced Dressing Station) on the Albert–Bapaume road about a mile outside Albert. Got there about 8pm. Took a party of bearers up St Andrew's Street (a communication trench) to the Regimental Aid Post at Kean's Redoubt near our old front line on Tara Hill. They had been shelling this place badly and the trench was all knocked about. Got some stretcher cases. Very slow getting back.

4th July. *At 8.30am a new attempt to complete the capture of La Boisselle was launched by 19th Division. Slow progress was made against a very determined enemy, but by the middle of the afternoon the whole of the village, except for some desultory ruins at the northern end, was in British hands.*

Smalley went up again about 4am. Several bunks in the dugout. Lay down for about an hour. Fairly steady stream of wounded coming in; car [*motor ambulance*] going off about every 10 minutes. Heavy thunderstorm and sheets of rain about midday. In the afternoon took 12 bearer squads and set off with Johnson to find Wibberley's aid post. [*Wibberley was the regimental medical officer of the 7th Battalion, Loyal North Lancashire Regiment.*]

Started off down a trench; still raining and the trench knee deep in water. Met an officer here in a rather awkward position. He was alone and following him about was an obviously drunk Tommy with a Mills bomb in his hand who was quite convinced that the officer was a German spy and was threatening all the time to 'do for him'. I didn't at all like arguing with a drunk man in a narrow trench with a bomb in his hand. Just then a sergeant and a couple of men with rifles came along and took charge of him. A little further on the Hun started shelling hard right on the trench, which fortunately was deep and we lay down for a bit. Apparently one or two of our men were hit and went back accompanied by most of the squads. A nasty big piece [of shrapnel] went 'smack' into the mud about 2 inches from my foot. After about a quarter of an hour they slacked off and we went on. I think it was meant for a battery just behind. After some trouble and a lot of wading about we found the North Lancs in our old front line (to the right of the Bapaume Road).

It was a nasty looking place in the wet – dead bodies of our own people lying about, some in the trench. Went to Wibberley's aid post. Just then the squads that had gone back turned up and we cleared his cases away. Went back across country round our batteries – rows of guns about a quarter of a mile long across the valley and about 5 deep – like rows of fences. We are having lots of 'prematures' now. [*Shells detonating prematurely – frequently in the barrel.*] While we were passing, one went off and wounded some people. Got back about 8pm.

About midnight a message came for bearers for the South Lancs (O'Flynn) in La Boisselle. Took all the bearers up St Andrew's Street – knee deep in mud and water. Trench full of ration parties and it took 2 hours to get through. Came down our old front line and then across the old No Man's land to the mine crater. Nasty damp morning.

Over the first few days of the battle, the 57th Field Ambulance had been under enormous pressure and had dealt with over 2,000 cases of wounded soldiers. The busiest day had been 3 July, when nearly 800 men were treated for wounds and injuries.

5th July. It was nearly light now – about 4am. Left the men on the chalk bank of the crater in a rough trench and went into La Boisselle with Sergeant Bloom to find the South Lancs. No signs whatever of a village, simply a labyrinth of battered trenches in the chalk with doorways and steep staircases leading down to dugouts about 40 feet deep. Wandered about and nearly lost ourselves and found a lot of people of other Divisions. Finally heard the 56th Brigade were on the left so went up a trench here and suddenly met Colonel Winser. Some Sherwood Forester's were coming through to do an attack on something and we were told to keep the trenches clear.

All this time it was very quiet and I heard very few Hun shells. Found O'Flynn in a dugout with Doherty. He had about 14 stretcher cases down there. After about an hour they said the coast was clear so we went back and fetched up the stretcher squads and got all O'Flynn's cases cleared. You couldn't possibly get them up the trenches so sent them off home over the open. Most of them went straight up the road which you could trace across No Man's Land. A few 'crumps' burst about the road but they all got through all right.

Walked back up Tara Hill where our dead were lying out as they had fallen, dotted about or in rows, faces blackened and ghastly. I think this was one of the most gruesome sights I ever saw. We got into St Andrew's Street and back to Bapaume Post about 8pm.

We were relieved by the 58th [Field Ambulance] bearers and went back to the Field Ambulance who were in the Hopital Civil in Albert. Had a wash and slept all afternoon. Had a hot bath in the evening and went to bed and slept like a top until 8am next morning.

6th July. Went up again to Bapaume Post in the morning. Smalley took up some bearer squads to Kean's Redoubt. They got shelled and had several casualties. Cawley [*one of the stretcher bearers*] was killed and 3 or 4 badly wounded. All this time the Hun seemed to reserve all his shelling for our front and support lines. The Bapaume Road for about 300 yards beyond our dressing station, nearly to the top of the hill, was crowded with men, cars, motor ambulances and the ground each side with infantry, but he hardly put anything over behind the crest of the hill. I don't think any shells came near us. He was putting over some shrapnel and high explosive about 400 yards further up the road. Our field guns were each side of us. There were some French 75 batteries as well and we had some Frenchmen in wounded by a premature. We had a good many cases in from prematures. About midnight, left Smalley up with half the bearers and went back to the Hopital Civil.

8th July. Began to rain about 9am and we had several very heavy storms during the day. The hospital was simply surrounded by heavy guns, big howitzers, 60 pounders, and two six inch long guns. In the gardens about 80 yards behind the house [there were] 3 or 4 very big howitzers. Every time they fired the whole place shook and the candles went out and if you were lying on the floor they jolted you about an inch off the floor. In spite of it I slept all night.

A terrific bombardment began about 7 or 8am, heavies all going off like rifles and field guns. Woke up to find half the ceiling in my room in chunks on the floor.

Heard we did very well – got Contalmaison and half of Ovillers. Went up twice to the Becourt Chateau in Becourt Wood (the 59th Field Ambulance Dressing Station). Smalley came back about 2pm.

Orders to move up to Bapaume Post again about 9.30am. Took up 8 bearer squads and relieved Hardwick (59th Field Ambulance). Got a message to clear the old German aid post in the far (Contalmaison) end of the La Boisselle. Set off up Sausage Valley as far as the big crater [*Lochnager*]. A lot of corpses were lying on the white chalk along the side of the crater. La Boisselle was marked by a row of shattered tree stumps sticking up along the sky line. We made for a point a little to the right of the last tree stump. The ground here was all torn up with shell holes and littered all over with dead bodies, arms, equipment of every kind, steel helmets, human limbs and our burst shrapnel shell cases. We had to walk through torn up barbed wire, in and out of deep Hun trenches, now full of mud and water and absolutely blown to pieces, some of them with dead Huns in them, dugouts all smashed up. It gave some idea of what our shell fire must have been like. It was hard to believe that anything could have possibly lived in it – I suppose nobody did.

We finally found the dug out – the trenches to the left of it and the space in front about 2 feet deep in mud and dead Huns lying all over the place, also with the usual litter of Hun machine gun ammunition, rifles, equipment, dressings and bandages and respirators in round tin cases. We got a little shrapnel and high explosive on the way up but nothing serious.

Found O'Flynn in the dugout and Proctor (MO 13th Royal Fusliers) and about 10 British and 20 German wounded – 2 of them officers. Typical Hun dugout – several rooms below with furniture, looking glasses etc and a couple of beds. One of the entrances had been smashed in and was blocked up together with a dead Hun. There was electric light in the place.

Very bad carry back. Ground muddy and very slippery. Shell holes and wire all over the place. Very hard to get down into trenches 6 feet deep and then hoist the stretchers up the other side – no easy job and there was a network of trenches here. After passing the crater there was a fairly good track. Got back about 4pm.

Smalley came up about 5pm with the rest of the bearers and we went up again, taking some water with us for the Aid Post. Half way up they put a good deal of shrapnel over and we had to duck into some trenches for a while. Got up there all right. While we were there some Hun prisoners were brought in, some of them wounded. The rest we made carry wounded. It took a long time getting the wounded out of the dugout and we sent the bearers off as soon as each case was ready.

It was getting dusk and we got several cases off, when the Hun began shelling pretty hard all about the place. And we had to wait. The bearers who had started had to lie low in some trenches but none were hit.

We finally got away in the dark with a lot of the walking wounded. We lost everybody and they all made their own way back; some got to Becourt Chateau. We got to the crater where there was a strong smell of tear gas that made our eyes smart. Here we found a wounded man in a trench and Smalley and I decided to carry him back. Till then I never realised what hard work it is carrying a wounded man on a stretcher. The Huns were shooting up the valley with shrapnel and tear shells and several [howitzer shells] followed us along rather uncomfortably close.

After much slipping up in the mud and frequent rests we finally arrived in the mouths of one of our batteries. We circumnavigated this and finally arrived at Bapaume Post about 1am. I was soaking wet half way up the thigh and jolly tired. Had a drink of tea and rum and rested till daylight.

9th July. I stopped at the dressing station and dressed cases. A fairly steady trickle of wounded coming through. We were relieved about 10am by the 104th Field Ambulance and went back to the main dressing station in Albert. Got back about midday. Glad of a rest.

10th July. The Division is coming out for a rest today. They have done very well. Among other things, they captured La Boisselle and the casualties were not so heavy as might have been expected. We marched back to our rest camp in Henancourt Wood. Passing through Millencourt I saw Colonel de Wiart looking very fit. Glad to see him safe and sound. They say he was simply wonderful and at la Boisselle led the whole Brigade in a bombing attack in person. [*Adrian Carton de Wiart, commanding the 8th Battalion, the Gloucestershire Regiment, won the Victoria Cross for his actions at La Boisselle on 2 and 3 July.*]

Pretty comfortable camp in the wood – rather dark and gloomy. In huts – one or two officers to a hut and a good mess room. Strolled to another part of the wood and heard the pipers of the 15th and 16th Royal Scots playing.

11th–18th July. We stopped in Henencourt Wood for over a week. Our ambulance was 'closed' and we had a nice slack time. We hacked about a little round the country. The men played 'house' all day long in little parties all round our mess hut. On the 12th went into Amiens by motor ambulance with Kidd and Smalley and did some shopping. Had a most glorious lunch and dinner in the evening at the 'Oyster Shop' (Chevalier Restaurant).

On the 17th, rode up with Smalley and Kidd to have a look at La Boisselle. A wet muggy day. One or two shells came into Albert just after we passed through. Left our horses at Bapaume Post and walked up the road to La Boisselle. The road had been made right into the village now and lorries can go as far as the village itself. Not much to see in La Boisselle now – still a few dead Bosch lying about. Walked up the communication trench that now leads to Ovillers but they were shelling up there so we came back and walked across to the German Aid Post at the other end of the village. It was rather interesting being able to walk about on top when before we had to keep down in the trenches.

We came back along the 'Sausage Valley' and had a good look at the crater there. It was far bigger than anything I had ever imagined. We walked over the lip of the crater and saw an enormous clean cut hole in the chalk with sheer steep sides and one or two men down at the bottom looked like ants. I believe it was 90 yards across. There was quite a good road right past the crater and a trolley line and lots of transport.

During the time Henry spent at Henencourt Wood, the British had made a significant advance through parts of the German second-line defences along the Bazentin Ridge. A night attack on 14 July had brought the Fourth Army over the ridge and into a position where it could mount further attacks on some of the commanding heights overlooking this part of the battlefield at High Wood, Delville Wood and Longueval. The battle was entering its attritional phase. Smaller, more localised attacks were directed against sections of the German line to gain tactical advantage. The fighting at these places would see some of the grimmest encounters of the war. Even the cavalry, in one of the most dramatic charges of the war, were deployed in a desperate effort to clear the Germans from their strong defences. Horses proved equally vulnerable to machine-gun fire as men. Gains were usually measured in yards and feet. On 18 July, the British launched a major attack on Longueval and Delville Wood which continued over the next few days, as control of this shell-shattered piece of ground ebbed and flowed. On the 20th, a further attempt was also made to take High Wood. Both attacks were supported by massive artillery bombardments from the guns sited near to Henry's position at Mametz Wood. This explains the heavy German counter-battery fire that Henry and his men experienced.

Both of these British attacks failed with disastrous losses. It would take another two months of heavy fighting before High Wood, Delville Wood and Longueval were eventually captured. Any talk of a breakthrough had, in effect, by now completely evaporated.

19th July. Got rather sudden orders around 7.15pm to move up behind the 56th Brigade to a spot just to the right of Mametz Wood. Got off about 8.30 and marched through Albert and on to Fricourt. It was a dark night. Fricourt was all knocked to bits – trees all bare and smashed, a few bits of wall left standing and in one or two places a few rafters of a roof still sticking up. Mametz was the same. After Mametz we turned down the road to the left for two or three miles and halted at the edge of Mametz Wood. A terrific bombardment was going on. The whole valley was full of guns all blazing away like mad. The noise was deafening. We simply couldn't hear each other speak or shout. In the middle of it all an occasional crump would land. We found the Dressing Station in a chalk pit on a road about 200 yards to the right running along the bottom of the valley parallel to the road we were on. We found an MO and went into a dugout where we could hear ourselves speak. He said they were very busy there and there was no accommodation for any more bearers. We decided to stop where we were at the edge of the Wood. Smalley went off to find Brigade HQ and I sat on some stores and waited. It was just beginning to get light.

20th July. 5.9s were dropping down on the road and in a little ravine the other side of it and some of the splinters were coming across to us. Smalley came back and said I should have to take some bearers up to the North Lancashire's Aid Post at Bazentin le Petit. As soon as it was light I took Sergeant Cross and 8 stretcher squads and got a guide from the Dressing Station and set off.

The Germans were putting a barrage across the top of the valley and 5.9s and big shrapnel were bursting right on the track we should have to go up. I felt horribly frightened but thought we had better keep on. I was walking in front with Sergeant Cross and our guide. The shelling slackened off and I thought we were getting through alright when there was a sudden crash overhead and something stung me in the leg. Sergeant Cross gave a yell and rolled on the ground. I looked round and all the rest of the men were on the ground, but they were only ducking. Sergeant Cross was hit in the abdomen and looked very bad. I dressed him and gave him some morphia and wrote him out a 'tally' with a very shaky hand and sent him back. A little further on, another man was hit in the foot by a splinter from a 5.9 and he had to be sent back.

In the middle of all this – crumps falling all about the place and shrapnel bursting – were shallow trenches and holes in the ground full of Tommies cooking tea and frying bacon quite unconcerned. A little further on we met an MO who said we were going the wrong way (to Bazentin le Grand) so we had to come back and then across to the left and got into Bazentin le Petit. This place looked cheerful – all smashed about – walls more or less standing, dead bodies lying about and a big Highlander lying in the middle of the street just gasping his last breath. Found a Company of North Lancs in a trench and after some trouble found the Aid Post together with battalion HQ in a Hun dugout in the wood just behind the church.

It was an enormously strong place, perhaps 30 yards long with an arched roof and concreted. There were rows of bunks all along one side, enough to hold 50 or more people. One of our 12 inch shells had hit it about the middle and knocked an enormous hole in the side. There were 4 or 5 dead Germans among the rubbish.

I thought I had got a 'blighty' in the leg but found it had only gone through my puttee and had made a mark on my leg as it went past. Smalley turned up soon after. I walked right down to the other end of the wood looking for the East Lancs Aid Post. 5.9s were coming into the wood. Smalley and I left the bearers at the Aid Posts and started to go back. It was an unpleasant place, shell holes everywhere. Lots of dead lying about, mostly British. Bazentin le Petit wood was a tangle of shell holes and smashed trees, a few trenches dug, large tree trunks smashed and lying on the ground. Hardly a square yard without a shell hole. A trolley line ran up through it to the Aid Post from Mametz Wood but this was smashed by Hun shells.

We went back through Mametz Wood to where we had left the cooks and the limbers. Got back about 10.30am. The Germans were shelling very persistently into and all around the little ravine on the other side of the road where there were a lot of 6 or 8 inch howitzers. The road here was crowded with people, motor ambulances going to and from the dressing station in the chalk pit, ammunition limbers and one or two staff cars. Several shells were landing on our side of the road and every now and then one would land right in the road and it was surprising that more people weren't hit. I saw one land in the road in the middle of a crowd of men and horses and I expected to see about 20 people laid out but only one of our men was hit and he got up and walked off. The little valley was simply full of guns, most of them not dug in at all, right in the open.

All day the ammunition limbers were coming up the road and turning up the steep bank to supply the field guns. I didn't envy them their job.

In the afternoon I got into a hole in the bank with a ground sheet over head and tried to doze a bit. All at once there was a fearful bang and I got up and saw Tracey was just killed or dying, the cook Cain was hit through the arm and had his brachial artery cut. I shoved on a tourniquet quickly. Hartshorn, the other cook, went on with his cooking as if nothing had happened. With one thing and another, I felt pretty rattled today.

In the chalk pit there was a pretty big crowd of wounded. Some bad cases. But there didn't seem any more room for any more MOs to work so I came back. We shifted our cooks, limbers etc back about a quarter of a mile where it seemed to be a bit more peaceful. While we were having supper, one or two crumps landed about 100 yards to the side of us.

1. Henry, as a small boy, aged 3

2. Henry, in his captain's uniform, Arras, 1917

3. Henry, demobilised, 1919

4. Henry outside the house at Long Stratton, 1920

5. Wounded British soldiers at an advanced dressing station behind the Somme front line, 1 July 1916

6. Bringing in a wounded soldier, Bazentin, 19 July 1916. German prisoners in the background helping the RAMC

7. RAMC officers tucking into lunch, September 1916, at a special facility for receiving gas cases on the Amiens road near Albert. Note the soldier standing ready to carve the roast joint of meat

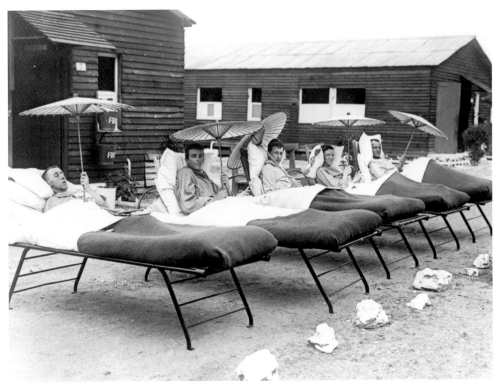

8. British wounded convalescing at a base hospital at Rouen, 1 June 1917

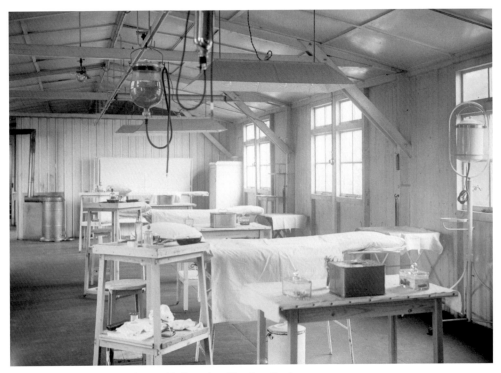

9. An operating theatre suite, at 23 Casualty Clearing Station

10. RAMC men preparing sandwiches for the wounded at Feuchy crossroads, Arras, April 1917

11. A dressing station in the mud, Boesinghe, on the first day of the Third Battle of Ypres, 31 July 1917

12. A doctor treats a wounded soldier at a regimental aid post in a captured German ammunition dump, Oostaverne, August 1917.

13. Crowds of wounded British soldiers at an advanced dressing station near Wieltje, on the road to Broodseinde, 1917

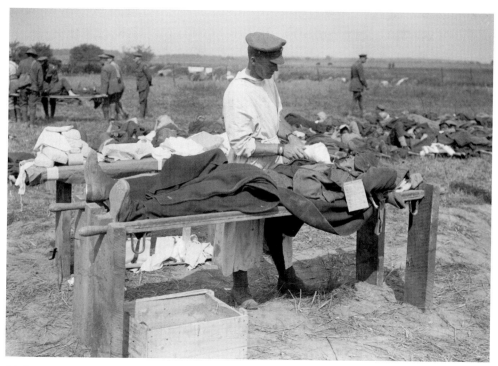

14. A surgeon attending to a patient at a dressing station at Le Quesnel, August 1918

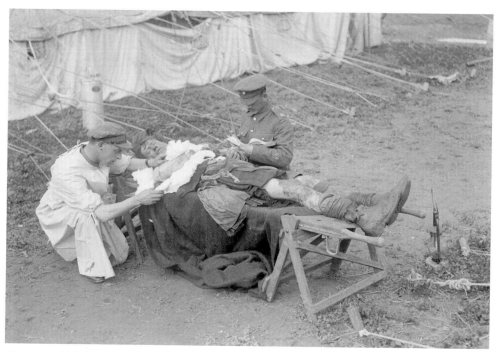

15. A very slightly wounded soldier of the Black Watch receiving treatment at an advanced dressing station, Bethune, 1917

16. British ambulance wagons, camouflaged against aerial observation, Ploegsteert Wood, October 1914

17. Wounded British soldiers being loaded on to ambulance wagons during the First Battle of Ypres, Gheluvelt, October 1914

It was a beautiful evening and there were crowds of planes up. We watched a very exciting airfight. A Fokker drove off one of our biplanes; one of our biplanes got above him and drove him down with machine gun fire. Rifles and Lewis guns blazed at him from the ground and all at once he dived straight down and crashed. Everybody cheered like mad.

Smalley slept at the dugout at the dressing station. I slept in a hole in the side of the road. I saw Elkington and Major Harding with the 8th Gloucester's going up. Smalley said they had had a lot of gas shells round them in the night, but none came our way.

21st July. Up at 6.30. Sent up bearers to relieve the others. Smalley came across and we sat in the sunshine and had breakfast. About midday, the Field Ambulance [was ordered] to act as Corps Main Dressing Station. We were to be relieved by 58th Field Ambulance and go back. We took the 58th MO up to Brigade HQ in a trench between Mametz Wood and Bazentin le Petit Wood. I think there were even more shell holes in the piece of ground between the two woods than anywhere I had yet seen. After tea, we marched off back. The whole country up here looks awful. From Mametz or Fricourt to Bazentin not a single habitation of any kind to be seen – no village, farm, cottage or anything. Trees all bare and smashed, not a green leaf anywhere, the grass all scotched and the ground torn up everywhere with shell holes ... the whole place looks brown and blasted.

We passed Fricourt and saw our wire and front line on one side of the road and the old Hun wire and front line up a steep bank on the other and we wondered how they even managed to get across. Got back to the Hopital Civil in Albert about 8.30pm. Our Field Ambulance was now taking in all the bad cases – practically all stretcher cases – from the Corps front. I slept in a tent in the garden.

The benefits of establishing corps main dressing stations became apparent during the early stages of the battle, particularly in the sector held by XIII Corps around Maricourt. Here two divisions held a narrow front of only one and a half miles. It made sense in these circumstances to concentrate the work of the main dressing stations at a suitable central location in each corps area, rather than have several working within close proximity to each other. By the end of July, all of the corps operating on the Somme front had followed suit.

23rd July. Heavy bombardment this morning. Up at 6.30am and were dressing cases practically all day till after tea when they slacked off. An awful lot of them seem to die simply of shock. Some bad gas cases. A lot of Australians in. Hear we took Pozieres and part of Martinpuich, otherwise the attack was rather a failure.

24th–30th July. In the Hopital Civil in Albert. Only busy at times. A number of shells come into Albert every day from a high velocity gun. Two or three more came into the garden.

31st July. The whole Division coming out to move up north. We were relieved by 2nd Field Ambulance and marched off about 12.30pm. Got to Behencourt about 7pm. Tents pitched in a meadow and got quite a comfortable camp made.

The 19th Division would now enjoy a two-month break from the Battle of the Somme and would be sent to a quiet part of the front at Ploegsteert, a few miles to the south of Ypres, to recover from its losses in July. Since it went into action on the night of 2/3 July, it had lost over 300 officers and 6,000 men.

3rd August. About 5pm the Brigade came past – battalions looked like companies. We marched behind them to Frechencourt to entrain. Train didn't start till 9pm. We got to Longpre at 2am and marched up to our billets at Heilly le Haute Cloche. Arrived about 5am.

Over the next few days, the 57th Field Ambulance moved further north and took over billets in St Jans Capelle, the same area where Henry had been stationed in October 1914.

8th August. Main Dressing Station at the Hospice at Locre. Went on with Smalley to our ADS in dugouts at Lindenhoek. Saw my old ADS, the estaminet, just the same as before in 1914. People still living there.

9th August. Nice peaceful part of the line, very quiet and very little gunning. There was some trench mortar shooting and we had in about 4 or 5 casualties a day. Country here quite pretty – quite untouched. Recognised the same cottages, farms and trees that I had seen two years ago. Must have been very quiet here. Very nice little ADS. 'Elephant' steel shelters well sandbagged, nicely fitted up. Dressing room and a ward to take 12–16 cases. Dugouts for 20 or so bearers. We had a mess with a sort of veranda where we always sat out and had our meals looking out over really charming country –

a little valley of waving grass and wildflowers and corn across to Kemmel Hill, covered with trees and pines, half a mile away. The fields are harvested almost up to the road where our dressing station is. The cottage chimneys are smoking and still inhabited.

Looking towards the line you see the country all dry waving grass, trees all in heavy foliage except along the actual front line. The Wytschaete Ridge forms the skyline. From here you see a few ruined buildings of Wytschaete on the left and the ruins of Messines on the hill top to the right. Far to the left, you can just see the tower of Ypres Cathedral.

The front line was about 2000 yards off. The Regimental Aid Posts quite good with a long carry of about 1000 yards. The communication trenches, boarded all the way, are overhung with all kinds of grasses and wild flowers of every kind. You could walk up to the right hand aid post over the grass all the way, keeping behind the hedges.

We had a comfortable dugout for a bedroom with bunks and had our morning bath outside in the sun. Nearly all dugouts and shelters are now made of the arched 'elephant' steel. They were used at first chiefly for gun emplacements.

12th August. Bailleul much improved. Shops much better – full of things for the British. The inevitable 'Burberry' shop.

28th August. Left the Ambulance and joined up with the 7th Loyal North Lancashire's now in huts between Locre and Dranoutre. Colonel Hill, Scots Guards commanding, Major Thorpe, 9th Cheshire's second in command, Anson, adjutant.

September. At the beginning of September we went into the line in front of Kemmel. My aid post was half way up to the front line. HQ was back on the Kemmel–Vierstraat road in 'The Doctors House' – quite a nice little house, apparently never been hit. It was quite unique as a front line Battalion HQ. There was no protection against shell fire but nobody ever shot at it.

The front line was pretty bad; only breastworks and rather dilapidated. From HQ it was a long walk of over a mile up the communication trench to the front line. After about three days in the line we were brought out and the Division sidestepped down to Ploegsteert.

Behind this front there were a good many preparations for an offensive being made – a lot of new gun emplacements and new roads, but no signs of anything coming off yet. We came out of the line and marched by companies to huts at Romarine for one night. Next day we came up into the line in front of Ploegsteert Wood.

The line here ran just in front of the Wood. Duckboarded paths ran all about the Wood and were continuous with communication trenches that took you up to the front line so that you could walk on perfectly clean duckboards all the way from the road at Ploegsteert through the Wood and up to the front line. You could ride a bicycle up to the start of the communication trenches. HQ was a wonderful collection of very nice clean elephant shelters, sandbagged over and all painted white inside. The spaces between the dugouts were laid out as a garden with grass and little flower beds. Behind the HQ was a summer house [which] looked out on the trees and bushes and just behind them was a patch of lawn and a rustic bridge. Altogether it was a very charming spot.

Occasionally, the Hun did shell the wood with 5.9s. I think they shot chiefly at the support battalion HQ about a couple of hundred yards to the right and at the main path up the wood. A few splinters clattered about near us once or twice. It was a little alarming as I don't suppose any of the dugouts would have stood a direct hit from anything bigger than a 'pipsqueak' [*a light field gun*].

My Aid Post was on the left, outside the Wood in a little group of elephant dugouts only about 300 yards off the front line. A tram line ran past it right back to the ADS on the road. I had a nice clean dugout for a bedroom. The space outside was concreted. I noticed it had been hit by a pipsqueak which had dislodged two or three sandbags. All the time I was there I didn't see a shell come near the place. It seemed so peaceful that I had all my kit up there, slept in pyjamas and had my morning bath every day. I could have lived there for months.

The battalion came out in support in dugouts about the Wood. The support battalion HQ had been in the Wood but we used some elephant shelters at Cinder Farm at the bottom of the Wood on the road. I kept my same aid post and bedroom all the time. I could get back to my aid post if necessary on a bicycle in about 10 minutes. My only trouble was the machine gun bullets that clattered about the trees at night, when I was going back to bed walking along the duckboards.

We were holding a wide front and holding it pretty thin. Two battalions in front and two in support. We were in the left sub sector. The line was very good. A lot of the front line and communication trenches were new – well revetted and boarded on 'U' frames just being completed. The Bosch used to send over rifle grenades and trench mortars that made a horrible bang.

The Tommies were very clever at judging where they were going to land and always seemed to get out of the way. They always looked to me as if they were going to land exactly where I was.

There were some very good assembly dugouts up here, about 30 feet deep and big enough to hold about a battalion.

We had a very quiet time here and hardly any casualties. At the same time it was rather gloomy and depressing living in the Wood.

12th September. Rode into Bailleul. Went through Nueve Eglise on the way to have a look at it. Hardly recognised the place. Church all smashed. The houses on two sides of the square had quite disappeared, except two or three and the place was all overgrown with grass and flowers like a meadow. Our old billet and the houses down there were quite untouched and the people still living there. The Hospice where our dressing station had been was a good deal knocked about.

It was nearly ten months since I had last had leave. Special leave was now open for the Division and I applied for 14 days. I got my warrant about the 15th or 16th. Stopped the night at 'The Faucon' in Bailleul and [left] next morning by train for Boulogne.

1st October. Left Victoria in the morning after a good fortnight's leave. Got two early mornings with the Harriers. Arrived at Boulogne at about 3pm. Saw Major West and Graham at No. 13 General Hospital. Both very fit. Got as far as Hazebrouck and stopped the night there.

2nd October. Arrived at Bailleul about 7.30am. Nasty wet morning. Found the Division had moved out of the line, the battalion in billets near Meteren. I was billeted in a house where Bainsfather, the artist, had been. The people there showed me several sketches he had done.

5th October. Entrained at Bailleul for Doullens. Left about 8am and arrived about 1.30pm. Had about a 10 mile march and got to Coigneux in the dark, the battalion in huts in a wet muddy wood. I got a tent. Nearly all the roofs of the houses in the village [were] off, some of them the result of a big ammunition explosion, the rest I think with the idea of claiming for a new roof.

6th–9th October. Awful weather – raining every day. Hacked about, on my old chestnut blood horse that I had brought with me from the Field Ambulance, over the stubble fields.

11th October. Went into the line at Hebuterne. [*Hebuterne was at the northern edge of the Somme front line and from here on 1 July the diversionary attack on Gommecourt was launched by two divisions of VII Corps under General Snow.*] Very quiet. Line not bad. Hebuterne quite a big village but in a state of ruins. The communication trenches start in the village and our front line lies just out in front. My duties as MO take me round the front and support lines every day to inspect the sanitation.

12th October. In the afternoon we were to simulate an attack by putting out a smoke barrage from our front line with the idea of finding where the Hun would put his SOS barrage [*a defensive artillery barrage designed to disrupt any British attack*]. After lunch went out to the cemetery with the Colonel, Thorpe and Anson to watch. We expected a tremendous shelling from the Hun. The smoke bombs were thrown out and our front line was beautifully mapped out by the margin of the smoke. Our guns put up a show and a piece from a premature hit Thorpe in the back and cut his coat but the Hun never put a shot over. So I suppose it was rather a failure.

   The village of Serre lies out on our right front and Gommecourt just in front to the left. We expect to have to attack Serre shortly.

13th October. Came out to Sailly aux Bois. The battalion in bivouacks on the hillside. Came out from Hebuterne with the Colonel and Anson. Got a lift on an ammunition limber. The Colonel found an empty house for the HQ billet.

14th October. The Huns were shelling some of our aeroplanes with the usual black shrapnel. Three or four came over and burst in the camp. One blew a bivouack up but no one hurt.

16th October. Sudden orders to move. Whole Division moving. The push on Serre apparently off. Had been tuning myself up for several days for a horrible battle. Moved to Rossignol Farm.

Haig was anxious to see further advances on the Somme front before the close of the fighting season and the onset of winter. During September and October the British had slowly and methodically pushed the German line back. But many of the first-day objectives of the battle had still not fallen into British hands, particularly at the northern end of the front in the Ancre Valley and around Beaumont Hamel and Serre. The casualties had been enormous – over half a million to date. Political concerns were being expressed at home about the overall direction of the British campaign. A clear victory would silence these critics as well as help secure a better front line from which to launch further attacks in the spring of 1917. The 19th Division, along with many other refreshed units, would be needed to prosecute this final onslaught of the year. Henry's battalion would be deployed along the Ancre River bank to make a push towards the village of Grandcourt.

17th October. Marched about 13 miles to Contay, battalion in huts in a wood half a mile outside.

19th October. Beastly morning – raining cats and dogs. Battalion marched off at 9am. Got about a mile past Warley and halted. Saw Colonel de Wiart who said they were going back. Soon after got orders to come back. Got into our same billets. In the evening got a motor ambulance from the 57th Field Ambulance and motored into Amiens with Smalley, Kidd and Anson and Hartwell (our Quarter Master). Had a good dinner there at a new place called The Savoy. Back about 10.30pm.

20th October. Ordered to remain where we were.

21st October. Marched to camp – tents – at the 'Brickfields' near Albert. Got in by lunch time. Very cold. Hacked over to Bouzincourt with Major Thorpe and had tea with his brother at 39th Division HQ. Very chilly night.

22nd October. Moved into billets at Aveluy. In the afternoon rode with the CO and Company commanders to part of our line above the little village of Hamel and looked over the Ancre, Thiepval and Grandcourt. Saw the bit of ground we should have to go down towards Grandcourt when we attacked.

Several tanks passed through the village in the evening going up to the line. Not so much impressed by them as I thought I should be. They were smaller than I expected and were going very slowly, about 2 miles an hour and took a long time to turn around the corner. But still, they looked rather alarming. Some carried four machine guns, others two 6 pounder quick-firing guns. The travelling band it moved on looked to me too smooth to grip soft ground.

23rd October. Foggy day. Walked up to see our battalion HQ in the line near Thiepval with the CO, Thorpe and Anson. Stuff Trench, which we were holding, had only been taken a day or two before. It was only about 300–400 yards in front but everyone was walking about over the top. Only a few machine gun bullets went over. Passed two tanks just behind battalion HQ lying there knocked out.

I never before saw anything like Thiepval. Nothing left of the village; no trenches left, everything smashed up and gone except a few tattered tree stumps. You didn't so much see definite shell holes as the ground was absolutely ploughed up over and over again with shells. Hardly a square foot left anywhere. Much worse than in front of Mametz Wood. As far as you could see, the ground was all brown and ploughed up, not a touch of green anywhere. Looking to the right you saw an undulating sea of grey mud stretching to the horizon. In front was the crest of the hill. To the left the row of tree stumps along a slight rise in the ground that marked the position of Thiepval. Looking back you saw a valley of mud going away back to Thiepval Wood. I never saw such a scene of desolation.

Very roughly dug and battered trenches. Still a good many dead bodies lying about – Huns and ours. We had a small but very deep and safe Hun dugout for HQ. The Aid Post was at Thiepval.

24th October. Went up to Thiepval and took over the line from the South Lancs. Holding Stuff Trench. Had several casualties.

The fighting around the high ground at Thiepval, with its commanding views over the Ancre Valley, and the capture of Stuff Trench, had been conducted by 39th Division in order to prepare the way for a more general advance astride the north and south banks of the Ancre River, which would be undertaken by General Sir Hubert Gough's Fifth Army. The main objectives for this attack would be the spur running north from Miraumont and then on to Serre. A subsequent advance would then push the line forward to Pys and Irles – in total an advance of about two miles. It was a limited set of objectives. The enemy would be removed from the high ground and a new front line, more easily defended, would be established for the winter.

Plans for this new attack had been severely impeded by the heavy rain that had been falling almost continuously since the middle of October. The main assault had been initially scheduled for 25 October. It would be regularly postponed pending more favourable conditions.

25th October. Started a new Aid Post in Bainbridge Trench – a new trench and the Huns had not shelled it much so far. The Hun was very fond of shelling Ransome Trench 50 or 100 yards in front of us with 4.2s and black 'wooley bears' and we used to stand and watch them. Had a party on digging – first a hole leading out of the trench and level with the bottom (about 5 feet deep) and 6 feet by 10 feet. Moved up to HQ dugout [*in Bulgar Trench*]. Awful getting about. Mud a foot deep. Almost impossible to get along the trenches and everyone going on top. No track or path from HQ to Thiepval – about 500–600 yards to the ADS – and you had to flounder along through the mud and shell holes. A rotten carry for the stretcher bearers.

Helped to clean up our dugout. We were all wearing Tommies clothes now as we expected to go over the top and also because of the mud. We excavated shelves in the walls where it was not boarded. The CO with his coat off and a wooley knitted cap on his head working away like mad with a little Hun spade and an entrenching tool. The CO and Thorpe had bunks, one above the other. Anson slept under the table and I slept on two planks at the foot of the stairs. The signallers and cooks were at the other end of the dugout through a passage.

About 4.45 next morning the Hun started a hell of a bombardment. We were about 30 feet down so were quite safe but he kept putting them on top of the dugout and the lights kept going out and he knocked all our trench about just outside. He was shelling the front and support lines as well. Wires were cut. The artillery Forward Observation Officer who was with us went out and tried to signal back SOS with a lamp but was promptly hit on the head. His tin hat saved him and he only had a scalp wound. Anson went up the stairs and gave a comic display with rockets – filled the dugout with awful smoke. Some seemed to go off alright and our own barrage opened just after.

26th October. The Bosch attacked on our right, where the East Lancs were but were driven off and left 40 odd prisoners. They said our barrage was very good. Went out as soon as it was well light. Quiet now. Everything smashed up. Went up Ransome Trench to see some wounded in D Company. Trench absolutely knocked in all along. Not many casualties after all as there were several useful deep dugouts in the support Companies. Had about 50 or 60 killed and wounded in the two days, most of them I think during the relief.

O'Kelly, 81st Field Company, Royal Engineers, came up after breakfast and we continued with the new Aid Post. Relieved after lunch by [9th] Welch. Fine afternoon. Back to billets at Aveluy. Beautiful fire in the mess room and bedrooms. Had a good hot bath in front of a fire. The colonel had a case of some good champagne and we had a very jolly dinner.

Made our house very comfortable. It was quite empty but practically untouched by shells and the rooms had nice wallpaper and open fire places. We made doors and patched up the windows, and got in the famous easy chairs (souvenirs from the Doctor's House or Kemmel Chateau that now always travelled with us). Colonel Trower [*CO of the 5th South Wales Borderers, the divisional pioneer battalion*] who lives in a very nice house on the east side of the village gave us some glass from his cucumber frame and the carpenters put us in glass windows.

General Jeffreys, CO of 57th Brigade came to lunch. Major Thorpe got quite a good car from his brother at Bouzincourt about 5pm and he, Anson, Bennett and I went into Amiens and dined at The Savoy. The battalion in tents on the windswept hill above Cruicifix Corner.

27th October. The show put off for another 48 hours. The Hun puts a few shells into Aveluy almost every night from a high velocity gun I think. We heard a few things clattering on the roof once or twice but they didn't worry us.

28th October. Rode into Senlis in the afternoon. General Sir Douglas Haig and his staff passed us riding. Got some money from the Field Cashier.

29th October. Cold wet day.

30th October. After lunch moved up into reserve at Wood Post in Aveluy Wood. Companies in dugouts in the old German Liepzig Redoubt. Pouring with rain. Whole place soaking. Lived in the wood in some dugout things that looked like Swiss Chalets. Bedroom pouring with water, so slept in the mess room with Anson. Started on a bench thing but the rats worried me so shifted on to the table and slept there.

31st October. Wet morning again. Fletcher got a nice blighty wound through the thigh – shrapnel. Found him very fit. He had an omelette and then went off on the trolley line.

1st November. Took over the same line [*Bulgar Trench*] from the South Lancs. Trenches in an awful state – parts waist deep in mud. Men all stuck.

2nd November. Relieved about midday by the 8th Welch. C Company in the front line had a rotten time and got badly shelled. Some didn't get back till midnight. The Welshmen all got stuck in the mud and then the Hun started shelling them. They lost a lot. We got about 20 casualties and Porter [*a junior officer*] got badly wounded. Had about 30 casualties in the 24 hours.

Back to the same billet at Aveluy. After dinner went round with the Colonel to the ADS (58th Field Ambulance) in a car and saw Porter. He was pretty bad. Wound in the back.

3rd November. Hacked over to the Special Hospital at Warloy to enquire about Porter. He died about 10 this morning.

4th November. Fine day. Went for a ride with Anson after lunch but so beastly and muddy everywhere we didn't go far.

5th November. Up to the same piece of line again. Wet weather. Aid Post completed – a hole about 6 feet by 10, flush with the bottom of the trench and about 5 feet deep, timber supports holding a splinter proof roof of corrugated iron with about 2 layers of sandbags on top and some loose earth. I used this to dress cases in. Some trench boards on the floor. Connected by a passage about 6 feet long was another shelter just the same with a frame to lay 4 stretchers on which I used to stow the wounded on after they were dressed. Had some braziers.

6th–8th November. Still in the line. Trenches awful. Had about 50 casualties for the three days and Bowers missing. Don't know what happened to him. Never saw such a place for losing yourself. Not a landmark anywhere – everywhere exactly the same. A sort of rolling sea of mud and you simply walk up and down shell holes all the time. If you go out at night and turn round three times you'd never know which way you were facing. Went out last night and got a wounded man out of a dugout in Splutter Road (D Company, in support). The orderlies lost their way and we wandered about till I decided to come home and start again, but coming back struck the place by chance. Had an awful job getting the man up the stairs – almost perpendicular. He had a wound and also a broken thigh.

Came out to huts at Crucifix Corner. The new Nissen huts, arched corrugated iron on iron frames, boarded inside and floored with match boarding. Very quickly put up. The solid ends with window and door holes come up in sections. HQ had one for a mess and one for sleeping in with stoves. Very comfortable.

On 6 November, Henry wrote a letter home to his sister Darcey:

Just got your letter dated 29th October. You are an ass! I had to tear it up immediately and burn it in case anyone read it, but it did make me laugh. It rather appealed to me, as we had just finished lunch here – that is the Colonel, the Adjutant and the Major who is very large and fat, and me, in a deep Hun dugout. Just room for 4 to sit and there is really very little room.

We had cold ham (very good), cold tongue, cold boiled bacon, a beautiful sort of brawn stuff with sort of jelly on it and truffles in it (very good), fried chipped potatoes, boiled cauliflower. I think there was some cold beef, tinned peaches, tins of mixed biscuits, whisky, Perrier water, bottled beer, port, old brandy (very good, the CO's) and coffee. Of course I didn't have everything, but for the present I've quite given up trying to keep down the weight. That will have to be done later. It's no good bothering at present. You would have chortled to see us here a few days ago when we first came in to this dugout. Table (made of sleepers) covered with bottles, port, whisky etc, glasses, maps, papers etc and the adjutant, mining at the other end – making a shelf and scraping out mountains of earth on to the other end of the table burying knives, forks, bread, maps etc. The Colonel at the other end excavating another shelf with a Hun spade and me holding sandbags while he filled them. The Colonel (who is a very smart Guards officer) with socks and little Turkish bedroom slippers and a woolly night cap. The mice are rather a nuisance outside. But it is quite safe down here. They [the Germans] put the lights out now and then.

Yes we are where mother said right enough. We've been here 5 or 6 weeks and no prospect of a rest in sight.

Alec Ficklin is not far away. I am trying to arrange to see him some time. Horse very well. Rather thin. Going everywhere is awful at present. Have had rather a bad cold but it is improving. Tell me when you are going up to Scotland. Could you ask mother to order another 2 more bottles of peach brandy to be sent out, also any cakes, shortbread etc would be very useful. Any more snapshots?

Best love to everybody,
Your loving brother,
Harry

10th November. Another fine day. After lunch had quite a nice ride with Major Thorpe over the stubble fields round Bouzincourt. Lots of hares and partridges there. Still got a rotten cold and can't get rid of it. The push on again for Monday [*the 13th*].

11th November. Still fine. Bombardment began. Show to start Monday.

12th November. Fine dull day. Still got a cold. Go up to the line (Stuff Trench) after tea and attack at dawn tomorrow. Rode up with the Colonel as far as Thiepval. Got up to the HQ dugout about 7.30pm. Took over from the 8th Gloucester's.

The Battle of the Ancre would start the following morning and last for a further six days. Haig and his staff were keen to ensure that the battle was fought under the most favourable conditions and wanted assurances about the prospects of success with the least possible casualties. Over the next few days, as the attack developed in the heavy mud which made movement so difficult, there were clear tensions between Haig and Gough over the wisdom of continuing with the battle. Gough had initially considered launching the battle with a night raid. This plan was eventually replaced by a more traditional attack beginning just before first light.

13th November. Got up at 5am and went over to the Aid Post. Still dark and a thick fog. Quiet. My medical staff there – Corporal Crossley, Saunders and Gough, a jolly good little fellow with very bandy legs. Dressed two or three wounded that had just come in. Zero hour at 5.45am.

At 5.45 exactly our barrage began. The 18 pounders suddenly all started and kept up a continuous crackle. Couldn't hear the other guns as the 18 pounders were so loud. About 6.10 the fist wounded came in from the Hun first line. After that, [the wounded] kept coming in steadily – mostly walking cases. About 9am a lot of Hun prisoners came in. Got hold of a lot and made them carry stretcher cases down. Some of them wounded. Our battalion took quite a lot – probably well over 100. A few wore the big Hun tin hats. Very quiet round us, hardly a shell came over until about 12 o'clock. Still foggy.

Sent all the wounded across to the ADS at Thiepval a bit to the left of Bulgar Trench which they shelled. No proper track and a very rough carry. I had several RAMC squads up with me working between my Aid Post and the ADS. A good many bad stretcher cases came in a bit later.

Bennett came down with a bullet wound through the left elbow. Saw him in the HQ dugout where he was having some grub and a drink. Very bucked up with himself. Says they got close up to the barrage, which was very good indeed, fog very thick and when they got to the Huns they were all taken by surprise – some had no boots on. Bennett killed several with a revolver and a pick handle. Says he had the best couple of hours in his life. He had to come back with his wounded elbow so brought back about 10 prisoners with his servant when they suddenly ran into a trench full of Huns. One of them came out and said 'you my prisoners'. 'No bloody fear' said Bennett and swiped him over the jaw with his pick handle and knocks him down and ups off with his servant into the fog.

We had very few casualties – only 60 odd came through my Aid Post up to the afternoon. They all lost themselves in the fog. Scoals and Ford [*two company commanders*] and their men found themselves down at the river (The Ancre) so came back and finally dug in along an old Hun trench about 400 yards in front of Stuff Trench. The men very pleased. The Hun never seemed to put up a fight. They killed a lot and took a lot prisoner. Tripp and Fletcher were killed. Hood had a slight wound in the knee and I sent him off to hospital. Bowers body was found out in front of our line.

About midday the Hun started shelling back and fairly hotted us up all the afternoon; put them all round the Aid Post, chiefly 4.2s. Had just cleared off all the wounded and sent Hood off during a lull when they started again. Suddenly the whole place was full of smoke. One had hit the dugout and knocked half the roof in. Fortunately nobody hurt, although Berry, my servant, was standing right under it. Thought it better to move so moved Aid Post into a deep Hun dugout a short way off in Midway Trench. Plenty of room inside but very difficult to get stretchers in and out, but fortunately didn't get many more wounded in.

Successful day. 39th Division took St Pierre Divion and the V Corps took Beaumont Hamel and Beaucourt. Slept in my Aid Post dugout.

Henry's battalion had been joined in the attack by the 7th East Lancs. The job of these two battalions was to protect the flank of the 39th Division attacking up the valley of the Ancre on their left. Owing to the fog, the North Lancs had overrun their objectives but later regrouped to form a continuous line. German shelling was erratic and they made no attempt to counter-attack. The fighting would continue for the next few days as the British tried to complete the capture of the German trenches from Serre to Grandcourt, which formed a salient in their line.

14th November. Good lot of shelling round headquarters. About 20 or 30 more casualties.

15th November. Misty morning. After breakfast walked down to our new front line with Anson. Had to bob and run a bit as they were sniping and we had to go over the open. Quite a lot of dead Huns lying about. Quite a good trench, in chalk and quite dry but no proper dugouts. Very cold and all the men wearing grey Hun greatcoats. Sun just coming through the mist. Got a splendid view of Beaucourt across the Ancre and the opposite hills. Some shells falling into the Ancre and sending up showers of spray. Very little shelling.

Found the mist had lifted and it was quite clear. Took back one or two souvenirs. Ran from shell hole to shell hole. One or two shells falling about. The way down from HQ marked by a white tape.

Very fine in the afternoon and we all watched a fight on the opposite side of the Ancre. Watched our barrage for (18 pounder shrapnel) fire beyond Beaucourt. Hundreds of little flashes and puffs of white smoke, spreading and forming a perfect wall of smoke.

16th November. Bright sunny morning. Cold with a hard frost. Hardly a shell came over. Ran about on top to get warm. Keeping on the deep dugout in Midway Trench as an Aid Post.

17th November. Frozen hard everywhere. Very cold wind. Relieved at night by the 8th Gloucester's. (Had 5 full days in.) Got away about midnight to huts near Aveluy.

Gough was determined to make one last effort to achieve the objectives he had set for the battle. He had managed to persuade a deeply reluctant Haig that it was worth one more attempt to push the British line forward and to snuff out the German salient around Grandcourt.

The last attack of the 19th Division during the Ancre battle was launched the following day in appalling conditions. Whirling sleet greeted the soldiers of all three brigades as they went over the top. This was soon replaced by driving rain. Men groped their way forward as best they could under heavy enemy fire, through the mud and slime that clung to their boots and clothes, making any rapid movement totally out of the question. The tanks were unable to provide any support for the attacking infantry in these conditions. Their objective was the village of Grandcourt. Although some of the attacking troops managed somehow to get into the village and its defences, it proved impossible to hold these hard-fought gains and the troops withdrew to a newly dug line just short of the village during the early hours of the following day. The fighting on 18 November effectively marked the end of the Battle of the Somme. For many who took part in this gruesome last day of fighting, the horrific conditions of 18 November would forever conjure up a nightmarish image of trench warfare. To this day, any mention of the Somme re-kindles this graphic and terrible image.

18th November. Snow on the ground. The 57th and 58th Brigades and the South and East Lancs attacking Grandcourt. South Lancs had very heavy casualties. Colonel Torrie (East Lancs) was killed. Got their objectives.

By now the weather had deteriorated again and with heavy rain obscuring the whole battlefield and mud everywhere, Gough finally conceded that any further offensive operations were out of the question. The Battle of the Somme was finally over. The medical casualties during the battle had been colossal. Between 1 July and the end of November, during the succession of major and minor engagements that made up the campaign, 316,073 wounded men were admitted to the field ambulances of the Third, Fourth and Fifth armies, and 120,000 men were killed. This was the equivalent of over 3,500 casualties every day that the battle continued. Casualties on this scale imposed a unique strain on the army's medical services.

Few of the territorial objectives for the campaign had been realised, with the British gaining a maximum of about seven miles of ground. But the battle had certainly had an attritional impact. German losses were probably much higher, although it has been difficult to quantify them precisely.

The losses amongst the RAMC were also high. Forty-eight medical officers and 340 other ranks of the corps were killed. A further 169 officers and 1,700 men were wounded. On every day of the battle, the men of the RAMC were sharing the same dangers and privations of those who needed their help the most – the men living and fighting in the trenches.

19th November. Nasty cold day. Beautiful fire in our mess room. Rather bad news – 57th Brigade apparently all chewed up. Just before lunch orders came in to move up to St Pierre Divion. Ten minutes later these orders were cancelled. About 6pm, orders in again to move up to reserve line at St Pierre Divion.

Rode up with the Colonel and Anson to Hamel. Very dark. Then walked on with them to Colonel Fitzjohn (7th King's Own) up a kind of morass which had been a road over the river to Brigade HQ at St Peirre Divion. Wonderful big underground passages and rooms. The battalion took over the reserve line (the Hansa Line), battalion HQ in a dugout about 100 yards from Brigade HQ. A little tiny entrance in the middle of shell holes up the hill. You couldn't see it until you were right on it. Very difficult to find in the dark – or in the light. Rations came up to HQ dugout on mules. Wonderful creatures! Very difficult to get there walking on your own feet, up and down craters etc.

Slept in Smalley's ADS, an old Hun dressing station a little further up the road. A lot of Hun dressings, sera, medicines etc.

20th November. Quiet day. St Pierre Divion absolutely vanished. Couldn't see where it had been. Nothing but a rising round of powdered earth and ups and downs of shell holes. The flooded valley of the Ancre on the left. Could see all the country very well across the other side. Some stray tanks lying about. The shelling seemed heavier on the other side. Opposite the ADS were the ruins of a house – the cellars covered in with iron girders and concrete – the only trace of the village you could see. An enormous 15 inch dud shell lay in the doorway of the ADS. Above here you began to trace the road again. Walked up the road half a mile with Smalley to one of the battalion Aid Posts, dug into the bank. A party was sent out tonight to bring in the Belgian gun taken from the Huns by the Gloucester's in Grandcourt. Didn't get it in.

21st November. General Rowley, 56th Brigade, gone home. Colonel Long, Scots Grey's who had been commanding the 6th Wiltshire's took over the Brigade. (Son of Walter Long the politician and nephew of Captain Long who had the Dunston Harriers.) He came into the HQ dugout in the morning to see Colonel Hill.

Relieved in the evening. Heavy barrage on Hansa during the relief. Had several casualties. Walked back over the Ancre to Hamel. Heard some big shells going over. Had our horses there but we missed them and went back in a motor ambulance.

22nd November. Division relieved. Thank God! To go back to rest. The battalion marched to Warloy. It was now so small [*in numbers*] that all the men were carried in motor busses.

23rd November. Beautiful clear sunny morning. Fresh breeze and a slight frost. Marched to billets at Vadencourt. Country looked topping after Aveluy and Thiepval. After lunch went out with Anson and we felt so bucked up by the country that we galloped right away over the open stubble fields, grass and woods to Beliencourt and back.

25th November. Marched to final rest billets at Berneuil. Beastly wet morning. Everyone soaked. Rather a dilapidated village, only ourselves in it. Will soon make ourselves comfortable.

Very nice country all round – no troops, no guns, no horse lines or camps, no mud and no row. Only rooks 'cawing'.

HQ mess was a nice big room in a farmhouse in the village. Got our furniture in – the Kemmel armchairs – got a sideboard made and a brick fireplace put in. Very nice having a bed and white sheets. The whole place seemed well away from the war and peaceful.

Henry would now have the opportunity to indulge his great passion in life – hunting. Away from the front line and with few calls on his time now that the battalion was out of action, he could devote himself to his favourite pastime.

We expected to be out at rest for several weeks and our first idea was to get hold of some hounds. I wrote home to try and get some beagles sent out, without success. A day or two after we arrived I walked into Domart, a little town close by to see if we could hear of any local hounds we could get hold of. After trying several shops we heard of a farmer in the town who had some very good dogs for the 'chasse'. We found they were shooting dogs – setters and spaniels – but this man told us of a farmer who lived at Barly, near Doullens who had some real hunting dogs, Basset hounds etc, who would probably let us have some.

1st December. I borrowed a car from Kidd, from the 57th Field Ambulance, and went over to Barly with the Colonel and Anson to investigate. We found the place, a rather dirty little farm at the top of the village. There was the usual farm yard with stables and cow houses and the usual midden in the middle and walking about in it were quite unmistakeable hounds. We found Monsieur Mallart was quite a sporting old chap. He had his hounds in the stables and cow houses on the other side of the farm yard. He let them out for us to see. I never saw such a mixed lot. Basset hounds, one or two specimens of several breeds of French hare hounds, deer hounds, some quite nice looking light coloured English Harriers from the Hadlow in Kent but most of them were of the Bricquet d'Artois breed. He must have had 50 or 60 couples altogether.

He said he wanted to show us something – couldn't quite hear what – and he opened another door and out rushed a ferocious looking wild boar which dashed through the hounds, frightened us to death and finally rushed in again. He also showed us a big eagle or falcon of some kind which he used for hunting. He was very pleasant and agreed to let us have some seven couple of the Bassets. We were to give him 100 francs and the price of the hounds which he would give us back when we let him have the hounds back. He also arranged some fox hunting or hare hunting for us over there with his own hounds.

We tried to get a lorry or something to get the hounds over in, but failed. So a couple of days later I rode over and saw Monsieur Mallart and he agreed to drive them over that evening in a cart. He arrived about 6.30pm and had dinner with us. We found he knew the mayor of the village – an old friend of his – so the mayor was sent for. The mayor had been rather opposed to the idea of hunting, but with the help of the Colonel's old brandy soon got very matey and all for the sport. They both got quite gay and finally noticed a fox in a picture on the wall and both began hollering and 'tally-hoing'. Monsieur Mallart finally went off home very pleased with himself and we had no more opposition from the mayor.

I undertook to hunt the hounds. I kennelled them in a stable in the village. We fed them on biscuit and bully beef. I had got a hunting horn from home. They were very wild at first and for two or three days just took them out by couples with one of the grooms. I took them out four or five afternoons a week.

As a pack they were not a success. They didn't hunt together well. I think the French use them chiefly for hunting hares out of coverts when they are shooting. The worst difficulty of all was the tremendous swarm of hares on the land. Hares used to jump up all over the place. One day they ran into the big woods near Gorges which are full of hares, rabbits, foxes and deer. We very soon lost the whole pack and only managed to get them back to kennels in driblets after it was quite dark.

We had better sport [*with the biggest hounds*] and after a bit we started riding after them and I hunted them on horseback.

I usually rode my old chestnut horse. Hunting was contrary to orders so we had to keep it quiet and as a rule only the Colonel, Anson and one or two of the battalion came out. Major Price, the Divisional Claims Officer often came out. On the last two days out quite a big field joined in, including General Long and one of the other Brigadiers. We had great fun and it kept us fit and gave us something to do and personally, I thoroughly enjoyed hunting them.

About once a week we had a day with Monsieur Mallart's hounds at Barly. We used to meet at his house at about 11am. His very charming little daughter did the honours at the meet. He didn't like a big field out and as a rule there were only 5 or 6 of us – usually Colonel Hill, Thorpe and Anson and one or two more. He turned out in his everyday clothes and carried a rough stick out of the hedge. He didn't use his big circular French hunting horn as it was wartime, but hunted them entirely by voice. We hunted over a wild bit of country to the north of the village through which ran two or three deep cut valleys. Along these valleys ran big beech woods. He had a good idea of how to hunt hounds; he let them alone and let them hunt and when he cast them he was usually right.

It was very jolly to see hounds hunt at all. It was very pretty to watch them and hear them hunting down the steep hillside into the valley and then up the far side. I used to like finding a fox – it always cheered you up to see one. They were fine red foxes of the ordinary English kind.

We used to make a full day of it, and about midday the mess cart always met us at a convenient point with cake and sandwiches and drinks of all kinds. Monsieur Mallart thought this was a splendid idea. He was very keen and never left off before dark. When we got back, Mr Mallart's daughter always had coffee ready for us by the fire and after that we hacked home in time for dinner. It was an old fashioned kind of hunting but those days in the hills and dales of Picardie were very pleasant.

When we were at Berneuil our mess was a really luxurious affair. A professional cook with a wonderful reputation, who was said to have been cook for the King of Spain, was asked to come and cook for Colonel Hill's mess as long as we were at Berneuil. He certainly justified his reputation. His pastries and soufflés were perfectly marvellous. For the next few weeks our menu and cuisine could have done credit to the Ritz or the Carlton.

The Colonel was determined that the whole battalion should sit down together under the same roof for their Christmas dinner. In the early part of December a wonderful structure – building or tent or tabernacle – began to grow up in a piece of spare ground in the HQ farm. The roof and walls were made of old aeroplane hangars supported by rows of tall pine logs. The floor was made of cinders and then boarded. Where all of these things came from was a secret. It was 20 or 30 yards long and 10 or 15 yards broad. At one end a stage was put up complete with scenery. The whole place was finally decorated with canvas and also with coloured cloth and flag and lit by a large number of Japanese lanterns.

The week round about Christmas was a succession of lunches, champagne dinners, concerts and rejoicings of all kinds and I think for a week the battalion band never stopped playing day or night.

On the 21st December the North Lancs won the Divisional football, some boxing events and the cross country race. By some extraordinary fluke I came in first in the race. The football and cross country teams were given a dinner in The Tent and we celebrated it with champagne in the HQ mess. Next day we had another champagne dinner in honour of Anson who was going home next day to be married.

At Christmas Eve, Colonel Hill entertained about 30 guests and the officers of the battalion, including General Bridges and 3 Brigadiers, to a really wonderful dinner in The Tent. Next day all the men of the battalion had their Christmas dinner at long tables in The Tent. Every man had turkey, beef, pork, plum pudding besides fruit etc and wine and beer, followed by a concert. The band by this stage was in a state of coma and happy collapse and had stopped playing. The sergeants had their dinner on the following night.

I think this was certainly the jolliest and certainly the most rowdiest Christmas I've ever spent in my life and it was a good thing we were beagling and hunting as well.

Chapter 5

The Year of Passchendaele and False Dawns
1917

The year 1916 had been one of terrible attrition on the western front. Firstly at Verdun and then on the Somme, over a million casualties on the Allied side alone furnished a grim and violent testimony to the bloody stalemate that had settled over the whole length of the line. More of the same looked inevitable in the New Year as the Allies sought to renew their attempts to expel the invader from France. An enormous effort had been made to find a way through the German defences in 1916 to no avail. The British had used tanks for the first time during the Battle of the Somme, but, although a fearsome new weapon, they had not proved to be the catalyst for a paradigm shift in fortunes. The tanks were slow, liable to breakdown and vulnerable to artillery fire. The German defences, although battered, remained intact and formidable. Trench warfare continued to paralyse the battlefield. There would be no easy path to victory.

Although the Allied losses were grievous, 1916 had ended with some encouraging developments on the battlefield. The French had scored a famous victory at Verdun in October under the leadership of General Robert Nivelle. Fort Douamont, the symbol of German success during the earlier fighting, was recaptured by the French Second Army in a dashing infantry attack backed up by an enormous hurricane of artillery bombardment. Further progress at Verdun, again under Nivelle, was made in December. The British too had ended the fighting season on the Somme with an important tactical victory and a boost to their morale by advancing up the Ancre Valley.

If progress on the battlefield was slow, at least the war of materiel was moving in the right direction at last. The level of armament production – particularly of heavy artillery and ammunition – had increased substantially during the year, to the point where the Germans no longer enjoyed any significant advantage over the

Allies. Already, the Allies had more men on the western front than the Germans. The BEF alone now consisted of fifty-seven infantry divisions, compared to the five divisions of the original force. Despite all of the hardship and endurance of 1916, the New Year might therefore be expected to hold out the prospect of at last finally breaking the enemy's resistance.

At a major Allied conference at Chantilly in the middle of November 1916, at which General Joffre, the French Commander in Chief, had presided, plans had been laid for a resumption of offensive operations from the middle of February 1917 onwards. The attacks envisaged at Chantilly were to be prosecuted with every means at the Allies disposal. The frontage of the Somme battlefield would be effectively widened, with the French attacking between the Oise and the Somme to the south and the British attacking from between Bapaume and Vimy to the north. The scarred and devastated battlefield of the Somme front itself would be held defensively as the conditions here effectively ruled out any major new campaign. After the conference had concluded, Haig and Joffre also came to an agreement about another major campaign for 1917 – a large British offensive in the Ypres area designed to fracture the enemy lines and capture the ports of Ostend and Zeebrugge from where the German Navy mounted its deadly submarine attacks against Allied shipping. This campaign would eventually mutate into the Third Battle of Ypres and would begin in July. It would prove to be anything but a breakthrough. Henry would be closely involved in its bloody execution.

Many of the outcomes of the Chantilly conference were effectively superseded by the resignation of General Joffre at the end of December and his replacement by General Nivelle. Nivelle, following his success at Verdun, believed he had found the magic formula to end the stalemate. Newly installed as the French commander and with the strong backing of a new French government anxious to bring the war to an early conclusion, the seeds were being sown for what was billed as a dramatically different strategy for 1917.

Nivelle was above all an artillery commander. The 'secret' of his success at Verdun was based on his skilful handling of this important weapon, which he used firstly to overwhelm the enemy's defences by a powerful opening barrage and then to lay down a 'creeping' barrage of real depth and intensity, permitting the infantry to maximise their advance. He now intended to apply this tactic, first used at Verdun on a rather limited front, in an attempt to bring about a breach in the German defences on a large scale. In truth, Nivelle's success at Verdun owed a great deal to the failure of the Germans to position their counter-attacking forces within a reasonable striking distance of the front – a mistake they would not make again the following April.

Nivelle's new plan involved the assembly of a new 'army of manoeuvre' of twenty-seven French infantry divisions which would break through the German lines at an agreed point after an enormous artillery bombardment organised along the same lines as Verdun. The British would assist in this plan by pinning the Germans down along the front originally agreed at Chantilly for an offensive between Bapaume and Vimy, and by taking over a twenty-mile stretch of the front line held by the French south of the River Somme. This would help release some of the troops required for the new attacking force. This extension to the British line stretched resources and manpower to the limit. The British Army would now hold a front of 110 miles.

Nivelle's dramatic new plans therefore represented a significant change in Allied strategy. No longer would the Allies' efforts rest on the continuation of attritional warfare and the gradual wearing down of the enemy. Instead, the plan would be for a quick and outright victory in one great decisive battle. The Battle of Arras, to be launched by the British Third Army in early April, was designed to distract the Germans and prevent reinforcements being sent to the main theatre of operations further south, on the banks of the Aisne River.

Nivelle's plans ended in almost complete failure and led to a widespread mutiny amongst many French Army units, plunging the French Army into an immediate crisis of morale and confidence. Heavy fighting on the Chemin des Dames and in front of Rheims in the middle of April produced many prisoners but no breakthrough. In the process, the French attack had succeeded in moving the front line forward a mile or so, but only at the cost of nearly 100,000 French casualties. In the meantime, the BEF continued with their plans for a major offensive at Ypres – a battle whose horrors would forever be etched on the British psyche by the word 'Passchendaele'.

The year 1917 also saw some other events of enormous significance for the conduct of the war. Revolution in Russia at first blunted the capacity of the Russian Army to wage war against the Germans and ultimately removed Russia from the Allied order of battle altogether. But the United States entered the war at about the same time, bringing in the prospect of significant troop reinforcements for the western front. The Germans had also been forced to surrender most of their front line on the Somme, and in March began pulling back several miles to the newly created Hindenburg Line – a defensive position of enormous strength, protected by huge swathes of barbed wire, deep bunkers and carefully sighted machine-gun nests that provided interlocking arcs of fire. This retreat offered some comforting supporting evidence to those who argued that the effects of the fighting on the Somme had yielded important Allied gains after all. And at Cambrai, in November, Allied hopes of victory were given a dramatic but eventually unfounded boost when the massed ranks of British tanks did finally succeed in breaking through the German lines on a large scale. Victory bells tolled noisily from English churches for the first time since 1914. Within a few days, all of the gains had been lost to German counter-attacks – brilliantly conducted operations which once again cruelly exposed the impact on British capabilities of the enormous losses and expenditure of resources of the 1917 campaigns. When the possible breakthrough beckoned, there were insufficient men and material to push home the initial advantage.

For Henry, all of these tribulations lay in store. For him, the New Year would start quietly. The 7th Loyal North Lancashire's, having enjoyed a relatively sumptuous Christmas sojourn, were still recovering from their efforts during the final stages of the Somme campaign. The winter would prove to be a harsh one. Temperatures plummeted. Conditions in the front-line areas became extremely harsh. The men shivered and waited for battle to begin again. Henry would spend most of the year with the battalion as medical officer. There is a sense of boredom that emerges from his diary during the first half of the year. He relieved this by spending a few weeks in the middle of the year working as a surgeon with his friends West and Graham at No. 13 General Hospital in Boulogne. Here he would be able to take on new responsibilities for the care and treatment of his patients. But his thoughts were always with the battalion and with its well-being. The pull would prove irresistible, and he would rejoin it in time for the later stages of the Third Battle of Ypres in September.

During the winter of 1916 and into the first few weeks of 1917, the army medical services began to gear up for the new military operations on the western front. The First and Third armies, on the Ypres and Arras fronts respectively, would be most actively engaged and so medical resources were concentrated on these army areas. The other armies would be required to retain as many of their sick and wounded in order to avoid strain on the ambulance trains and motor ambulances needed for the active fronts. The chief anxiety of the RAMC commanders at the turn of the year centred on the number of hospital beds available in the rear areas. During the Battle of the Somme, up to 70,000 sick and wounded men were being shipped back across the Channel to England for treatment. During the winter, however, this steady flow became more of a trickle, with less than half this number being evacuated during the first few weeks of 1917. As a result, the number of permanently equipped beds which remained vacant gradually reduced to only a few thousand. Casualties from the planned campaigns in 1917 would far exceed the number of free hospital beds in France. A crisis in medical care loomed.

It was averted by radical measures. The numbers of patients being sent back to England rapidly increased again from March onwards, freeing up hospital beds in

France once again. In addition, seven new general hospitals of over 1,000 beds each were rapidly assembled and dispatched to France. All of these new resources would be required to manage the flood of wounded and injured men which would begin to flow again as soon as battle re-commenced.

9th January. Cold snowy day. Marched out of billets at Berneuil to Beauquesne and billeted there for the night.

10th January. Marched on to Authie. Beastly dirty place. Rotten billets but improved them and they were soon pretty comfortable.

11th January. Very cold; hard frost. Rode over to the inn at Le Bon Air, near Doullens with the Colonel and the padre and had lunch there. Bought wall paper for the mess room in Doullens.

12th January. Billet fresh painted and papered. Rotten cold weather – snow.

21st January. Moved from Authie into huts at Couie. Hard frost and snow on the ground.

22nd January. Into billets at Sailly aux Bois. Two Companies at Hebuterne. Ground hard frozen. Very nice mess room in a nice little red brick house that had never been hit. Room papered with canvas and tastefully decorated with pictures from 'Colour' etc. Slept in some very good dugouts behind – an old Brigade HQ, Chesters Castle.

I walked up the road to Hebuterne to see the two Companies in The Keep. The road was quite quiet when we went up but they shell it a lot and also the batteries all over the open ground between Sailly and Hebuterne. There were a lot of fresh shell holes about the road. They shelled Sailly occasionally. A lot of heavy howitzers were about and behind the village. One night when I was up in the D Company billet they suddenly put two or three bursts of shrapnel over and the Company Sergeant Major and two or three men were wounded. At the same time I was sent for as they had sent several 5.9s into the other end of the village round HQ. Two gunner officers and one or two men were killed and two or three wounded. An aged woman still lived in a little cottage all alone among the ruins in the east end of the village. I don't think there were any other civilians.

25th January. Moved up into the line at Hebuterne. Very cold and everything frozen hard. Battalion HQ in a very nice clean stone cellar under a fairly complete house. It was 'propped' inside and had a good thickness of bricks and sandbags on top and was fairly safe. It had a good brick fireplace in it and was quite warm and when we had our candles with pink shades on the table and drinks put out on the sideboard it looked very cosy.

The Aid Post was in a room in the adjoining house and I slept in a deep cellar underneath.

The 57th Field Ambulance was in cellars and dugouts in the village about 300 yards behind.

26th January. Walked round the line. (We were now holding the left sub-sector alternately with the South Lancs.) Everything frozen hard and you could walk along all sorts of old trenches usually full of water but now frozen solid. We were holding the line very lightly, with posts, relying chiefly on Lewis gun and machine gun fire and holding only the main support line – the Red Line which was in fair condition, although the parapet in places was very low. We had some posts out in the old front line which could be reached only at night. There were some good deep dugouts in the support lines where the men were very warm in an atmosphere of pungent brazier smoke.

The weather was clear and sunny and the ground was covered with three or four inches of snow which gave the place a nice clean look uncommon to the trench area. You could look across to the Hun line and Gommecourt Wood in front of our left Company. All four Companies were in the line with two platoons in the second support on Yellow Line in dugouts which were being re-boarded and revetted by the Royal Engineers and very good. Three platoons were in cellars in the village.

It was really very quiet in the line. The Hun used to snipe at you with Whizz Bangs to a certain extent and shelled it occasionally. He used to shell all about Hebuterne a good deal, especially around 'The Pond' but very little just where our HQ was. He was usually most active soon after dark when he thought reliefs were going on and rations coming up. Rations came up during the day and the Company cookers were in the village.

28th January. Still, clear and frosty weather. Made my morning round of the trenches. Had just left B Company HQ dugout in the Red Line at the top of Yankee Street [*a communication trench leading up to the front line*] where there was an artillery observation post and was going along the Red Line to the left when the Hun started shelling with 4.2s which made a nasty big burst on the frozen ground. One set off a box of Verey Lights. I said to Gough (my orderly) it must have hit the trench. When I got back to HQ I was told that General Long had just been killed at B Company HQ, also

Brien (B Company CO) and Sewell (Brigade Major) had been slightly wounded. They were standing in the trench just outside the dugout, talking, and the shell hit the back of the trench and the General must have been killed instantly. I saw his body afterwards. [*Brigadier General Walter Long, the son of cabinet minister Walter Long, MP, was the commanding officer of 56 Infantry Brigade. He was 37 years old when he died.*]

After dark we came out to the reserve Battalion billets at Bayencourt. Anson and I slept in an Armstrong hut outside. We had a stove in it but in the morning everything was frozen hard. Brigade HQ was in the village a few yards off.

29th January. General Long's funeral at Coiun. A lot of people were there including Prince Albert of Connaught. His death came as a great shock to everyone in the Brigade, especially as the line was so quiet. He was very popular.

31st January. Into the line again. Snow still on the ground; about 20 degrees of frost. Very cold walk up. My ears ached. Next day went down the big underground caverns in Hebuterne, about 80 feet deep and big enough to hold a battalion. I think they are old stone quarries. The South Wales Borderers (Pioneers) had made tunnels down to them. Would make a good Advanced Dressing Station in a 'push'.

3rd February. Out to Sailly again. A lot of gas shells about. Still fine and sunny, but still freezing hard. Everything frozen – sponge, shaving brush, bath towel etc.

4th–21st February. Still in the same place of the line. We did three days in the line, three days in support at Sailly, and then three days in the line again and then three days in reserve at Bayencourt. When at Sailly we had two Companies in The Keep at Hebuterne.

The men in the posts, including the advanced posts, were relieved every 12 hours and hot tea and stew were taken up to them in thermos containers. All the Companies had their food cooked at Hebuterne and sent up in these containers which kept it beautifully hot for several hours. The men, when not actually on duty, were very warm down in the dugouts and cellars and all kept very fit. I think I only had 2 or 3 cases of 'trench foot' all the time we were there, in spite of the cold.

It was very quiet in the line. I used to see coveys of partridges come over the line from No Man's Land. As we were holding it lightly and the dugouts were deep, we had very few casualties – I think only 15 or 20 wounded all the time. A man killed close by HQ was the only [fatality]. They got a direct hit on a post in the Red Line when the South Lancs were in and killed or wounded them all. I saw it next day. There was a heavy trench mortar – that fired 'flying pigs' – about 200 yards to the left of HQ and the Hun used to shell it sometimes with 5.9s. Once when I was coming back from the left Company HQ along the duckboards (Thorpe Street) two flights of 'pipsqueeks', evidently meant for it, burst all about the trench about 50 yards in front of us.

We made a raid from the left Company (The MouseTrap) one night into Gommecourt Wood. I went up and stopped in D Company dugout until it was over but they found no Bosch and had no casualties. There was a bright moon on.

We had a nasty walk to and from the line. They used to shell the road very badly between Sailly and Hebuterne and we took to going by cross country tracks where all our field batteries were. They used to shell these a good deal too, especially with gas shell, but you could always avoid a particular area they were shelling. We often walked through fresh shelled areas with the snow all blackened, which stank of gas. Walking across this plain the wind used to cut like a knife.

16th February. I was in my aid post in Hebuterne seeing the morning sick. I heard several planes overhead and a lot of 'Archies' [*anti-aircraft fire*] bursting. All at once there was a tremendous shouting and cheering. I went out and saw one of our planes and two Bosch and a lot of archie smoke. One of the Hun planes was clearing off, the other had one wing off which was floating away. He was only at a moderate height. He seemed to try and balance himself for a few seconds and then lurched over and rushed down like a stone at a terrific pace. As he got near I could see the big black cross on his wing. I thought he would fall right on top of us but he hit the ground with a crash about 80 yards away. The plane was smashed to fragments and the Hun pilot looked – as one of the men said – like a pot of jam smashed. Apparently two Hun fighting planes came over and tackled one of our old artillery spotting planes, but he got his machine gun onto them and cut the wing clean off.

19th February. At Sailly. Rode over to 18th Division HQ at Bouzincourt and rang up Alec Ficklin with the 8th Norfolk's and found Pop was at Martinsart. Found him there. Very fit and grown tremendously. He seemed to think the war great fun. Had tea and dinner with him and rode back to Sailly. Thick fog and pitch dark.

About the last day we were in the line it began to thaw and we just avoided all the horrors of mud and water after a frost.

21st February. Relieved and left Sailly. Went into Nissen huts at Bus. Bad camp, just put up. Mud awful.

25th February. Sudden orders to move up to Courcelles. Hear the Huns have evacuated Serre and Miraumont. Had just made our huts comfortable – very annoying. Was in Courcelles 3 or 4 days. The Companies were in Nissen huts. The battalion was working on railway lines. The Hun sent over a few shells somewhere not far off. After 3 or 4 days, I got my warrant for special leave. Hacked into Acheux and got down in a hospital train. Lay on the floor of a rest hut at Etaples for about 3 hours in the middle of the night and got to Boulogne about 6am. Got across to Folkestone that morning.

Good weather [at home]. Everybody very fit. Got a good day with the Dunston Harriers – had a 3 mile point in the morning – and a very cold and chilly day with the Henham.

11th March. Returned from leave. Arrived at Boulogne about 4.30pm and went up to No. 13 General Hospital and found Major West, and Graham. Had dinner there and stopped the night.

12th March. Caught the 7.30am train to Abbeville. Arrived about 11. Had to wait until 6pm for the next train so went up to No. 2 Stationary Hospital after lunch and saw Gladys Dalrymple. [*Gladys was a nurse working with the Womens Voluntary Aid Detachment. Henry knew her from Norfolk days and his mother's network of Church contacts. Gladys and her sister Valerie had been looked after by Spencer Fellows, the vicar of the neighbouring parish of Pulham St Mary while their parents were living and working in China.*]

Uncomfortable journey. Got to Bouzincourt about 2am and found Divisional HQ here. Division on the move north and the Brigade have gone on. Couldn't get in anywhere so slept on the floor in an office. Weather fairly warm. Borrowed a blanket and slept fairly well.

13th March. Up at 7am. Had some coffee and an omelette with Lionel Gwynn. Found Higgins and got a lift in a staff car to St Pol and on to where the battalion was billeted at Cauchy a la Tour (near Auchelles). Nice billets – electric light etc.

14th March. Wet day. North Lancs beat the South Lancs at football, 18-1. General Bridges watching.

15th March. Battalion marched to Estree Blanche – same billets as in April last year. Expected to stop a fortnight.

There would be no immediate rest for Henry and the battalion. Over the next few days they continued moving north to take up a position on the Ypres front.

20th March. Marched about 22 miles to Mentque. Started at 7.15am and halted for lunch just outside St Omer. Had a jolly good lunch in an estaminet – potage, omelette, ham and beef. Beastly afternoon – cold wind and rain. Arrived about 4.30pm. Men tired and a lot falling out towards the end.

Fairly good billets but B and C Companies a long way off. The Brigade to do a fortnight's training. Had very nasty weather most of the time, snow, sleet and rain.

2nd April. Very cold wind and 2 inches of snow on the ground. Left our billets and marched to Arques.

3rd April. Marched to Hazebrouck. Awful morning. Snowing and blowing and four inches of snow.

4th April. Moved on to very good billets at Castre. Sent in an application to be transferred to No. 13 General Hospital. Arranged it with West.

6th April. Marched through Bailleul to camp near Reninghulst. Began to rain as we arrived. Nothing there except some tents badly put up in a muddy field. We got a wooden hut built for HQ mess. I got a bedroom in a little refugee cottage about 300 yards away. Awful weather still – snow, hail, wind and frost.

All this country is very different from what it was in 1914. La Clytte is a mass of camps, huts, permanent horse standing and stablings, railway sidings and ammunition dumps. There are also lots of little new houses for refugees built chiefly out of old ration and ammunition boxes. Light railways and baby engines run up to the trench system and there is also a good service of tram and trolley lines. Lots of gun emplacements and a fair number of guns up – lots of 60 pounders and 6 inch howitzers, but not many big things. There seem to be plenty of preparations for a big push but apparently it is not expected to bring it off for a month or two. The Hun is said to have a lot of guns concentrated on this Army Front.

18th April. Relieved the 57th Brigade in the front line. Our sector is just south of St Eloi, opposite the Nag's Nose. Walked all around the front and reserve lines. Pretty rotten trenches – nice and dry but only breastwork and no parados. Comfortable Aid Post – sandbagged 'elephants'. Brigade HQ in sandbag shelters and dugouts behind Vierstraat. Very quiet walk. The reserve line was good with small 'elephant' dugouts for all the men.

20th April. Nice fine sunny day – warm. During the morning the Hun was ranging on one of our batteries across the road with high explosive shells bursting high. In the afternoon he put over 200–300 5.9s on to the battery. He kept it up for an hour or two and we all watched. Don't know if any damage was done.

Just after dinner a lot of shelling began on our reserve companies and on our left. Gas alarm went. Put on my box respirator and went up to the Aid Post. Apparently he was sending a lot of gas shells on to our reserve line. There was also shrapnel bursting over Ridge Wood. Our guns started a devil of a row and kept up for half an hour. I had no casualties.

Battalion relieved by the East Lancs and went into support in Ridge Wood in rotten little 'elephant' shelters with about two thicknesses of sandbags on top.

21st–24th April. In Ridge Wood. Nice warm sunny weather. Spring at last. All the swallows back. The Hun was doing a lot of counter-battery shelling on our gun positions behind the Wood, otherwise it was fairly quiet.

24th April. Took over the left sub sector from the South Lancs. My Aid Post in the cellars of the old brasserie at the cross roads – a good deal of bricks and stuff on top and fairly safe. The wounded were sent down to the Advanced Dressing Station by tramway. Front line bad. All tumbled down and overlooked by the Hun everywhere. No parados, only a breastwork in front; worse than the right sector.

27th April. Very busy building new mess room. Got a lot of timber from the Royal Engineers, also girders etc for the roof. Burst with the Colonel sandbagging. After tea the Hun started strafing the cross roads. Sent over a lot of pipsqueeks and 4.2 high explosive. One shell went through the brasserie roof and several all round. He also sent some black Wooley Bears over HQ but didn't follow it up with anything. No one hurt. About 10pm there was a huge crowd round the cross roads – ration parties and working parties. And at 11pm he started shelling again. Fortunately most of them had gone and no one was hit.

28th April. Went round the companies, front and reserve lines. Came back to lunch and found a new MO there, sent up to relieve me, and orders to report to the Deputy Director of Medical Services at Boulogne [*the principal medical officer for the lines of communication*]. Handed over to the MO, Captain Smeall. Had tea and said goodbye to the CO and everyone. Had to wait a bit as the enemy was shelling the cross roads again, then went down to the Advanced Dressing Station. Got a car down to our transport lines at La Clytte. Got my kit here and went down to Bailluel and stopped the night there at the Officers Club. This is quite a good place. Lots of beds, baths and haircutting place.

29th April. Posted to No. 13 General Hospital at Boulogne. Major West and Graham were here.

The hospital was in the Casino near the harbour. After two or three weeks I got charge of half of one of the surgical wards – about 30 beds. I had some very interesting cases and got a lot of help from West who had charge of the surgical division and was doing very good work. Also [got help] from Graham who was doing all the head cases.

We had a nice house on the seafront to live in; plenty of bathing also tennis in very good courts under the ramparts.

In June we got the news of the brilliant capture of the Messines–Wytchaete Ridge by the Second Army, where 19 gigantic mines went up. The 19th Division were in the first fight and had only light casualties. I got 2 or 3 of my old battalion in my own ward. It all sounded rather pleasant and I began to get rather keen on getting back to the front again.

Soon after this I heard that the hospital was to be taken over by the Americans. This meant that we should probably all be split up and I decided I would try and get back to the 19th Division again. Besides, I was getting rather tired of the base. The front isn't always very pleasant when you are there, but after you have been down at the base for 3 months you begin to feel rather out of it.

I happened to meet my old Assistant Director of Medical Services, Colonel Hinge and he very kindly arranged to get me back to the Division.

Things were fixed up by the 27th July. I said goodbye to Graham and West and next morning set of to re-join the 'butterfly' Division.

Henry would find himself joining up with the infantry at the very moment that final preparations were being made for a major offensive at Ypres. The attack was designed to break through the German lines on a wide front and seize control of the Belgium ports. The first phase of the operation had been initiated with the capture of the Messines Ridge, strategically important high ground overlooking the battlefield three miles to the south of Ypres in early June. The capture of the Messines Ridge and its successful defence against German counter-attacks represented a significant victory for the British and set the stage for one of the bloodiest battles of the war. For many who took part in it, the fighting at Ypres would bear an uncanny and depressing resemblance to the slogging match of the Somme a year earlier. The fighting at Ypres over the next few months constituted a series of battles at Pilkem, Poelcapelle, along the Menin Road, at Broodseinde and Polygon Wood and finally at Passchendaele itself, over a morass of water-logged, shell-devastated country where all distinguishing features had been completely obliterated. The British tried heroically to dislodge the Germans from their dominating positions on high ground. The attacks were severely hampered by appalling weather, which reduced the battlefield to a quagmire. Progress was painfully slow and the casualties appallingly high as the attacking troops threw themselves against hundreds of reinforced concrete pill boxes. No breakthrough could be obtained. The Belgium ports remained firmly in German hands.

The fighting at Ypres did, however, at least allow the British to maintain pressure on the Germans in the aftermath of the mutiny and ill-discipline that had erupted in the French Army following the failure of the Nivelle strategy in April.

The medical resources available to treat the wounded had been carefully husbanded in the run up to the battle. Fifteen casualty clearing stations were deployed behind the front line. Thirteen hundred tents and over sixty large huts were provided for the sick and wounded, providing accommodation for over 14,000 cases at any one time. A further 25 per cent could be added to these numbers without any great inconvenience. At St Omer, there were three general hospitals open as well as three Canadian stationary hospitals at Arques and Longnesse. Eleven advanced dressing stations were established along the Yser canal with six corps main dressing stations near Dickebusch, Poperinghe and Elverdinghe, which were formed from the personnel of several field ambulances. Extra surgical teams were also attached to the casualty clearing stations, allowing them to take on much more complicated cases.

Zero hour was set for 3.50am on 31 July.

28th July. Up at 3.45 and caught the 4am train to Hazebrouck. Reported to the Director of Medical Services, Second Army. Had arranged an exchange with Fry back to the 57th Field Ambulance. Got my orders and went on by car to Locre. Had lunch at Divisional HQ on Scherpenburg Hill and got the Ford car down to the Field Ambulance at Locre Convent. Very hot day. Country looking very pretty.

Colonel Powell, Kidd, Smalley, Fry Cochrane and Bennett the Quarter Master still here. After tea we walked up to the top of Kemmel Hill. Rather hazy but we got a good view of the Messines–Wytchaete Ridge. The villages were entirely gone. It was quite extraordinary to see from here the effects of our shell fire. All the ground between us and our side of the old No Man's Land was quite green. On the Bosch side right away as far as you could see it was brown, just like a ploughed field and the line of demarcation perfectly clear cut. We could see some of the big mine craters. Now our heavy guns are mostly along the hollow below Kemmel village.

29th July. Thundery day; rained a good deal. Smalley went up with the ADS party to the Advanced Dressing Station on the Damm Strasse to the left of Wytchaete after tea.

30th July. Another dull, wet day; muggy. Am going up to the ADS at 5pm. Took 6 stretcher squads up by car as far as Voormezeele. Passed the 8th Norfolk's at Dickebusche but of course had no time to stop and look for Arthur. Walked on past St Eloi. Passed Anson and Forster Sutton (North Lancs) riding back. They were to be left out tomorrow and were going back to their transport lines. (I heard afterwards that 3 or 4 minutes after passing us they were both wounded by a shell that went right back and burst in the road close by them.)

We passed the Bois Carre on our right and our old front line, across No Man's Land and up to the Damm Strasse where we found Smalley and the ADS. From here you could see how completely the Hun had overlooked our old positions before the June push. Pretty quiet. A few shells falling about but none near us.

11pm. Have just been up to the North Lancs Aid Post in Ravine Wood with some extra stretcher squads. Saw my old orderlies and servant. Went down to the HQ dugout and had a drink and some supper with Colonel Hill and Thorpe.

So far very quiet. Looks like more rain coming – bad for our push. The ADS is a pretty strong Hun built concrete dugout or pillbox on the ground level, built into the Damm Strasse (a raised road about 10 or 12 feet high) on the 'wrong' or German side. Fairly safe – ought to stop a 4.2, possibly a 5.9. Padre Archer (North Lancs) stopping with us. Turned in about midnight. Very hot and muggy. Tried to sleep but every time I got drowsy the Hun put some shells over, meant for a battery just behind us. Two or three came pretty close and put our lights out. Apparently no gas shells.

The Fifth Army under General Hubert Gough would launch the main assault against the Germans around Ypres on a front of about fifteen miles on 31 July. The original battle plan drawn up by General Rawlinson involved a cautious initial advance of about a mile, allowing the guns to take new positions as the infantry moved forwards in a series of further limited steps, driving the Germans from the high ground in the process. The cavalry would be ready, as ever, to exploit the breach when it happened. Gough, renowned for his attacking zeal, had persuaded Haig to back his much more ambitious plans for an advance of about 5,000 yards. Instead of a succession of deliberate blows aimed at destroying the enemy's reserves and morale, an all-out assault on the first day would be attempted.

Gough had around 750 medium and heavy guns and over 1,300 field guns and howitzers at his disposal – a field gun for every twelve yards of the front being attacked. The preliminary bombardment was begun on 16 July. The gunners faced a difficult job. Facing the entire front of the Fifth Army, the German defences, except for a forward line of observation posts, lay on a reverse slope which was out of sight of ground observation. Counter-battery fire proved particularly difficult as the Germans constantly switched the locations of their batteries. The mass of enemy artillery assembled behind the Gheluvelt plateau at the southern end of the front being attacked remained largely intact and maintained its striking power – something that would be evident on the first day of the battle. But in terms of both the number of guns and the amount of ammunition expended, the battle would set a new record. Over 4,000,000 British shells would land on the enemy.

The first day of the campaign saw some important gains to the north. The four assaulting corps of the Fifth Army overran the outposts. The initial objectives were taken on the Pilkem Ridge, which was captured – an advance of about a mile. But around Gheluvelt there was much more limited progress as the infantry struggled against the effect of machine-gun fire from numerous undestroyed pillboxes as well as the massed ranks of German artillery. Heavy German counter-attacks limited the depth of the British advance. The British were only halfway to achieving their first day's objectives and had already lost between 30 and 60 per cent of their fighting strength Most of the casualties were received not on the advance, but in holding their new positions as they came under heavy machine-gun and artillery fire.

The ground over which the men attacked imposed an additional cruel burden on the troops. Days of unceasing shell fire and steady rain had converted most of the battlefield into a lunar landscape of shell holes and cloying thick mud. The focus of the fighting switched to the Gheluvelt plateau and the need to sweep the Germans from this strategic high ground, over which they continued to pour fire down into the British lines. The Fifth Army would need time to gather up its strength again.

The Second Army held the line to the south of Ypres. It joined in the main attack of the Fifth Army by launching five divisions against the enemy line in a subsidiary attack designed to improve observation over the German positions and consolidate the line achieved after the Battle of Messines. The 19th Division, part of IX Corps, held the line at the foot of the Messines Ridge, and advanced about 500 yards on 31 July.

31st July. Up at 3.30. Had some tea. At 3.50 our barrage started. It didn't seem to be very heavy on our particular front but of course we are quite on the right of the attack and don't have to advance very far. Watched the flashes and sparks. A good many Hun SOS rockets going up.

About 5am a few wounded came in. Could now hear very heavy drumfire to the north. All along behind Ypres was a continuous flicker of gun flashes. Stretcher cases began coming about 7am. The North Lancs came in for a lot of machine gun fire from a strongpoint. Priestland (North Lancs) came through wounded in the forearm.

Very dull, overcast day. Heavy clouds hung very low in the sky. Could see our planes flying very low over our front line, coming in and out of the clouds. About 7 I went up to the North Lancs Aid Post in Ravine Wood to see if they wanted anything. Very little shelling by the Huns on this side of Ravine Wood. Corporal Dooley got hit on the back by a big piece but only bruised. We had got all our objectives but the Division on our right had been hung up and our right had to come back to conform. Had only about 100 cases through the ADS and very few really bad ones. Justice (North Lancs) was killed by machine gun fire. He was an awfully nice fellow. He had just got his Company (D Company). Hun seemed to retaliate very little on this front. Wet evening. Quiet night. Went to bed at 9.30pm.

1st August. Up at 6. Raining steadily, ground a swamp. The wounded all coming in soaked. Quiet day. I suppose this beastly weather has stopped our offensive. Didn't see a single plane up all day. Have got 6 Hun prisoners carrying, but very few wounded coming in.

After lunch left Smalley up here and walked down to Dickebusch and found Pop with the 8th Norfolk's transport. He was acting transport officer. Hadn't seen him since February at Martinsart. His battalion went over yesterday and were fighting in front of Hooge. Had tea with him.

Coming back passed the 1st Cavalry Field Ambulance. Went in and found Ward there in a tent – very fit and a Major commanding the unit. Walked back to the ADS. Rained steadily all day. Apparently no fighting today. Quiet night. A few shells coming about somewhere near and some gas shells. When you are lying in a good strong concrete house the 'sigh' of shells coming over seems to sound rather soothing and pleasant.

2nd August. Very cloudy and still raining. After lunch Smalley went off on leave and Fry came up instead. Rain stopped but still very cloudy. Walked around the Aid Posts in Ravine Wood, Godsel Post and Oostaverne Wood. Pretty quiet. After dinner fairly heavy firing away to the north. Some shelling round the ADS about midnight.

3rd August. Rained steadily all day. Orders to return to the Main Dressing Station at Locre in the afternoon.

4th August. After lunch rode over to Reninghulst to find Arthur.

Was told he had moved to Dickebusche. Went there and found he was still in camp at Reninghulst. Began to rain, got soaked and went home. All the roads a mass of mud. Crowds of sick coming in.

5th August. Fine day, big clouds about. About 150 sick came in. A good deal of gunning tonight.

6th August. Arthur came over for tea and dinner.

8th August. The Division coming out. Handed over the hospital and marched to camp near Berthen.

10th August. Up at 6. Marched down to Bailleul. Entrained 150 personnel and 2 limbers. Train started at 12.30. Heard some shells whistling miles overhead towards Hazebrouck. The train stopped 10 minutes in Hazebrouck station. Just as we arrived a big shell dropped among some cottages about 20 yards from the line and a few minutes later another fell in a field about 100 yards further away. And Hazebrouck is about 18 or 20 miles from the front line!

Detrained at Wizernes and marched off at 3.30pm. Beautiful afternoon. Marched through very pretty country. Halted for tea at the roadside and got into billets at Quesques at 10pm.

11th August. Marched to our final billets at the Chateau Fresnoy near Allingthem – only 8 miles from Boulogne. We each had a beautiful bedroom and free use of a very nice garden. The surrounding country was very pretty – hilly and well wooded with green meadows and green hedges and the whole place to ourselves. No sign of troops or war anywhere, only the sound of pigeons and woodpeckers calling.

14th August. Went temporarily to the North Lancs to relieve Jones who was going on leave. Colonel Hill was leaving the battalion and Maule and I rode into Boulogne in the afternoon to see him off. Anson has left and Thorpe has transferred to the Tanks.

22nd August. Very hot day. Marched to fresh billets at Nielles. On the march received my leave warrant and returned to the Field Ambulance at the Chateau Fresnoy. Slept the night there and next day took a car down to Calais.

Stopped there for the night and got onto the leave boat next morning. The first person I saw on the boat was Arthur, also going home on leave. A fearful gale blowing – was horribly ill for an hour and a half. However, as Arthur remarked, it was worth it.

Henry returned to France on 7 September and rejoined the field ambulance, which was now billeted in a farmhouse between Dranoutre and Kemmel Hill, the following day.

9th September. Ambulance closed – nothing doing. We now have an American doctor attached to us for duty. A jolly good fellow and quite amusing. After tea we walked up Kemmel Hill to look at the view.

11th September. After breakfast, went up the line to take over the Advanced Dressing Station and bearer posts from the 37th Field Ambulance. Took a party of over 20 NCOs and other ranks by car to St Eloi and went on foot and found the ADS in dugouts in the north bank of the Ypres–Comines Canal at one of the lock gates called Norfolk Lock. On the north and east side of the lock was deep water but below, on the other side, was simply the dry bed. Went into the ADS and saw the MO there and decided to take a squad up to each of the bearer and relay posts and take them over.

We had to walk up the canal bank for about three quarters of a mile. There were a good many shell holes plumb in the middle of the path. We had an uncomfortable walk as he was shelling it now. First they [landed] well ahead of us then he lengthened and they went well over behind us and then one or two came rather close. Then I heard one coming and I thought 'I believe this one is going to get us at last.' I instinctively crouched down. Wooff!! I was hit by a hot puff of air and covered with mud, stones and smoke, but that was all. Sergeant Dooley said the hole was 5 yards from me.

We left the canal bank and walked up Oaf Avenue a communication trench about a mile to a Regimental Aid Post in a concrete pillbox in Fusilier Wood. Quiet all along here. Came back along a duckboard track up the high ground past two more relay posts – concrete pillboxes in Battle Wood. Of course there is no wood left. From the high ground here you get a wonderful view over the Boche lines to the south east. You could spot Boche gun flashes quite easily. Coming back over The Bluff we passed the two old front lines, about 15 yards apart. A few yards further you got a view of the ruins of Ypres and Zillebeke Lake and nearly the whole of the salient.

When we came down the hill and saw the canal bank we found he was simply basting the Norfolk Bridge and the bank all around the ADS with 5.9s. Three or four shells were coming in every 15 seconds or so. One went into the water and sent up a white column of spray a hundred feet or so high. Waited until they stopped and then went down to the ADS. One shell had dropped just in front of the door and had sent a lot of filthy black mud over everything.

Smalley turned up about 4.30pm with the rest of the bearers. The ADS was a pretty safe place dug right under the canal bank which is about 30 feet high here. There was room for about 10 stretchers cases. We had a room for ourselves with two bunks and the place was fitted with electric light. A tunnel runs from here right up the canal bank over half a mile to the top of Oaf Avenue. I never went up it.

The line here is held by a series of posts – no continuous trench – with a support trench line behind. As it was a very long carry back to here we have to have several relay posts. From the Regimental Aid Posts to here is about one and a half miles.

12th September. Fine morning and a cool breeze from the north. In the afternoon I walked round two relay posts on the south side of the canal opposite the pontoon bridge. I think this piece of country just here beats anything I've ever seen for sheer destruction and obliteration of nature and the work of man. I think even the Thiepval country was less strafed. From St Eloi below on the left as far as you can see to the right, or east, it is a waste of shell torn ground, mine craters, old trenches and dugouts partly overgrown with coarse grass and weeds. Not a green tree or shrub in the whole of it. This bare, scarred undulating region now baked white in the September sun, was once thickly wooded. Ravine Wood, Battle Wood, Fusilier Wood and the woods away towards Hooge and southwards to Oostaverne have all disappeared. Only a few little splintered stumps stick up here and there. A few hundred yards from here a fine white chateau used to stand, with elaborate gardens laid out and a private road running south along the Damm Strasse and north to an iron bridge over the canal. Every trace of all this has now vanished, except at one place where a little mound of rubble which may be on the site of the chateau and the smashed and battered iron bridge lying in the canal bed.

Standing on the high ground near the White Chateau and looking north you see the high canal banks all bare and cratered with shells. Just over the far side [there is] a big jagged mine crater, somewhere about where the old line ran. Behind this the high ground of The Bluff and a few ragged stumps of Ravine Wood and behind this and a little to the right a slightly raised knoll of bare earth which is the famous Hill 60. All this ground has been ploughed and pounded with shell for nearly 3 years. To the left of The Bluff in the distance you see the ruins of Ypres and the low ground of the salient which runs south to St Eloi. Facing round to the south on the right you see Kemmel Hill, tree covered and standing up sharp and high over the surrounding country. To the left, facing it and separated from it by a shallow valley, you get the long bare rise of the Wytchaete Ridge.

All the low ground round St Eloi is thick with heavy guns – 8 inch, 9.2 and 12 inch howitzers, while the 60 pounders, 6 inch howitzers and field guns spread right away up Ravine Wood and The Bluff nearly down to the railway and Fusilier Wood. I never before saw such a mass of concentrated light and heavy artillery.

Good roads have been made over this rough ground, also plank roads or corduroy, good enough to take a lorry and these run as far as the advanced gun positions. Up them come all the ammunition and all the material for the front line. There is also a good system of train lines and light railways. Light engines run right up to Battle Wood.

13th September. Met Maule in the morning and we walked up to our C post with him. The Hun was chucking over 4.2 howitzer shells in salvos of 4 between here and B post. Went on to the RAP in Fusilier Wood. Saw Young. Our front line of posts is about 400–500 yards in front of here. Our guns were pretty noisy in the evening. Had very few casualties though.

14th September. Bennet came up at about 4pm with the rations. Walked back with him to Voormezeele. The ground between St Eloi and Voormezeele simply black with heavy guns – all blazing away. Watched a 15 inch howitzer firing in Voormezeele. The shell going away looked just like a black rabbit hurling through the sky. Parties from 58 and 59 Field Ambulances are working under Royal Engineer supervision on a new ADS on the St Eloi mound, to be ready by the next push. It is to be 2 long elephant shelters about 15 yards long dug into the side of one of the big mine craters. They will have 4 or 5 feet of earth and sandbags on top and some concrete slabs and are supposed to be 5.9 proof. I doubt it.

15th September. The Boche sent some 5.9s near us about 5am. About 7.30 we had a practice barrage. Beastly row for half an hour. Walked round the RAPs and relay posts and painted up red crosses as bag marks. Came back down Oaf Avenue and the pontoon bridge. About 6pm there was an intensive bombardment from all our heavies for about half an hour. Tremendous noise, ground shaking. A lot of 60 pounders all round us. Sat up on top of the canal bank watching it. In the afternoon he shelled about here a bit and further down the canal. Put a 4.2 just outside our door.

16th September. Another beautiful day. Another concentrated bombardment from our heavies from about 10 until 10.30. About 11.30 the Hun shelled the canal 100 yards below us and smashed up our trolley lines – got direct hits in 6 different places. Our heavies burst again in the evening. The whole ground away to Voormezeele darting all over with flashes.

About 9pm he sent some shells right back near Voormezeele and set off a cordite dump or something. An intense orange flare lit up the whole country side for 15 minutes.

18th September. Relieved by the 59th Field Ambulance. Went down with the bearers and Smalley in the afternoon to The Hospice at Locre and spent the night there. The rest of our Ambulance is running the Main Dressing Station here. The attack is the day after tomorrow.

The first few weeks of the battle had seen the British inching their way forward in conditions that defied description. The soldiers were asked time and time again to attack heavily fortified positions, under heavy artillery bombardment and machine-gun fire in a sea of mud that made rapid movement absolutely impossible. Discontent was palpable. There were nearly 70,000 British casualties by the end of August. However, very large numbers of German troops were being drawn into the fighting at Ypres and they too were suffering terrible losses. The mutinous and disillusioned French Army was thus saved from having to face any serious fighting.

Back home, the politicians were beginning to get cold feet. The high casualties and lack of real progress led Prime Minister Lloyd George to propose that the battle be discontinued. Haig managed to persuade the government to press on. However, he now faced growing manpower pressures as the number of new drafts arriving in France dropped to a trickle.

Fresh attacks were planned for September. The Gheluvelt plateau remained in German hands despite repeated efforts to take it. Now the resources of the Second Army would be massed against the German stronghold, which would be captured by a succession of assaults or steps with limited objectives, enabling the troops to continue to enjoy the full protection of their own guns. Second Army, under General Plumer, would be tasked with the capture of the eastern end of the plateau. They would have to advance a total of 4,000 yards through some of the most heavily defended ground on the western front. Plumer planned to take the plateau in four separate attacks with an interval of six days between each to allow time to bring forward artillery and supplies. Plumer intended to land a huge blow on the German line at Gheluvelt. Compared to the first day of the battle, double the force was to be employed to cover half the frontage. The infantry would attack in small parties of skirmishers who would outflank the enemy pillboxes and fortified shell holes.

The 19th Division would be in the first wave of the attack at the southern end of the battlefield. The job of IX Corps would be to establish a defensive flank for the main attack of X Corps to the north. The Fifth Army would attack simultaneously on the left.

Success would depend, once again, on the accuracy of the artillery barrage.

19th September. Had a good night. Beautiful morning. A photo group of the unit (officers) was taken. Our bearers went up in the afternoon. Smalley and I rode up about 2.30pm. Smalley went on with the bearers to the Hun concrete dugout in Oaf Avenue. I stopped for the night at the ADS on The Mound, which was to be our ADS for the attack tomorrow, with Colonel Preston (now commanding 58th Field Ambulance), Burton and Andrews. Pretty continuous gunning all night. A lot of 60 pounders just on the edge of the crater making a beastly row. Slept on stretchers but didn't sleep much before 2am. A good deal of rain fell in the night. Zero hour 5.45 tomorrow.

20th September. Got up about 5am. Just beginning to get light. It was still pretty dark at 5.45 when our barrage started. It really was a wonderful sight. The whole countryside all around us from Voormezeele to Ypres to the skyline – The Bluff, Ravine Wood etc. blazed and flickered incessantly with flashes which showed up blurred and yellow against a dark blue background.

The Hun seemed to be putting over a bit of a barrage to the right of the canal about our front line. Nothing was coming our way. About 7am it cleared up and the sun came out and shone rose coloured on Kemmel Hill behind us. Our planes came over and observation balloons went up. About 7.45 the first batch of Hun prisoners came past – about a dozen. Then a big storm came up. Clouds very low. Visibility bad. Stretcher cases began coming in about 8.45am. Busy dressing cases all day. Passed through about 250 stretcher cases and 200 walking wounded. Very little shelling near us.

Beautiful evening and sunset. Hear everything has gone well and we have got all our objectives. Rhodes came in about 11pm (MO, 88th Brigade RFA) and carried on all night for us. Turned in and had a good night.

The 19th Division had a successful day. They moved forward about 600 yards on a 1,600-yard front and, despite some stiff resistance, reached their objective along the eastern edge of Hessian Wood. About midday, Major General Bridges, who had gone forward to congratulate his brigadiers, was injured in a shell explosion and lost his right leg. The division as a whole sustained nearly 2,000 casualties on 20 September. Overall, the day saw British gains all along the front being attacked.

21st September. Up about 7am. Went up the relay post in Oaf Avenue and relieved Smalley. He had had a rather uncomfortable time. They shell rather a lot along the communication trench and 2 or 3 of his people were wounded and one killed. Things pretty quiet up here this morning. Walked up and saw the MOs in Fusilier Wood. Everything alright.

Spent an interesting afternoon in a gunner Observation Post just the other side of the communication trench with two gunner Majors who were working two 60 pounder batteries by telephone. From here you got a splendid view over the low flat ground in front where the Boche lines were right away to the town of Werwick in the distance. The Boche seemed to have any number of batteries in and around Werwick, and you could spot a number of gun flashes. Looking through glasses you could see each house quite distinctly and could even see shell holes in them. When you saw a gun flash you could get a pretty good idea where it was. These two 60 pounder batteries were the only guns dealing with these Hun batteries.

It was very interesting picking up a new target. He would ring up a gun, say No. 2 gun, give the map co-ordinates of the target and order '1 round shrapnel'. A few seconds later they would ring up 'No. 2 gun ready'. He would send back 'Fire No. 2'. Then you would hear the familiar double 'bang-thud' of the 60 pounder and hear the shell whistle over and see the white shrapnel burst in the air somewhere near the target. He would correct this with the next shot and then tell them 'repeat No. 2 gun, high explosive'. Then you'd see a fine black burst, perhaps plumb where you thought the gun was and see things flying up in which case he'd say perhaps 'repeat, high explosive, 6 rounds at one minute intervals'. They were also using the new 106 or instantaneous fuses. With this fuse the shell, instead of burying itself before detonating and making a deep crater, goes off on the very instant of contact with any more or less solid object. It makes only a very shallow crater and the splinters fly out laterally in all directions and are very destructive against troops in the open. The Boche is using the same thing now in a lot of his high explosive.

I'm afraid if any gunner happens to see this he will say it's all entirely wrong! But as a casual outsider this seems to me to be roughly the way they usually work these things.

After a bit the Hun began to make it rather uncomfortable out there with shrapnel and so I retired to my little concrete house.

About 7pm, I heard a lot of shooting going on, especially from 18 pounders which weren't far behind us and went out to look. The Hun was making a counter attack and we were putting a barrage along our front on the low ground below us. It was getting dusk and you saw numbers of bright little flashes followed by a little puff of dense white smoke which gradually thickened into a curtain of smoke. The Hun began chucking shrapnel at us so I bolted in again and heard nose caps and splinters spattering about outside all over the place.

About 10pm Hogg came in and said I was to relieve him in Fusilier Wood. He was going off to Australia! Had an uncomfortable walk. He had a nasty little 4.2 gun or howitzer shooting along the trench steadily at about 15 or 30 second intervals. Got into the Aid Post and found about 14 people crowded into it. Inter-Brigade relief going on. About 8 MOs there, 2 other officers and as usual, 4 padres. No room to lie down. The 56th Brigade relieving the 57th Brigade with only 2 battalions in the front line. There had been 6 battalions in the front line which meant 3 RAPs with 2 MOs in each. We are right on the right flank of the push and apparently our part of the work is now finished.

Soon after the Hun started shelling we got two direct hits on our house – only 4.2s fortunately and this place is pretty strong. It had 3 arched compartments in it and a double all on the Hun side, each wall 3 feet of concrete. One compartment was the dressing room, one for bearers and orderlies and one for ourselves. They went on shelling most of the night. By early morning there was only padre Willis and the South and East Lancs MOs and myself left. Got an hour's sleep.

22nd September. Went round to the King's Own Aid Post. Quite quiet. Came back and had some breakfast. Went out again and walked up Oaf Avenue to the relay post there. He was still shooting at the trench with 4.2s. Had one or two rather near but it is wonderful what an ostrich-like sense of security a trench gives you. All well down there so came back to the concrete house in Fusilier Wood. This was still being used as an RAP by one of the MOs I was suppose to run the bearers and look after things from there instead of back at the ADS.

About noon they began shelling all round us again. Got inside and glad I did so as they got 6 direct hits on our house in 10 minutes. They seem to be 4.2 howitzers and come every 15 seconds – as soon as one bursts you can hear the next one coming. They kept this up for about an hour and then left off for half an hour. We went outside to look at [the house] and saw the chipped marks where the shells had hit. The shelling began again and got some more direct hits on us. On the end of our concrete dugout we had put up an elephant shelter fairly well sandbagged to dress cases in. One shell hit this plumb in the middle and biffed the whole of the roof in – bent it down to within 3 feet of the ground. Four of the bearers were inside but weren't hurt. This shelling continued, off and on, all afternoon. Luckily no casualties came in. Sergeant Watson was messing about outside in the afternoon and got hit in the leg and had to go down.

I hear the ADS at The Mound where I was yesterday morning, got a shell right through it and there were about 7 killed and 15 wounded – RAMC men and patients. The trolley line from the pontoon bridge down to The

Mound has all been smashed up again and we have to evacuate down the canal bank to Norfolk Lock.

23rd September. There was an 18 pounder barrage about 7 this morning and the Hun retaliated round about Fusilier Wood again. When it was quiet I looked out. Misty morning. We seemed to be in a deserted looking spot. We were in a little shallow gulley. There was a low bank in front with tree stumps and torn up roots sticking up. Looking right and left along the gulley you saw a few old dirty smashed up dugouts and a straggling duckboard track hit in several places. The rest was closed in by mist. There was not a sound and not a soul to be seen.

Went down to the relay post again. When I got back to the King's Own Aid Post he started slinging a lot of 5.9s about, along Oaf Avenue and one right into the trench near us [which] wounded some men. In the afternoon some enormous [shells] burst about 50 yards in front of the dugout – made an appalling crash, blew down our gas curtains and put out the lights. I think they must have been 8 inch shells. Our place wouldn't stand anything much bigger than a 4.2.

Sending down about 20 stretcher cases a day, but most of the casualties are from working parties and ration parties coming up at night.

24th September. Fine morning. The Hun still making the place very unpleasant. Got orders to go down to Norfolk Lock. Walked down the canal bank. Found the cookhouse at Norfolk Lock knocked to blazes and several fresh shell holes in front of the doors. He shelled us again pretty hard in the afternoon also the timber road just over the bridge.

25th September. More shells bumping about. One of our car orderlies was killed down by the Spoil Bank. After lunch Fry came up to relieve me. Glad to get away. Went down by car to Kemmel. Left the bearer squads here. They were all very done up – working hard all last night.

Walked over Kemmel Hill. Perfect autumn afternoon – beautiful air and sunshine. Got back to the Locre Hospice about 5pm.

By the way, the usual dress for heavy gunners seems to be trousers, boots, tin hat and nothing else. They strip to the waist and are burnt to a bright mahogany colour.

26th September. One of the bearers died during the night. Weak heart and too much hard work.

After tea, went out towards Dranoutre with Padre Luck and his dogs. Found several hares in the root fields and had good courses.

27th September. Maule came through badly wounded, but as usual in good spirits. A shell came right into their dugout in Fusilier Wood and knocked out 15. Dyke was killed. Busy night. Cases coming in all night. Lots of gunner casualties coming in. Shelling the back areas a lot.

29th September. In the afternoon played tennis on cement tennis court at the Club at Locre. In the middle of a set, a Boche plane was going over and a dud archie, the entire shell, come whiffling down out of the blue and landed bang in the court – in one corner. Very alarming. The hole in the ground went down further than you could reach. During dinner, a Boche plane came over and dropped 7 bombs about 300 yards from the Hospice. Awful crash and half the glass in the place smashed.

30th September. A lot of bombing again tonight. Some lorries were hit near the white chateau at Locre and did in a lot of Army Service Corps people. Had about 15 badly wounded in. 5 died.

October–November. Scherpenberge. For the next few days we carried on more or less uneventfully at the Hospice at Locre running the Main Dressing Station, taking in the wounded and sick of the Division. Except for the fellow who happened to be orderly officer, we weren't uncomfortably busy. We had some beautiful, sunny, misty early mornings with a heavy dew. I often went for a ride before breakfast round one of the numerous cross country tracks. We also had some good fun coursing hares with Padre Leech and his two dogs. There was a good deal of aeroplane bombing at night.

One evening, the 4th October, I walked up Kemmel Hill and had a look at the view. It was about 7pm, just getting dark and was rainy and windy. There was an attack on that morning by the 5th and part of the 2nd Armies towards the Passchaendale Ridge. The sight was really quite wonderful. An incessant flicker of brilliant darting flashes ran up and down the distant gun positions all along the line. It looked like the effect of electric lights reflected on rippling water – and yet you couldn't hear a sound.

On 4 October, the British launched fresh attacks against the German lines along the Gheluvelt plateau. Numerous pillboxes stood in their way. The still-fiercesome

German artillery barrage provided an additional obstacle. The 2nd Anzac Corps of Second Army and the New Zealand Division made steady and valiant progress and carried all of their objectives. The IV Corps of Fifth Army joined in the attack further to the north with the aid of a number of tanks. They too were successful, although a high price was paid for these modest territorial gains. All told, another 12,000 men had become casualties.

One day I walked down to Wulverghem with Fry, the village where we had a dressing station on 1st November 1914 in a little estaminet. The pave road was still there, more or less intact, but every trace of the village and the houses had vanished. A few little bits of the walls of the church were still there and a few tombstones. I noticed a cross put up to Captain Macarthur-Onslow (16th Lancers), killed on 5th November 1914.

I also visited some old friends of ours at Noote Boom near the Monts des Cats, where 1st Cavalry Field Ambulance were billeted next door to us at Christmas 1914. The children were getting very big. Marie and Germaine were now grown girls of 17 and 19 – I hardly recognised them. They were very hospitable and talked English almost as well as their own language. They had a surprising command of English slang!

On the 14th October, I once more got shifted from the Field Ambulance and was sent to take over the medical charge from Captain Pole of the Divisional Royal Engineers, ie the 81st, 82nd, and 94th Field Companies and the Signals Company Royal Engineers. This is considered quite one of the nicest medical jobs in a Division. You live at Divisional HQ and visit the camps or billets of the Signal Company and Field Companies each day. You don't have to go up into the line at all as a rule, as the various working parties are scattered along the whole Divisional front and get medical attention from the nearest RAP or ADS.

I lived in the Commander, Royal Engineers (CRE) mess at Divisional HQ in huts on Scherpenberg Hill. The Scherpenberg is a high isolated hill, one of the range that starts at Cassell and ends at Kemmel. It is grass covered and at the top is a picturesque farm house and a wooded windmill. From it, looking east, you see the wooded Mont Kemmel separated by a valley about a mile wide of fields and trees, the whole landscape just now a blaze of red, gold and brown.

In the mess were only the CRE, Colonel Hodgson, his adjutant MacDonald and myself. The CRE was one of the nicest and most interesting men I have ever met. He was an extremely competent and keen soldier. He was a very intellectual man and took a great deal of interest in many other things, especially artistic things – music and literature. He had spent most of his service in India, Burma and Tibet.

The work just filled in the morning. I saw the sick at Divisional HQ and then rode my pony round the Field Companies at RE Farm, Bassiege Farm and Vierstraat. All this country just behind the front or shelled area has an atmosphere quite its own. It is a mass of dumps, horselines and camps – tents and huts of every description and a few dilapidated farms dotted about. It has its own peculiar set of sounds. The sound of the gunfire is rather distant – the heavies are only a little further on. The anti aircraft archies are usually firing as the Hun is pretty enterprising in the air on this front. Bugle and transport camp calls are played and rims, fifes, bagpipes and brass bands are practising all over the place. The general effect of the mingling of these various noises is peculiar to this area.

I saw several exciting airfights here. On the 17th October I saw 2 Boche planes about 12–15 thousand feet up with the archies firing at them. Some of our planes attacked them and immediately one of them burst into flames and fell straight down, breaking to pieces as he went. The other was driven down by our planes who kept on top of him and he fell near Ouderdoun. Pilot and observer were both killed.

All this October the nights were fine and the moon clear and every night our planes, showing lights, went out by scores to bomb the Boche. In return, we were bombed every night. All the railway sidings, dumps, camps and horselines round about us were tempting targets. We never had a bomb actually into our camp, but bombs are noisy things and Nissen huts don't give you much sense of protection. We had some rather disturbed nights. General Geffries who used to command the 57th Brigade now has command of the Division.

On November 10th the Division was relieved by the 37th Division and went back to rest in the Blarringhem area. The Field Companies were left where they were in the Corps area to work on horselines and stables for the winter. The CRE's mess moved to Fermoy farm between Scherpenberg and Kemmel. The civilians were living in the house but we had our bedrooms there and messed in a Nissen hut close by. I rode over to Poperinghe several times and met Pop there and had lunch or tea with him. Also met Phillips there. The fighting around the Passchendael Ridge was still going on. The guns sounded very loud down our little valley and when a big shoot was on the glasses on our sideboard were clattering all day long.

On 12 November, Henry sent a quick letter to Darcey:

Many thanks for your letter – some weeks ago. I have just been in to Pops [Arthur's nickname] and met Phillips and Arthur and had tea there. Both quite fit. I know where Arthur is now and have arranged to meet again. He is a very long ride away from me – almost 12–14 miles but I hope to see him again this week.

My love to all,

Harry

The Third Battle of Ypres was now drawing to its conclusion. On 10 November, the Canadian Corps with support from II Corps finally reached the Passchendaele Ridge and held it against German counter-attack. In the final days of the battle, and with the Canadians acting as the spearhead of the British Army, the Canadian Corps alone sustained over 12,000 casualties. A few days later, beset with manpower shortages and keen to open an attack at Cambrai before the weather conditions ruled it out, Haig ended offensive operations on the Ypres front. Total British casualties amounted to over 240,000 men. It is probable that the German losses were even higher. The misery caused by the atrocious conditions in which the men fought would, however, be impossible to quantify.

No great victory had been achieved. German submarines were still free to use the Belgium ports as a base for their attacks on Allied shipping. The battle had at least maintained the pressure on the Germans on the western front, at the same time as keeping it away from the weakened French army. And at last, after three long years of domination, the Germans had been pushed off the high ground around the salient.

All of the ground won at such a huge cost would be given up again in the following spring as the Germans launched their own massive operation to win the war. Russia, under Bolshevik rule, was by now out of the conflict altogether. Large numbers of German troops, freed from their responsibilities in the east would soon be poured into an attack of unprecedented ferocity. The Allied cause would, once again, hang in the balance.

Henry was also struck by the unintentional humour of the front-line soldier:

The Tommies' way of twisting words about is amusing. I think almost every Tommy calls an incinerator an 'insinuator'. The other day the sanitary orderly at the 82nd Field Company was talking about an 'absolution' bench for the men to wash at.

In the spring of 1917 the Germans had pulled back from their positions in and around the Somme front to newly constructed defences known by the British as the Hindenberg Line. The Allies would have to break this line of defence at some point if they were to defeat the Germans on the battlefield. Throughout the spring and early summer the British had launched a series of attacks against these formidable fortifications. The Hindenberg Line consisted of an outpost zone, with a strongly wired forward edge of at least 100 yards in depth, deep trenches and an interconnecting network of heavily armed strongpoints. The support system to the rear consisted of a front and a support trench, each protected by three or four belts of barbed wire and numerous dugouts. All of these trenches were connected by communication trenches which were themselves protected by belts of wire on both sides. Behind the support system there was a further line of defence. Its construction represented the very latest German concept of active defence in depth. The depth of the whole defended area was between 6,000 and 8,000 yards. It was a serious obstacle.

Despite its obvious strengths, Haig felt that if the Hindenberg Line could be breached between Banteux and Havrincourt then a short advance northwards could threaten the whole of the German salient which bulged into the Allied lines as far as the River Sensee. A simultaneous advance towards Cambrai would seriously disrupt enemy transport and communication lines.

Various plans for the attack were formulated during the spring and early summer. A radically new plan of attack was finally settled on early in the autumn. This would dispense with the long, drawn-out preliminary artillery bombardment as this destroyed any element of surprise. Using new techniques to identify the location of German batteries and defensive positions, the artillery would, instead, launch an enormous protective barrage as soon as the attack commenced. The assault itself would be made by a massed formation of tanks which would crush the barbed wire, allowing the infantry to follow through and get into the enemy trenches. The RFC would join in with low-level strafing and bombing. The objectives for the attack were simple: to break the Hindenberg Line, push the cavalry through north and east and do as much damage as possible.

The plan represented a significant break with the past and began on 20 November with a stunning and unprecedented success. The surprise was complete. The British tanks terrorised the German defenders and crashed through the Hindenberg Line. The British were able to advance over four miles into German territory. But the tanks were far from reliable machines. After the initial attack, many were either broken down or stranded, or knocked out by enemy fire and could not therefore press home the advantage that had been won. And after the heavy losses during the Third Battle of Ypres, there were few reserves of infantry to reinforce the gains that had been made. Most significantly the British were unable, despite several heroic attempts, to capture the strategically significant high ground of Bourlon Wood, which Haig had insisted be secured before there could be any prospect of sustaining the offensive. Haig closed down the battle on 27 November and sought to defend the ground he had gained. Massive German counter-attacks, which began on 30 November, saw virtually all of the gains lost. It was a crushing disappointment given the euphoria of 20 November.

Henry would now be sent to the Cambrai front, which had now settled down for the winter.

4th December. Sudden orders to join up with the Division. Transport to move off this afternoon and the Companies to entrain at Dickebusch tomorrow. A few days ago we got the news of our attack across the Hindenberg Line towards Cambrai, the ringing of the 'joy bells' in England and the Boche counter push into our positions around Gouzancourt. I suppose we are going down to that front.

5th December. Sunny day; hard frost. Went by lorry with the CRE and MacDonald to Blarringhem. Very cold. Billeted there for the night.

6th December. 16 degrees of frost, but fine. Went down with the DADMS in the Ford ambulance via Aire, St Pol, Doullens and Beaumetz to Basseux, a little south of Arras. Nobody arriving there yet so went into Amiens and spent the night there.

7th December. Back to Basseux. Divisional HQ arrived in the morning. This village was only about a mile behind our old front line, but seemed entirely untouched. Must have been a very quiet front.

8th December. Division moved to Achiet le Petit. Rode there with the CRE. Very desolate country. Long rolling stretches of grass, few trees and all the villages and houses entirely in ruins and except for a few troops not a sign of human life anywhere for miles. This was the country the Boche had laid waste when he retired in the spring. Every house was systematically destroyed – knocked down or blown up. A lot of the fruit trees cut down and lying there. Spent a chilly night in a little hut camp just outside the village.

A few little houses or huts have been built in some of the ruined villages and a few lonely civilians are living there trying to get the country under cultivation again.

9th December. Division moved to Etricourt to relieve the 6th Division [*which had been involved in the initial attack at Cambrai*]. Nasty rainy day.

Rode there with the grooms. Passed through Bapaume. The whole town a ruin. Didn't see a single house you could possibly shelter troops or even a horse in.

Billeted in a pretty good hut camp at Etricourt on the banks of the unfinished Canal du Nord.

12th December. Division moved to Neuville-Bourjonval. The Division, two Brigades in front, holding the line just west of Marcoing and just in front of the famous Hindenberg Line. We have the advantage of good deep Boche dugouts. Saw one of our observation balloons brought down in flames by a Boche plane. The observer came down in his parachute.

Very depressing dreary country here. This village like all the others completely in ruins and only a few walls standing. The trees are quite untouched. The ground is a rolling neglected waste covered with dead grass. Straggling groups of trees here and there mark the positions of villages. There is an unnatural sort of silence too, as there is not a farm with a dog or cows or sheep for miles and miles behind us. There seems very little bird life either. Our quarters were not too comfortable. Our mess was a corrugated iron hut with a mud floor and heated by a stove improvised from an oil drum. MacDonald and I spent two shivering nights on the floor of the office Nissen but then spotted a 40 foot deep dugout and fixed this up as a bedroom. It was in chalk and fairly clean. It was warmer than a hut and moreover down there you were entirely safe from bombs. Once we were in our bedroom we didn't mind if he bombed all night.

Most of the sections were living in dugouts in the Hindenberg Line. I was pretty busy here as I had to see the sick of Divisional HQ, the whole of the Divisional train (Army Service Corps), the reserve Brigade transport lines and a road construction company, besides the RE units. I very often saw about 80 sick a day.

I went up past Trescault one day and I had a look at the Hindenberg Line a bit south of Ribecourt. The Hindenberg Mainline consisted of a front and support lines – big wide trenches 8 to 10 feet deep with a wide fore step and I should think 8 to 10 feet broad across the top. They were not revetted. There were plenty of good deep dugouts well fitted up. What I noticed most was the tremendous thickness of wire in front – 3 and 4 bands each from 10 to 30 yards deep. I saw where our tanks had cut lanes through the wire and also where they had crossed the trenches by throwing into them enormous fascines (or bundles of sticks) 4 to 5 feet in diameter and bound round with chains and then crossing over on top of them. The fascines filled up the whole of the lower half of the trench. Further on were the main Hindenberg support lines. And beyond these again the line we hold at present. The ground was white with snow and the effect of the hoar frost on all the wire was quite pretty. It seemed very quiet. I hardly saw or heard a shell.

There was a good deal of bombing at night and we had several casualties close by. One day, December 13th, the Boche shelled the cross roads at the top of the village with a high velocity gun. He did a small attack that morning. I also saw 4 or 5 Boche planes brought down, one by archie fire.

On December 24th I dined with 57 Field Ambulance at Bus. They were running the Divisional Rest Station and had a very palatial mess and bedrooms. Christmas day we spent at Neuville. Two to three inches of snow fell in the afternoon and we had a rather chilly dinner in our hut.

Chapter 6

Victory

1918

The British Army in France had spent the whole of 1917 on the offensive. It had been a gruelling year of pain and sacrifice. The battles of Arras and Ypres had been fought to ease the pressure on their French allies who, after the failure of the Aisne attack in the spring, were no longer in a position to mount large-scale operations. The ability of the French Army to withstand a heavy onslaught was also in serious doubt. The BEF had therefore, by virtue of necessity, taken on the role of senior partner on the western front. As a result, the casualties had been enormous. Territorial gains, however, had been miniscule. The German defences remained robust and intact. Prime Minister David Lloyd George was becoming increasingly concerned over Haig's conduct of military operations and his failure to bring about the promised breakthrough in the stalemate of the trenches. The flow of new recruits from Britain began to dry up as the politicians tried to minimise the grim toll of casualties. Of necessity, the fighting strength of each British division was reduced in size from twelve battalions to nine. The strain on the BEF of carrying the principal weight of the Allied campaign in France was beginning to tell.

Despite all this effort and sacrifice, by the end of 1917 the tables on the western front were about to be dramatically turned. Russia had succumbed to revolution and had dropped out of the war altogether. This began to release vast numbers of German soldiers from the eastern front. During the last month of 1917 and the first few weeks of the new year, over forty fresh divisions were re-deployed to the western front. The Italian defeat at Caporetto in October imposed a further strain on British resources on the western front, when two corps of five divisions were sent to bolster the Italian war effort. The Allies' numerical superiority had dramatically evaporated. The ground was ripe for a major German offensive. It was now just a matter of time before the hammer blow landed. The only question was where would the Germans strike? The tables had effectively turned. As the New Year began, it would be the turn of the British to assume a defensive posture.

The tactics of defence on the western front had also been gradually changing. It made no sense to place large numbers of defending troops in the front line as this made them highly vulnerable to artillery and machine-gun fire. Instead, a system of defence in depth had emerged, whereby layers of increasingly strongly held positions were created, sapping the enemy's strength as he advanced and thereby making him more vulnerable to counter-attacks. A new 'forward zone' a mile or so in depth would be lightly defended. Behind this a strongly wired 'battle zone' several miles in depth would be the main line of resistance. A third and final defensive line would be sited behind the 'battle zone'.

A German attack looked likely to come sooner rather than later. There was, however, some good news for the Allies. The American Army was on its way to France. A few divisions had already arrived but were not yet combat ready nor fully equipped. In any event, the US commander, General Pershing, not unreasonably wanted his troops to fight as an American army and not as plug-in replacements to weakened British and French formations. All this meant that it would be several more months before the American divisions made their presence felt on the battlefield. The Germans knew this and would need to attack before the Americans joined the British and French armies in the trenches.

The intelligence picture was not entirely clear, but it seemed most likely that the attack, when it came, would probably be launched against the Third and Fifth armies, and would be designed to sever the link between the French and British forces with the ultimate aim of securing the Channel ports. This would effectively cut off the British armies from their lines of communication and supply. The war was thus entering its deadly final stages.

Towards the end of January, Henry had managed to get home for another fourteen days' leave. En route to Boulogne he travelled through the shell-torn Somme battlefield of 1916.

In the old Somme battlefield of 1916 we passed little crosses marking graves, singly, or in twos, threes or in groups – everywhere, thousands of them.

When he returned to France in early February, he would find the 19th Division at Neuville, on the Cambrai front, six miles to the south east of Bapaume. Neuville was about ten miles behind the British front line. It was part of the Third Army and stood almost directly in the path of the prospective German advance. Once again, Henry's job was to attend to the medical needs of the divisional Royal Engineers and other supporting troops.

15th February. Division relieved by the 63rd, Royal Naval Division. Divisional HQ moved back to camp near Haplincourt. Fairly comfortable here. Had an Armstrong hut to myself and we had a double Armstrong for the mess. The Brigades, Field Companies in camps round about.

4th March. [Still in camp] near Haplincourt. Last three days beastly cold; very rough north wind with snow and sleet. 'Wind up!' Huns expected to attack any time.

The general position as it appeared to us was roughly this. When Russia dropped out of the war last autumn the Boche was left with a useful superiority in numbers. This numerical superiority he still maintained at the present moment. American troops would be coming into the fight soon, probably by the early summer. At what rate they would be able to get over and what numbers the Americans would be able to maintain in the field at first we did not know. But they were certainly coming and from the moment they began getting into the field the Boche superiority would begin to lessen and might very likely soon be entirely lost.

What would the Boche do then? He might remain strictly on the defensive and nurse his forces, hoping by these tactics to prolong the war until the allies, seeing the hopelessness of obtaining a decision for a very long time, might propose an inconclusive peace. Or he might collect every available man and gun and put every ounce of his strength into one colossal attack, hoping to give us a knock out now, while numbers were still on his side. If he succeeded he won the war; if he failed he would probably be too exhausted by his effort to offer much resistance when it became our turn to attack. It was a gamble. All the same, everybody thought it was 10-1 he would take the risk and attack. Apparently this was the view of our Higher Command as well. Hence the 'wind up'.

7th March. Having beautiful weather just now; slight frosts at night and warm sunshine all day long. A slight wind from the north east. Went to the 'Duds', the 17th Division Variety Show. Very good show indeed, very clever and amusing. Very good orchestra, good costumes, scenery and very well stage managed. The best little imitation 'girl' I've ever seen. They perform each night in a big hut between here and Bertincourt. Dined with the 57th Field Ambulance about three quarters of a mile behind our camp.

10th March. The Division is now re-organised on the new three battalion per Brigade system. The 56th Brigade was broken up and reformed out of the 8th North Staff's, 8th Cheshire's and the 4th King's Shropshire Light Infantry from another Division. The machine gun Companies have been formed into a divisional machine gun battalion, Colonel Winser (South Lancs) commanding them. My old friends, the 7th North Lancs have been broken up.

17th March. Still having quite abnormally fine warm weather. Country dry and dusty. Everybody sitting out in the sun just like summer. Frosty nights. The goslings on the willows all out. No Hun attack yet, but the 'wind still up!' We were to have gone into the line on the 6th but the relief was postponed as the Hun was expected to attack and our Division was supposed to do the counter attack.

The Hun sent some high velocity shells over our camp the other day. He sent about a dozen or twenty; they burst 400–800 yards behind us in some ploughed country. We are ploughing up quite a lot of country round here. Some of it is sown with wheat or oats already. MacDonald has gone temporarily to Corps (V Corps, Villers au Flos) as staff officer to the CE and Heaney is doing adjutant. [*V Corps had three divisions in the line, the 47th, 63rd and the 17th.*]

19th March. 'Wind' apparently subsiding. We expect to relieve the 17th Division in the line on 21st–24th. Divisional HQ at Bertincourt. Fine moonlight nights lately, but very little bombing by the Hun.

20th March. Went for a stroll with Smalley. We were looking at some of the Corps or Army reserve lines and wondered if the Boche would ever get as far if he attacked. Any amount of wire but the Corps line that runs along in front of Haplincourt [*the final defensive line*] is only marked by boards and just marked out with a spade.

A wire came round to say that the Boche would probably attack tomorrow! For the last few mornings we have been putting up heavy 'counter-preparation' barrages as a precaution, ie heavy barrages on points where the Hun might be likely to be massing.

The Germans were to launch their main assault the following day on the whole of the front of the Third and Fifth armies. It would be the biggest attack of the entire war to date. A crashing artillery blow landed on the thin and weakened British positions. More than 6,000 guns took part in the bombardment, firing a mixture of gas, shrapnel and high explosive. No one had ever seen or heard anything quite like it before. Whole sections of the British front line, along with its defenders, simply disappeared under the unprecedented violence and ferocity of the German guns. Camouflaged by heavy fog, wave upon wave of assault troops – specially trained 'storm troopers' – then hurled themselves against the remaining defenders who were holding out in small pockets in the battle zone. Chaos reigned as the fog of war descended. Numbed by the onslaught, the British line began to crack wide open. The outcome of the war itself began to look suddenly in the balance.

21st March. A good deal of gunning in the night. At 5am the thing started with a crash! I jumped out of bed, found it very chilly, so got back and listened. Every gun we had seemed to be firing as fast as they could let them off. A lot of our heavies were only a mile or so up the road and their repeated crashes resounded above the general din. I could hear a pretty persistent bursting of big Hun shells. A lot of high velocity shells were coming over into the back areas. A regular stream of them were passing over us and bursting in Haplincourt and down near our stables about 400 yards to the rear. The whole place was shaking.

After a bit I went and saw Heaney in the next hut. A tremendous lot of heavy Boche stuff was coming over and with all this shelling of the back areas there was no mistake about the attack having come at last. We both dressed. We all had an early breakfast about 7am.

We could get no news. All was reported quiet on the Corps front – no attack so far. The din went steadily on. About 10 am I rode round to see the Companies. Shrapnel was bursting up the valley by the 81st Field Company where the 'Duds' had been performing last night and a lot of horses and transport were moving back away from it. A lot of shells had fallen all about the 82nd and 94th Field Companies at Bertincourt and were still bursting all along just north of the Haplincourt–Bertincourt road and about Velu Wood. No one had been hit. There were no sick! As I came back there were more shells round where the 'Duds' hut was and one or two into the 81st people's camp. The transport were moving further up the valley. I could hardly believe it! This was a back area! But they certainly were real shells. I looked in at the 57th Field Ambulance. They had no news. They had had one or two shells in to their camp. The bearers were all ready to go up. The bombardment seemed to have slackened off about 11am.

As I rode down towards our camp I saw black smoke blowing away from it. Then two or three fresh puffs. Could they be shells? It seemed hard to realise it, but they certainly were – not big ones, but still shells.

Henry returned to the 57th Field Ambulance.

When I arrived most of the shells were bursting a little further up the road and about General Monkhouses's (artillery) Headquarters. Suddenly – fizz! One swished past my head and burst about 15 yards off. I got off my pony and gave her to my groom and went to the mess. People were sitting about in an uncomfortable sort of way trying to look as if they thought it was funny. The CRE was sitting in his office distinctly annoyed at being shot at there. The shells stopped soon after. They were only small 'pipsqueeks' and 4.2s but after all, there isn't much protection in an Armstrong hut.

The news was vague. The Boche seemed to have come through a good way – 1st and 2nd systems – on some part of the front. These shells seemed to be field gun shells. As it was quiet now, we had lunch. Between 2 and 3pm he shelled us again for 20 minutes or so. Quite a lot of shells came into the camp but only 4 men were hit. I dressed them – they were not serious – and sent them off in a car.

I could get no more definite news and I hung about the camp in an aimless sort of way. It was quiet here now except for a few high velocity shells that went two or three hundred yards over the camp. The 57th Brigade were to do a counter attack in the evening at Doignies supported by tanks.

People began drifting back from the front in an ominous kind of way. A crowd of heavy gunners with an officer were sheltering in a hut. He said the Boche were nearly up to their position. They fired off all their shells and then smashed up the breach mechanism of their guns – 9.2 howitzers – and came away. Just as they came away one of the guns got a direct hit from a shell. About sunset it got very chilly and a thick fog came up. I heard no news about our counter attack.

The CRE and I began preparing a slit to sleep in for the night. We thought they would be sure to shell us again and it would be more comfortable sleeping in a slit outside than inside in an unprotected hut. But about midnight Divisional HQ moved back to a spot just south east of Bancourt. It was a grass field and there was a thick wet fog. It was very chilly. After an hour or two we managed to get a few bell tents put up and got a few stretchers and blankets and managed to get an hour of chilly sleep.

The Germans had fought their way deep into the battle zone of the Fifth Army to the south and, in places, were almost through it altogether. Further to the north, in the Third Army area, the 51st Highland Division had eventually given way under the force of the German attack. The V Corps was just about managing to hold the ground in-between and the counter-attack of the 57th Brigade, supported by tanks and despite grievous losses, had at least for the moment checked the enemy's advance. Just after midday the 19th Division had been transferred to the

IV Corps on the left of V Corps and, minus its artillery, engineers and pioneers, was ordered to move forward to take up a position behind the 51st Division. The Royal Engineers of the 19th Division were put to work preparing the defences at the rear of the battle zone. However, with the Germans advancing to the north and the south of V Corps, a retirement had to be effected. The IV and V Corps had been forced back to the rear defences of the battle zone on the whole ten-mile front between the Bapaume–Cambrai road and Fontaine les Croiselles. A complete breach in the British lines looked highly likely.

22nd March. Foggy morning and quiet. Got up and had some breakfast. He was putting some high velocity shells into Corps HQ at Villers au Flos. During the morning the sun came out and it got very hot. The Division was all in the fighting now. I asked the Assistant Director of Medical Services if he could give me anything to do but he said I'd better stop where I was for the present. Not much news. In the afternoon [the enemy] put some nasty big black high velocity shells just short of the road (8" guns I think). You couldn't hear them coming and the splinters were flying about all over the place.

About 6pm we all moved back to Grevillers. I rode back with Heaney. He was putting some shells into Bapaume as we came through. It was a nice camp – huts – and had been a Corps HQ. Now there were three divisional HQs in it so there wasn't much room. A few shells were falling somewhere between us and Bapaume – on the road I think. Slept in a hut with the CRE and the adjutant. People coming in and out all night and I didn't sleep much.

23rd March. No news, but the situation rather serious apparently. Asked the ADMS what I could do. He told me to go and help the Highland Field Ambulance (51st Division) who were running Corps Main Dressing Station at the old CCS camp up the road towards Bapaume. A lot of 60 pounders were alongside and firing hard. The CCSs (two of them) had cleared off two or three days ago and had apparently left most of their equipment behind including all the beds, blankets and sheets etc, including a complete X Ray plant.

Things were pretty busy here. Dressed cases all the afternoon until about 9pm. Kept up all night to relieve the other men but not many cases came in. The Huns were putting over some pretty big shells trying to get the 60 pounders – splinters were flying about the huts and one or two of the shells came into the camp. Bright moonlight again but I only heard one lot of bombs dropped.

No. 48 Casualty Clearing Station in an advanced position at Ytres on the opening of day of the battle, had been forced to pull back during the course of the first evening and had been forced to abandon some, but not all, of its stores. The Lucknow CCS had also been forced to abandon some of its stores. Generally, the medical services of the Third Army lost very little equipment during the battle, notwithstanding the rapid nature of the retreat.

24th March. Fairly quiet in the morning – misty. The Field Ambulance was preparing to move off, having cleared most of their cases, so I went back to Divisional HQ again. In the afternoon we moved back to some huts on the road to Achiet le Petit and Miraumont. Rode over with Heaney and got there about 4pm. We seemed to be coming back a tremendous long way. I wondered how much further we should have to go back. At any rate we probably shouldn't shift from here for a day or two.

The ADMS sent us two or three hundred yards down the road to help Colonel Preston to fix up some huts as a dressing station. Found Preston at the huts near a railway siding at the bottom of the hill and helped him fix the place up as the Divisional Main Dressing Station. All three Field Ambulances turned up about an hour later. We had a good meal and I lay down for a couple of hours but couldn't sleep.

At 10pm cases began coming in from Bapaume and Grevillers. The bearers had an awful carry and were dead beat. Smalley, Kidd, and Cochrane turned up dead beat, also Burton. They had had a pretty rough time. The shelling at Bancourt, Bapaume and Grevillers had been bad.

A mass of transport filled the road between Miraumont and Achiet le Petit and on to Bucquoy. It could make very little headway and only seemed to move on about 100 yards in an hour. All night long the road was full. It recalled the retreat from Mons in 1914. I expected every minute that Hun planes would come over and bomb the whole road and column to blazes, but I never heard a single one.

By now there were not many cases coming in. Towards dawn I lay down on the floor and dozed a bit.

25th March. We cleared our cases in some Motor Ambulance Convoy cars which turned up and had some food. About 9am the Ambulances moved off to a new dressing station at Bucquoy. Smalley and I walked back to Irles to investigate a road where cars might run from Miraumont up the valley past Irles and pick up the odd wounded. Very little shelling from the Hun. It looked just like manoeuvres on Salisbury Plain. The 18 pounder batteries were in action in the open along the top of a ridge in the old text book way and along the skyline in front we could see lines of extended infantry retiring and then lying down. A few Boche shells were bursting along the skyline. Saw Trescott [a sapper officer] in Irles on a bicycle going to blow up a bridge or something.

We saw nothing of the cars so came back through Miraumont. He was putting some big shells about our last night's dressing station and some very big – 8" or 12" shells – into the back end of Achiet le Petit. A whole mob of infantry – I don't know who they were – they looked fed up to the last degree, were plodding away up the railway line in the valley towards Puisieux. Some infantry of another Division were coming up the road towards the line.

It seemed awful to think of the British Army retiring like this. The troops were done in; their morale was gone and they had no more fight left in them. They had been fighting for 5 days and were frightfully thinned out so it was only what you would expect. But why had no re-enforcements come up? Why were Divisions made to fight on until they were dead beat? Was it because the Allied Army was fighting all out and there were no fresh Divisions to send? Or was Foche sacrificing the troops on this front so that he could concentrate on another part of the front where the Hun was weak – say the Ypres–Dunkirk front – and make a tremendous counter offensive there? The whole thing seemed a puzzle. We had heard no news of any fresh Divisions coming up here or of any kind of counter push of ours anywhere. It was all very depressing.

We found the new Main Dressing Station in a big hut at Bucquoy. We went into a tent they had put up and had some lunch. In the afternoon, a good many cases came in and were dressed. A tremendous lot of transport was collected just around here but began to move off. It was getting dark and cloudy and the wind was very cold. I borrowed a spare coat from Preston. I only saw two Hun planes over but swarms of ours were up. I was told that we brought down a Hun plane that was trying to machine gun the road in the morning, just up the road.

Smalley and Kidd went back to our old dressing station of last night to try and collect any stray wounded and to fix up some bearer relay posts. Divisional HQ had moved back to Puisieux but were now away again. About 5pm I started back with Colonel Powell and Burton and the 57th and 59th bearers. They had been shelling Bucquoy before we left. We got back to Puisieux and there met one of our MOs who said the Boche were in Miraumont. A battery of 18 pounders came back past us in rather a hurry. I suggested going back to give Smalley and Kidd the tip but he said they had left so we went on over the old battlefield of Serre and Gommecourt and arrived about 9pm at Hebuterne.

Recognised all our old haunts here where we used to hold the line last winter. There was a big hut here that was being used as a dressing station and we dressed a few cases, then went into one of the few remaining houses and had some food. Cochrane, who had been missing all day turned up here and Smalley and Kidd soon came in.

About 11pm we all went to bed – that is we lay down on the floor. I had no coat. I lay on some damp straw but in a few minutes was so cold that I got up again. I thought I would walk across to Divisional HQ who were said to be at Colincamps, 2 or 3 miles off, and try and find my kit and come back here in the morning. We had now come back such a long way, surely we could hardly move back again for a day or two? I started off about 1am. I arrived at Colincamps and was told HQ had moved back to Courcelles. At Courcelles I was told they had gone to Souastre. This was another 5 or 6 miles. So I plodded off past an ancient billet of ours at Sailly aux Bois and finally reached Souastre. It was very quiet. I didn't hear the sound of a gun or a bomb. At Souastre I was told DHQ had gone to Foncquevillers. The 51st and 41st Division HQs were here. Luckily the 59th Field Ambulance were here as well so I broke into their house and woke up Hardwick and got some grub and borrowed some blankets and had 3 hours good sleep. By the way, this was the first village with real houses in it that I had been in for months.

26th March. Very quiet this morning. Couldn't hear any shooting. Transport went back to St Amand. Smalley and Kidd came in and had a bath, intending to go back to Hebuterne after.

About 10am a fearful panic started. Nobody quite knew who started it. Apparently two staff officers (Boche spies?) were responsible. At any rate we were told to clear all our cases the best way we could at once. Transport and gun wagons all came dashing through the village, went the wrong way, tried to turn and got jammed. The civilians got excited, some began to weep. One old woman with an eye to business ran among the traffic with a brush and dust pan and swept up quite a lot of corn which was spilling out of a sack on a wagon, and which no doubt fed her hens for a long time.

A nondescript collection of infantry, Army Service Corps and other oddments were paraded and served out with rifles and ammunition to defend the village to the last. Never having probably seen a rifle loaded before they then proceeded to try and load theirs with the result that bullets began popping off in an alarming way. They finally took up a position behind the village and began to dig in. We had cleared all our cases and began fixing up an Aid Post in a sunken road just behind the village. The Boche cavalry were said to have broken through and were expected at any moment.

In the middle of the excitement the mail arrived and Hardwick was presented with a nicely bound volume on 'Ferrets' – how to breed them, feed them, train them etc. Hardwick and I fully expected to be killed or captured in the next hour or so and decided that at all cost if we were captured we should keep together for company. And we could also have the book on ferrets to read.

After waiting about for two of three hours in a very cold wind with nothing to eat, nothing more seemed to happen, so we returned to our house and opened up there again. About 1pm I was sent back with Gregg and the 59th Transport and bearers to Coullemont. The 57th were also here. We got some tents up for the men and got into a small estaminet close by where they had a good fire and some hot coffee.

The panic was caused by a false alarm. A Hun patrol got into the outskirts of Hebuterne and started machine gunning. A panic started among some transport. The transport and the panic soon spread down to Souastre!

It was nice and peaceful back here. No war had ever been as far back as this. We all slept on the floor of the bar room with a huge fire burning and had a long nights rest. Strange to see cultivated fields again.

The retreat of the Third Army effectively ended on 26 March. For the next ten days of the German offensive the line held by the Third Army remained practically unaltered. It had been pushed back all the way to Albert, losing all of the ground gained since the spring of 1917. The offensive had inflicted grievous casualties on both armies. But the attack had spent itself. Many German soldiers took advantage of the abundance of food and drink they had discovered during their advance. Discipline suffered as a result and progress slowed. Through a combination of extraordinary bravery and resilience, coupled with the difficulties the Germans experienced in re-supplying their troops over long distances and the breakdown of discipline in many places, the defenders had prevented a wholesale breach of the British line. But if the High Command thought the immediate peril was over, they would be very much mistaken.

27th March. Very quiet again. Went back to Souastre and found Colonel Mackenzie and Burton there. Hardwick up at an improvised dressing station near Chateau de la Haye.

28th March. Heard more gunfire again and several casualties came in. The Boche evidently getting his guns up again. Hardwick came in about 2pm. The Division is coming out of the line. The rest of them went back after lunch to Coullemont and I joined up with the CRE at Divisional HQ at La Cauchie.

29th March. Up at 4.30am and rode with Heaney to Doullens. Entrained about 11.30am and arrived at Strazeele about 5.30pm. We got some coffee and omelettes at an estaminet at the station and rode to our new camp with Padre Railton. Bailleul had been badly shelled. It was quite empty; all the civilians had gone and the picturesque old tower of the town hall was completely smashed. Our camp – Nissen huts – called Ulster Camp was just behind Dranoutre. My kit arrived about 3am and I went to bed and had a good night.

The 19th Division, exhausted after its heroic labours of the last few days had been moved further to the north in order to recuperate. It had sustained very high casualties and needed time to gather up its strength again.

The German offensive was, however, far from over. Plans were already developed for an equally powerful blow to be landed on the front of the First and Second armies holding the line around Ypres and down to Armentières. This time the Channel ports were the objective. Far from finding a quiet resting place, Henry and his colleagues had been moved almost directly into the path of the second German hammer blow.

In the meantime, the British government was forced into rushing all available troops to the western front in order to bolster the line. It rescinded its promise not to send boys below the age of 18 into combat. General Foch was placed in overall command of all the Allied armies in France, giving him 'full control of the tactical employment' of the British, French and American forces.

30th March. Got up about 10.30am. A nice camp – comfortable huts. The Division had an awful time last week. As far as I can make out they did well, but I believe the fighting strength of the Division when it came out of the line was about 1000 bayonets. The RAMC were very lucky and had comparatively light casualties. I think there were no officer casualties except two MOs captured on March 24th. The Division is apparently to be made up to strength again with drafts immediately and is going to take over the line in front of Messines. It seems to be very quiet up here except for some long range shelling by the Boche on Bailleul. The 57th Field Ambulance are at

Dranoutre. Colonel Powell is leaving – going to get a job at the base. Rained all day. It seems the Boche push down at the Amiens front has come to an end.

2nd April. Divisional HQ moved to Westhoff farm. Behind Neuve Eglise. 82nd Field Company at Fort Victoria near Lindenhoek, 81st at Wulverghem, 94th at Moroka Camp on the Wulverghem–Neuve Eglise Road near La Hutte. The Division is holding a front of about 3000 yards in front of Messines. Our Brigade, plus 6 Companies from the other 2 Brigades are in the line. The 57th Field Ambulance are clearing the line. Advanced Dressing Station at Kandahar Farm at Wulverghem – rather a long way back. Smalley and Humphries there. Quite a good place. Defended to a certain extent and accommodation for about 30 stretchers and bunks for 60.

Colonel Powell left this morning for Etaples. Sorry he's gone. The 59th Field Ambulance are running the Divisional rest Station at the Hospice at Locre. Went over and dined with them. The sisters are still running the restaurant for officers. 'Jane' was still there. All the way round the wall of the dining room was a kind of frieze of British regimental badges painted on the wall very nicely. Any number of different regiments were there and I thought how interesting it would be for British people visiting the place after the war. All the civilians were nervous about the Boche attacking up here. But the Boche are apparently very thin up here and have not many guns and there seems to be no sign of any attack on this front.

The second major offensive of 1918 opened on 9 April with a huge bombardment along the front from Lens to Armentières, using a large quantity of gas shells. Shortly after 8am, nine full-strength German divisions attacked through a thick and heavy mist. The Portuguese 2nd Division holding the line around Neuve Chapelle and Laventie broke and ran almost immediately, leaving a gaping hole in the British line, which was only just held until fresh troops could be brought up. The 40th Division on the left of the Portuguese at Bois Grenier also buckled under the weight of the German onslaught, although the Lancashire battalions of the 55th Division on the right stoically held their ground, putting up a fierce and formidable resistance in a remarkable act of defiance against vastly superior forces.

The 19th Division now formed part of the reserve to IX Corps. Its brigades would be detached to various parts of the line to try and bolster the defence. All three field companies of the Royal Engineers to which Henry was attached would fight as infantry over the next few hectic days, plugging gaps in the line at short notice.

The German assault on 10 April would also push the weak and under-strength 19th Division, holding the line further to the north, back several miles. The fighting was desperate and bloody. It consisted of a wild confusion of attack and counter-attack. Steadily the British line was forced further and further back. By the end of the first day the Germans had advanced up to six miles, forcing the British back behind the River Lawe. Another crisis loomed. It would lead Field Marshal Haig to issue his famous 'backs to the wall' order of the day where he called on the British forces to hold every inch of ground to the death.

9th April. Foggy morning. Very heavy gunfire this morning a good deal to our right, south of Armentieres. Nobody seemed to know much about it. Later I heard that the Boche had attacked on the Armentieres–La Bassee front and were said to have penetrated to Fleurbaix. That is a good way behind our front.

10th April. Still foggy. Very heavy firing again extending all along our front right up to the Menin Road. He is shelling the back area with high velocity guns. He was putting big shells into a camp half a mile behind us on the road over Ravelsberg Hill and huts were flying up into the air. There is evidently some pretty big show on.

The Boche apparently came over all along our front in the fog this morning and have got through nearly to Wulverghem. The Field Companies are all up in the line acting as infantry. Major Smith, OC of the 81st Field Company, was badly wounded this morning. The Boche are said to have come through a long way on our right where they attacked yesterday. The Portuguese were holding the line here and let them through. In the afternoon the civilians were all clearing off from Westhoff Farm and other farms round about taking away everything they could and driving away their cattle. A lot of heavy guns began coming back, also transport. A regular retreat seemed to have started again. Divisional HQ are going back. The Boche are getting quite close on our right and seem to have gone right through to Estaires. No more definite news from our front.

About 9pm we moved back to Ulster Camp at Dranoutre. Neuve Eglise and all the back areas were all badly shelled during the day.

11th April. Did nothing all day. The Boche put some big shells into Dranoutre, smashed the road up. About 10pm the ADMS told me to join up with the 58th Field Ambulance who were running an Advanced Dressing Station at Kemmel. Found Preston fixed up in a hut camp at Little Kemmel, the old Brigade HQ camp just on the left of Kemmel Hill. Nothing doing at present so we slept.

On 11 April the Germans captured Merville. Heavy fighting took place on the Messines Ridge and the 19th Division was obliged to withdraw to positions east of Neuve Eglise and Wulverghem, leaving Hill 63 and the Messines Ridge in the hands of the enemy. The German attack had created a huge salient, twelve miles long and six miles deep into the British line.

12th April. Went by car to the old ADS at Vierstraat and joined Preston who had gone on to fix it up. The 58th Brigade were in reserve at Rossignol Camp. I went and saw them about arranging to clear their wounded etc. I also visited various units and Aid Posts at Byron Farm and Ruined Farm at St Eloi. Pretty quiet everywhere. Went back to Vierstraat. Moved back with all the bearers at night to a hut camp behind La Clytte. Had a good night there.

It had been a day of chaos and confusion as well as intense fighting. The front of the IX Corps had come under great pressure and a gap had opened up on the left where the 148th Brigade had fallen back, but the enemy had not managed to penetrate the line.

13th April. About 1pm I got orders to join Colonel Preston who was running the Divisional bearers at Little Kemmel. The Boche has been shelling the crossroads at Canada Corner at Locre but it was quiet when we came through. Our line has now come back roughly to the Neuve Eglise–Wulverghem road, just covering Wytschaete then just in front of the Damm Strasse to the canal. In the confusion of the last three days' fighting the different divisions and brigades had got mixed up. We had to arrange to clear from 8 or 9 different aid posts and from brigades of other divisions besides our own, Gregg was out reconnoitring some of these aid posts near Wulverghem. Preston sent me up the Kemmel–Neuve Eglise road with two bearer squads to find the 4th King's Own Yorkshire Light Infantry and the 4th Yorks and Lancs (148th Brigade, 49th Division). Pretty heavy shelling up here. 'Daylight Corner' (the corner where the road goes to Wulverghem) had been all smashed up. Enormous 8" and 12" craters blocked the road and one had taken half one of the houses away. Further down he was shelling all about and some were going just over and just short of the road. I found one of the MOs in a house just short of Neuve Eglise. He was landing some nasty big shells just here and the windows had just come in. I left him one squad and went on and found the other aid post in Neuve Eglise. Our line was just outside the village. Left the other squad here and came back to Kemmel. We were using some of the huts as a dressing station. The main dressing station was now at Westoutre. We also had a forward car post at Lindenhoek on the Kemmel–Neuve Eglise road. I dressed cases in one of the huts all night until 5am. We had a lot of wounded in. The Boche was putting a lot of shells just beyond us – trying for some batteries I think. Some of the splinters were flying back and hitting the huts. At 5am I turned in and slept until noon.

The German attack on the 13th was vigorously prosecuted against the ten-mile front held by the XI, XV and IX corps. The enemy enjoyed a superiority in numbers of almost three to one. The Germans made their biggest gains along the front held by the IX Corps. They had pushed the line back over two miles between Bailleul and Neuve Eglise. The enemy wanted possession of the high ground around the Mont des Cats and Mount Kemmel.

14th April. Up at midday. Surprised to find it so late. Had some food and then went back to reconnoitre a track by 'Butterfly farm' back to Canada Corner with a view to carrying cases right back there if the road through Locre became impassable for cars. Lots of batteries about in action. I saw some batteries of French 75s also French infantry in their light blue uniforms who had come up and were in reserve trenches near Scherpenberg. When I got back Colonel Preston was there. The French were expected to make a counter attack at dusk. This apparently was a mistake as I don't think there was any counter attack.

Busy evening. The Huns attacking on the Neuve Eglise front. About 11pm I went up to the old ADS at Lindenhoek, now a Regimental Aid Post with 5 MOs there to see about some cases from the 7th Sherwood Forester's.

The 14th saw more fighting but not a lot of movement in the line. For the 19th Division it was particularly difficult day. It was heavily shelled and its right flank near Neuve Eglise was in considerable difficulty.

15th April. Left Lindenhoek about 5am and came back to Kemmel Hill. The Boche has got Neuve Eglise. Our line now runs in the valley between Neuve Eglise and 'Daylight Corner', behind Wulverghem to Wytschaete. Preston and the ADS moved back to Canada Corner. Gregg, Jones and I stopped where we were at Kemmel with the bearers and one or two dressers running the place as a car loading post. We kept two large cars standing there. During the morning the Ford car up at Lindenhoek got knocked out and the orderly was wounded. The Regimental Aid Posts came back to the brasserie in Kemmel village which had some good fortified cellars.

We put the bearers in the big tunnels dug in the hill on the opposite side of the road. There were also some handy dugouts close to the road which we used for dressing cases in or putting them while waiting for a car. We stopped in our steel shelter on the side of Kemmel Hill. It was just about 'pipsqueak' proof. The Germans kept shelling the other side of the road and had smashed up several of the huts there. These shells came over the hill from the direction of Neuve Eglise.

In the evening the Germans suddenly started shelling us with 5.9s. The first one landed just outside our house near a hut where the cooks were working and they all scuttled off into a dugout. 40 or 50 [shells came over] in rapid succession. They were coming unpleasantly close. I sat on the floor of our room and inwardly quaked. Fortunately we were just out of their direct line. The shells came all through the camp and fell within 5 or 6 yards of us. They blew in the window and splattered the walls with splinters; several huts went up. When they stopped we went out and saw one of the cars knocked out and blazing all over. The other had been hit but could be got away. Gregg went out to speak to a despatch rider who had just come up. He had just come back into the house again when a 5.9 came over and burst in the identical spot where he had just been standing. More came over and we had another dose of it for the next few minutes. Fortunately we had no wounded in. The hut we were using for dressing cases yesterday was simply riddled with splinters. These shells come from quite a new direction, ie from the direction of Wytschaete. Our car was completely burnt out, but they managed to get the other away. We slept in our same house that night but weren't much disturbed.

The Germans captured Bailleul on the 15th.

16th April. The camp was shelled on both sides of the road more or less all day. Not many cases came through. In the afternoon I went back to look at some dugouts a little way down the road behind Kemmel Hill. When I got there I found the crater of an 8" literally in the doorway of our house – the middle doorway. It had blown in the door and piled up about two feet of earth into the doorway of the hut so that you stepped directly out of the room over this earth into the crater. I thought I wouldn't sleep there at any price. I suggested the tunnels across the road. Gregg wasn't very keen on moving as the tunnels were very crowded. We went and looked at a dugout just behind. I didn't like it. It was dug into the bank and had timber over the top with 5 or 6 feet of earth over the timber and the doorway faced the Huns. It was the sort of place you would likely to be buried in, so we decided on the tunnels and moved in there for the night. Unfortunately a couple of bearer squads that had just been relieved were put into the dugouts that we had decided not to sleep in, for a night's rest.

The Germans continued to make headway on the 16th and captured Wytschaete.

17th April. When we woke up the Germans were giving the area an awful shelling. We could hear them crashing about outside. Some gas shells were coming over as well and we had to put on our respirators. The enemy evidently knew of these tunnels and was enfilading the entrances. He probably expected a brigade HQ or something of the sort would be here. Our cars were standing further up the road in a cutting and we were getting them down when we wanted them. Luckily we weren't getting many wounded. I went out to see a man who had just been hit by some splinters in a dugout close by. I had just got into the dugout when another shell burst right on the lintel of the doorway. It blew in the door and fetched down about half a ton of sandbags and filled the place with smoke and pungent fumes. I think it must have been mixed gas and high explosive.

Soon after I got back someone came in and said 8 or 9 men had been buried in the dugout across the road behind our old elephant shelter. A party turned out at once to dig them out. Gregg and I went across. It was quiet just for the present. The little hollow was an extraordinary sight. The whole camp – there had been perhaps a hundred huts in it – was reduced to a litter of splintered matchwood,

An 8" shell had landed bang on top of the dugout and knocked the whole thing in. It was a frightfully slow business digging them out as big beams of timber had to be sawn through to get at them. One or two of the men were miners and had done the same kind of thing before and knew the best way to set about it. While we were digging I heard another 8" howitzer shell coming. It made a row like a train coming. It fell among the trees about 100 yards short of us. Then another fell in the tree just to our left, then another about 5 yards off our elephant, then 2 or 3 more. I heard one coming and I thought 'this one's going to get the lot of us.' It went just over us and earth and lumps of mud were showering down on us for nearly half a minute. The crater was only 6 or 8 yards from where we were. It was very unpleasant.

The men worked [hard] and after a bit we had got them all out except three. They were all very badly shaken, some were badly bruised and crushed and couldn't walk. The other three were dead. I could get my hand down and touch two of them and they were stone dead. The other had about a ton of beams and earth on top of him. The men didn't want to leave off working but we got them to stop and they got the three dead bodies out in the afternoon when it was fairly quiet.

We heard that we and the French were to do a counter attack in the morning, but apparently there wasn't one.

Cochrane came up about midnight and relieved Gregg who went back to the Main Dressing Station at Reninghelst. Brigade HQ were in the big tunnels on the main Kemmel Hill. The Boche was making their tunnel entrances pretty unhealthy as well.

The 17th turned out to be a day of successful resistance in the face of persistent and heavy German attacks. The attacking waves of infantry were cut down by machine-gun and rifle fire and British gun fire inflicted heavy casualties amongst German soldiers sheltering in their own trenches and dugouts. The failure very nearly led the German High Command to break off the battle.

18th April. Quiet day. The Division to be relieved by a French division tonight. [*Almost certainly the 28th Division.*] In the afternoon, Cochrane and I moved down to a dugout in the sunken road where the cars had been standing. As we walked down the road two or three shells swished over the road and burst just over the bank. I was getting rather sick of shells. The cars had all gone down and they didn't send them back for a long time and we had some cases to clear. We spent the night in the dugout at the roadside. Quite a lot of French soldiers drifted in asking the way. They looked a smart lot of fellows. They had been in the defence of Verdun but had not been in the line for quite a long time. Quiet night.

Between 19 and 24 April there was a lull in the Flanders fighting.

19th April. Quiet morning. Relief completed and all squads in by 11.30am and we moved out in driblets. Cold morning, snowing. We passed Smalley at Butterfly Farm with the 57th bearers. He was left there to clear the French temporarily. A few shells burst around Canada Corner as we passed. The Germans had been shelling Reninghelst and dead horses were lying about. We found the rest of the ambulances at Remy Siding near Poperinghe. They were in huts here. An old CCS I think and quite comfortable. Had a wash and a shave – the first for nine days.

In the evening I walked into Poperinghe with Kidd. They had been shelling the east side of the town a lot. We saw some French battalions detraining. They looked smart and workmanlike. They looked much bigger and older and tougher than our present infantry. They had very neat, light, 2 wheeled transport. All three Field Ambulances were here. There was some bombing somewhere in the night, but we slept well.

20th April. Rejoined the CRE's mess in a farmhouse near Abeele.

25th April. Kemmel Hill was taken by the Boche this morning. [*French troops were defending the hill.*]

27th April. The Brigades moved up forward yesterday. In the morning I went up to 57th Brigade HQ as medical liaison officer. Cochrane up there as well with 56th Brigade. Fairly quiet day. There were some shells going over a bit behind us. All the roads round Poperinghe are pretty badly knocked about. Still quite a lot of civilians in front of Poperinghe. The Brigade came out in the evening to Tunnellers Camp. Came back in a car with the Brigadier (T A Cubitt) to a very nice little camp near the Houtcove Chateau near Proven. Proven was shelled tonight. The Division in the line between Dickebusche and La Clytte.

28th April. In the afternoon, rejoined Divisional HQ in a camp near a farm house east of Wattou. Dull mild weather still. Swallows all back. Pretty heavy shooting all day. It got heavy about 4pm and about 7pm there was a terrible bombardment on the Zillebeke–Locre front which continued most of the night. This was chiefly our guns. A Boche barrage started about 3pm.

29th April. Slept in a tent. Had a good night, Still a terrific shoot going on. The Boche attacked on the Zillebeke–Locre front this morning and was completely repulsed all along the line. Of course we have got a tremendous lot of guns of all kinds along this front now.

8th May. Beautiful warm weather. Living at Wattou at Divisional HQ near Wattou. The Field Companies between Busselboom and Vlamertinghe. Went up to see them two or three times. Scherpenberg Hill is now an absolutely bare rounded summit – wind mill and farm quite gone. French divisions are now holding all the front from about Vierstraat to somewhere about St Jans Capelle. Heavy firing yesterday. The Boche attacked the Brigade on our right (33rd Division) and took Ridge Wood and advanced as far as Gordon Farm. The 100th Brigade counter attacked in the evening, also the French on their right and entirely restored the line.

The other day a French aeroplane came down for some reason or another and crashed right onto the ADMS's hut and completely wrecked it. Fortunately the ADMS was out! Both pilot and observer fell out and were killed.

On 11 May, Henry wrote home to his sister Darcey:

Many thanks for your letter. I also got another of yours a day or two ago that had taken about a fortnight to come. I heard from Phillip's family recently – I can't quite remember when. He was somewhere away south and was quite fit. We have had beautiful weather for the last few days. The country is beautifully green, all the trees are green now except the Ashes. The Hawthorne is out.

Tell [Mother] I sent home one of my tunics a day or two ago. It had better be done up by the tailor and it will do for next winter. I am not expecting leave this side of Xmas. I don't think the war is ever going to stop. I have tried it by counting plum-stones and they always make it come to 'never'.

I'm sorry I have no news. Please thank Mother and Father for their letters dated 8th May.

Best love,
Harry

12th May. The Division comes out of the line today. Relieved by a French division. Our Division is already being made up to strength with drafts.

13th May. The Division is going down south into the French area, probably near Chalons sur Marne. It is to have a spell of rest and training and then go into a quiet sector of the line somewhere about the Argonne. That is the latest semi-official rumour.

14th May. Rode over to Bergues and had tea there. Interesting old town, surrounded by moats and earthworks fortifications. There is a beautiful old belfry tower there.

Yesterday I watched a lot of big shells bursting on the Mont des Cats. The monastery on the top of the hill seems to be getting pretty badly knocked about. Our old home, the Hospice at Locre must be a complete ruin by now as it has been taken and re-taken several times in the last few days. We must have wonderful observation from the Mont Noir–Mount Rouge line of hills on all the Boche positions between Bailleul and La Clytte.

We entrain tomorrow for the Champagne country.

16th May. Beautiful day. The Division entraining for the south. The train to carry Divisional HQ to start about 4pm. Rode down to the station with Heaney and got on board. Our carriage very hot and crowded so got on to an open transport truck with a general service wagon and found it much more pleasant. Passed Bergues, Calais, Boulogne and Etaples. At night I found my Maltese cart and got my kit off and spread my blankets on the floor of the truck and slept pretty well.

17th May. Heaney came and lived on my truck and we had our food and drinks fetched there. We passed through very pretty country – beautiful poplars all along the valley.

Stopped at Pontoise near Paris. The train was supposed to stop for 40 minutes. We went outside the station and got some coffee and came back in about 30 minutes to find the train had departed without us. Fortunately we got the loan of a motor box car from an American Flying Corps officer – about 8 of us – and dashed like mad after the train through St Denis and just caught it about 15 miles further on at Pantin. All the way through the outskirts of Paris the civilians were wildly enthusiastic, waving flags and hander kerchiefs everywhere, kissing their hands, cheering.

We went on up the beautiful Marne valley, crossing and re-crossing several times the big windings of the river. Pretty red-tiled, white villages and beautiful woods along both banks. We still stopped in our open truck.

18th May. About 3.30am we arrived at our detraining station (near Chalons). By the time we had got the horses and transport off the sun was up. The most perfect early summer morning. We rode on 5 miles or so to our billets at St Germain, a village on the Marne about 10 miles south of Chalons. [The people] seemed delighted to see British troops. The country looked perfectly beautiful – red and white Hawthorne out everywhere.

The vin ordinaire here is quite drinkable. We got some red wine and an omelette followed by coffee. It was a blazing hot day. Later we bathed in the canal that runs alongside the river. The river itself is rather too swift to be safe.

19th May. Left the CRE's mess and went to live with the 81st Field Company at Pogny, a village about three miles further up the river as all three Field Companies were together here. It was a nice clean little town. Our mess room was at the post office. They had a nice daughter aged seven, a pretty little thing who soon made great friends with everybody in the mess. I had a comfortable bedroom in a farmhouse at the edge of the village. Apparently only one old lady lived here and did most of the work about the farm yard and the house herself. Her brother was a General in the French Army

This was of course a French area and all the billeting arrangements were systematic. The whole area was allotted according to units – Divisional HQ, offices, Battalion HQ mess, orderly room, company messes, company billets etc. Everyman had a bunk. In each village there was also a small infirmary with beds for 20 or 30 where cases from units could be treated and detrained if necessary.

I was pretty busy here as I was the only MO in the village and besides the Royal Engineers I had to look after the Divisional Train (Army Service Corps), the motor transport company and the signal school. Also an epidemic of a short and sharp variety of influenza ran through several of the units.

During May influenza of a mild type had been more or less prevalent in the First Army but was beginning to spread around the BEF. The outbreak was of a highly infectious nature. Later in the summer it would begin to affect the ability of some divisions to fight at all.

We stopped here about ten days. All the time we had the most perfect weather, baking hot. The country was a mass of sweet smelling May bloom and all night long the nightingales sang by the dozen. I bathed every morning in the canal. We kept away from the river as much as possible as the place swarmed with the fiercest variety of mosquito. The surrounding country was the usual rather bare rolling corn lands with terraced banks on the hillsides, a few fruit trees straggling about and the main roads lined with trees, usually witch-elms.

The Division was doing intensive training and we expected to go into a quiet part of the line in a few more days east of Rheims. We were under orders of a French Corps.

A number of British divisions, including the 8th, 21st, 50th and 25th, weakened by the strenuous fighting over the last few weeks, had been transferred to the French-held part of the western front to replace the French divisions that had been sent to support the British behind Amiens and in Flanders.

By now, there were no quiet places in the line. Three of these divisions mistakenly thought they had found a peaceful place in which they could recuperate. Unfortunately for them, the Germans launched another massive attack along the whole of the Aisne front on 27 May. The British troops had been crowded into the narrow front-line defences, where they sustained heavy looses under the German artillery barrage that preceded the infantry attack. Once again, the Allied line looked like crumbling under the weight of a terrific onslaught. The enemy broke through and reached the Marne once again, less than sixty miles from Paris. On 6 June, however, the French and British (with the help of some Italian troops) managed to check the enemy advance. The great gamble was beginning to look like it had failed.

28th May. We got sudden news of a big Hun attack between Rheims and Noyon. About midday orders came in to 'stand to' ready to move. No definite news. The Boche said to have come through a good way. About 11pm orders came in to turn out at once. The Division was to be moved up to the battle in French motor buses. The right number of buses was ready for us in the village and by about midnight we started off. We joined up with the main column on the main Chalons road.

29th May. It was a very chilly journey. I sat on the front of a bus and only had a waterproof on. We passed through Chalons and got to Epernay in daylight about 6am. People were just going to work in the champagne factories – Moet & Chandon etc. After that we left the valley of the Marne and the road wound up steep hillsides covered with grape vines. The column of motor buses stretched away as far back as you could see. About 10am we arrived at a pretty village called Chaumuzy. This was to be Divisional HQ so we got out. The Brigades had de-embused somewhere near and went straight up into action. Thus the Division, which last evening had been over 50 miles back in rest billets, had been moved up by road in about 12 hours into the fighting line.

Some of the civilians here showed signs of clearing off, the rest were going about their daily work much as usual. It was getting hot now and we had had nothing since dinner last night so I thought I'd try and get a cup of coffee. I found the billet allotted to us as a mess. It was a clean little house where an old lady of about 60 lived [together with] a decrepit nice old man about 10 years older. The old lady was only too pleased to make us some coffee and was anxious to do anything she could for us.

About an hour later she came in again in tears. She said the Mayor had just ordered all civilians to leave by 6pm that evening. This was the second time she had had to leave her house and everything she had, she said. She had lived here for nearly four years but her home was at Rheims. In 1914 the Germans had shelled the town and everybody had to leave. Her husband was hit by a shell and had both his legs cut off. He was taken away to a hospital and she had never heard of him again.

The old man said nothing. He either didn't realise it or was too dazed by the news to talk about it. Out in the street I saw a distracted woman imploring a French soldier driving a staff car to take her and her family away. She ran into the house and came out again with her purse which she emptied – offering him all her money. They didn't seem to realise the terrible necessities of war.

The 21st Division were passing through – what was left of them – going out of the line. I saw an MO of the 8th Division. Nearly the whole of his Field Ambulance had been killed or captured. All those Divisions, 21st, 8th and 25th, had been frightfully thinned out. The barrage the Boche put down was so annihilating that practically everybody in the front system was killed and the Boche simply strolled through. The 8th and the 25th remained in the line with our Division.

It really seems that the only way to meet an attack of this kind with one of these modern barrages is to bring everybody back out of the front system and then counter attack later with fresh and unshaken troops. On this occasion the front system seems to have been a smoking inferno of bursting shells. Company commanders found it quite impossible to get in touch with their companies and later saw Boche strolling over with no one to oppose them.

The Field Ambulances opened up a Main Dressing Station in some big sheds or huts about half a mile in front of the village. An entire Casualty Clearing Station was said to have been captured near Fismes with all the motor ambulance cars. [*In fact the speed of the German advance resulted in the capture of both of the casualty clearing stations attached to the IX Corps. No. 48 Casualty Clearing Station, which had left Boulogne on 16 May, had set up at Montigny sur Vesle on the right of the IX Corps front, only seven miles behind the front line. The unit was abandoned early in the morning of the 28th. All of the medical personnel escaped. The Germans captured No. 38 Casualty Clearing*]

Station at Mont Notre Dame, which was seventeen miles behind the front, a few hours earlier. Many of the personnel were taken prisoner, including its commanding officer, Lieutenant Colonel Gray. As a result, and until the German advance was checked, British wounded were received into French hospitals during the different stages of the retreat. RAMC personnel were attached for duty in these French hospitals.]

The Boche have not come in very far on our right, near Rheims, but are going right away through on the left. They were well over the Aisne and had passed Fismes. Late in the afternoon our old couple trudged off with all their belongings in a little wheel barrow. The little cottage where they had lived in was now ours. There was their furniture just as usual, the cooking utensils, the photographs on the walls and the grand father clock ticked away drowsily and peacefully. But the old people would never come back. Tomorrow or next day this place would probably be shelled and the house looted and ransacked and very likely a ruin.

I went out into the little garden behind the house. It was neatly kept with flowers and vegetables. The village lay in the valley of the river Ardre, a small stream. On each side were hillsides with green cornfields blowing in a gentle breeze and a few vine fields stretching away to the edge of the woods. No troops were to be seen. It was hard to believe that by tomorrow or the next day this peaceful valley would be smoking and stinking with bursting shells.

30th May. We slept in our billet last night. No definite news. Our line has come back a bit. The ADMS lunched with us. During lunch the first shells arrived. They whistled overhead and burst somewhere down by the church. The place was crowded with transport and troops and there were still a good many civilians in the place. Some splinters were flying about and scared mothers ran out to drag indoors little children playing unconcerned in the streets.

In the afternoon, DHQ moved back to Nanteuil. About 4pm our kits and the office stuff was packed and Heaney and I went off on a motor lorry. The shelling had stopped but when we passed the crossroads at the end of the village we saw that some dirty work had been done. Several dead horses and a burnt out motor lorry were lying there. This was the A mess lorry. Some people were killed and wounded and several officers' kits had gone west. French troops, especially Algerian troops, were cheerfully looting everywhere and were carrying out systematic hen hunts round the farmhouses.

Preston and the 58th Field Ambulance had opened a main Dressing Station here at Nanteuil in a couple of long wooden huts. I was sent up to help. We were pretty busy here as a good many wounded were coming through. There were several of us so we could take reliefs. We had a good mess in a farmhouse close by and lived chiefly on fowls as the farm people were expecting to have to leave and were anxious to sell anything they couldn't take away with them.

I stopped here 4 or 5 days. It was a pleasant place and the hilly country around was pretty. One night, when the incinerator had not been properly put out, a Boche plane dropped a load of bombs about a hundred yards away. One morning, quite early in daylight, three Boche planes came over pretty low and one of them chucked a comic little bomb at us about as big as a Mills bomb. It burst 30 or 40 yards away.

4th June. The three Field Companies were now holding a reserve line and were all quite close to Chaumuzy. The CRE thought I had better go up there and look after them. In the morning I rode up to Chaumozy with him. I went round the three Company HQs. The 82nd were about three quarters of a mile up the hill on the left and the 81st and 94th were down in the valley by the stream. They were living in slits in the ground. The reserve line they were holding ran just in front of the village. Some of the sections were back with HQ and doing work on the line – wiring etc. It was a pretty valley full of poplars. The village looked very picturesque running up the side of the hill. They were putting a good many shells into it, also along the valley. A lot of dead horses and some human corpses were lying about the village. When I went past them I wore my box respirator.

I decided to fix up in a very nice house that had not been hit, near the church. Three battalion MOs were using it as an aid post and the Field Ambulance also had a car post here which cleared cases to the ADS at Marfaux, the next village. Smalley was there when I arrived. We lived in a small room on the ground floor. The walls were pretty thick and there was a good deal of protection. If the shelling got bad we retired to the cellars. We used the garage as a dressing room for the wounded and the cars stood under the lee side of the house. The garden was full of flowers and I filled our room with beautiful red and white peonies and pink roses.

The village was an unhealthy place to walk about in. The Germans used to put frequent bursts of shells into it, perhaps 20 or 30 in 3 or 4 minutes and you never knew when they were coming. In the morning I was just walking up the street with Padre Willis. Padre Robertshaw was walking about 50 yards ahead of us and suddenly there came a sound from heaven as of a rushing mighty wind, and the street about 40 yards in front of us was filled with crashes and smoke. We dived into the nearest house. Robertshaw appeared out of the smoke with a slight scratch on the neck and nothing worse. I thought he was destroyed. Like the Holy Family avoiding Herod, I returned by another way.

The old curé was still living in the village in spite of the shells. I suppose he had a good cellar. My servant used to bring me some bottles of very good Burgundy. I never asked him where it came from. There were also some ripe strawberries in the gardens. We had fresh milk for a day or two but one day a civilian came up and took the cow away. There was also a good supply of pork.

5th June. Walked round to see the Companies. The Hun is doing a lot of shooting, especially up the valley where the 81st and 94th were, and they had several casualties. Yesterday a shell dropped right into a little dugout place under the bank of the road near the 82nd HQ and killed four RAMC bearers. Burton came up in the evening and slept in my cellar. He told me Preston was knocked out by a high velocity shell that morning right back at the Main Dressing Station at Nanteuil. He didn't think he would recover. Only a day or two ago we had been talking about our hospital days at Poplar and he was telling me all his plans for after the war. He was going out to British Columbia. He was married during the war.

6th June. Woken up at 3am by heavy shooting. Our batteries were going hard and the Hun was sending a lot of stuff over, also a lot of gas shells. It was only 'Blue Cross' I think [*lachrymatory*] but we had to wear our respirators for about two and a half hours. A good many casualties came through. Major Godsall, OC 82nd Field Company, was slightly wounded. The French on our right fell back and our right Brigade lost the hill west of Mont Bligny. He was shelling the village hard, but fortunately was still only using fairly light stuff. He was also shelling all the way up the road to Marfaux and Marfaux itself which made evacuation difficult. Walker (MO Cheshire's) and Fry (King's Shropshire Light Infantry) were shelled out of their aid posts and came down to our cellars. The Boche weren't very far from our village.

About noon it grew quiet and I went round to see the Companies. I saw the poor old curé making off at last up the road to Marfaux. I suppose the gas had been too much for him. The ground round the 81st and 94th was simply peppered with shell holes, mostly gas shells. They had a good many casualties and Baker was killed. During the lull MacFarlane and Ellis appeared with my Maltese cart which I had been waiting for. I didn't want MacFarlane or the cart so I sent them back. MacFarlane was not sorry to go.

In the afternoon the 56th Brigade made a very good counter attack and retook all the lost ground. The French also came back to their original line. The French method seems much more sensible than ours. If their front is being badly shelled they simply come back out of it and go back when it's quiet again. If there are any Boche there they kick them out. They get nothing like so many casualties as we do.

7th June. I lived in Chaumuzy four more days. I went round the Company HQs each day. The Boche continued to knock hell out of the village but for some reason never seemed to hit our house. One day he smashed the roof of the house over the kitchen and a splinter came through my window. Another day I went into my room and found a lot of shrapnel or splinters had come through the ceiling and the room was full of plaster.

10th June. The 81st and the 94th went back to the Bois de Courton, a big wood on the hill a mile or two back as they no longer had to hold the reserve line. We lived and slept in the open. It was very pleasant as the weather was still fine and warm. We had slits dug in case of emergency but we camouflaged ourselves very carefully against overhead observation and kept all the men well out of sight in the bushes etc. Except for a few bursts of shells close by probably meant for the farm at Espilly we had a peaceful time. The sections went up each night for their various work on the line. I walked over to Chaumuzy each day to see the 82nd. Orringe, who took over command after Godsell was hit, was killed last night by a shell. I slept one night in my cellar again in Chaumuzy as an attack was expected to come off, but nothing happened.

After all its casualties the Division is acting as a composite Brigade, which together with Brigades formed from the 50th and 25th Divisions forms a composite Division. The 8th Division has gone out of the line more or less washed out. There is even talk of breaking up Divisions and we are afraid we may be broken up and sent to make various other Divisions up to strength. The troops are all thoroughly sick of it all and their morale is certainly not good. The line seems pretty firm now. We have a lot of guns up – French and British. French troops are on our left and an Italian Division is on our right.

From the edge of our wood you get a wonderful view over Marfaux and Chaumuzy up the valley to Mont Bligny and the German positions.

The issue of manpower was now a major point of friction between the French and the British. By May, out of the fifty British divisions on the western front, ten were considered to be exhausted and eight of these had been reduced to merely a cadre. All this was before the offensive against the French on the Aisne and the further heavy British casualties sustained by our divisions on that front.

At a crucial Allied conference on 1 June, Foch had pointedly asked Lloyd George exactly how many divisions the British intended to sustain on the western front. Foch believed that the strength of the British Army was decreasing at a faster rate than the newly arriving American Army, threatening the outcome of the war itself. The British reinforcement programme began to significantly improve after this point.

The question of morale was altogether more difficult to assess. Clearly Henry felt that morale was declining rapidly in the 19th Division, which was perhaps unsurprising given the three huge battles it had been required to fight over the last two months. The BEF was now very much a conscript army and it was bound to reflect some of the deepening mood of concern over the way the fighting was going. But as events would confirm, the British Army, including the 19th Division, was far from being on its knees.

14th June. Went back to advanced HQ at Nanteuil to look after Divisional HQ and Signals etc. Still some flu about. Messed with Signals and lived in a tent in the woods above the village. The Germans did not shoot at the place at all while I was there.

15th June. Rode over and saw 57th Field Ambulance about a mile north of Epernay. They are running the Main Dressing Station. They are surrounded by vine covered hillsides. They are also living on a light kind of sparkling wine, a kind of miniature champagne, not unlike bottled cider and they get if for a franc a bottle. We walked into Epernay in the evening. The enemy had put a certain number of long range shells into and just beyond the town but seems to have done very little damage.

19th June. The Division relieved by the 8th Italian Division. I lunched with Heaney in Epernay and rode on to our billets at Cuise about 2 miles further south overlooking Epernay.

The French Corps commander is very pleased with the work done by the Division. There was a big parade today and he presented several officers (including the CRE) and other ranks with French decorations while the Divisional band played daintily.

21st June. Moved back with DHQ to billets at Mondemont Chateau, about 20 miles back to the west. This was a rambling old place and had been badly knocked about in the Battle of the Marne in 1914. It contained a large courtyard in front and at each corner was a quaint circular stone built tower each of which had carried a cone shaped red tiled roof. Two of these had been completely destroyed.

The Chateau marked the limit of the German advance southwards in 1914. To the north all the villages show marked signs of recent war but to the south they are untouched. This was the most pleasant and most peaceful place I billeted in. We were in the depths of the 'campagne'. The Chateau was surrounded by beautiful shady trees. I used to ride around the Companies billeted at Oyes and Broussy. The 57th Field Ambulance were at Reuves.

Big re-enforcement drafts arrived for the Division and I did a lot of never ending inoculating for typhoid.

We expected to go into the line on the Marne near Chatillon but we soon found we were to go back to the old British area again.

1st July. Beautiful hot day. The Division entraining for the north. I was sorry to leave the champagne country. Everything was charming; the country, the villages, the people and even the weather. I rode about 20 miles with Harris who was acting adjutant to our entraining station at Sommesous. It took 32 trains to move the Division with [its] artillery. Our train didn't go until about 8am next morning and we had to sleep under a hay-stack. Some Welshmen, the 9th Royal Welsh Fusiliers were waiting for their train and they passed the time in singing. They sang old fashioned airs in harmony. They sang very well and the effect was melodious.

The series of German offensives were by now grinding to a halt. German casualties were probably well over a million and yet, despite these losses, no tangible strategic advantage had been secured. One last great effort was made in the middle of the month at Chateau Thierry. It was a complete failure. Successful French and American counter-attacks using large numbers of tanks and artillery drove the enemy back along more or less the whole length of the front. The enemy's bridgehead across the Marne had to be given up.

The resolve of the Allied armies remained undiminished. Throughout the early days of July, the French, British and now the American forces began to take the initiative with a number of successful operations. A joint Australian and American attack at Le Hamel was a textbook example of the new mood of confidence sweeping through the Allied ranks. The pendulum was about to swing again – this time decisively against the Germans. The resilience of the Allied forces would now bring spectacular results.

We entrained on 2nd July, passed Paris and arrived at Amien about noon on the 3rd. Went by road and got to our billets at Fauquenbergues about 7pm. The Division is now up to strength again. The Royal Engineers have had pretty heavy casualties. Since March, they have had 21 officer casualties alone. Everyone is now wondering where the next Boche attack is coming. We quite expect it on the Ypres–Arras front but at any rate there are plenty of good reserve lines dug right away back nearly to the sea and reserve ammunition dumps etc.

On July 10th I went on [9] days leave with Smalley to Dinard in Brittany. We spent a day in Paris on the way but they were still shelling it occasionally with 'Bertha' and it looked very deserted and dull. While at Dinard we heard the news of the great Boche attack along the Chateau Thierry–Verdun front, its complete failure and Foche's counter push on their exposed right flank.

When we got back on July 21st, DHQ were a few miles further east at Bouy. We stopped here another two or three weeks. The three Field Companies were up near the front working under the Corps or reserve lines near Bethune and Berguette and I had only DHQ, Signals and a company of the Train to look after. We had a lot of heavy rain while we were here. A splendid harvest was coming on and it looked as if it might be spoilt.

6th August. The Division went into the line just north of Bethune. DHQ moved up to Labeuvriere. The village has been shelled a good deal recently with a high velocity gun and several of the houses have been hit but the civilians are all living there still. The Field Companies are at Vendui, Annazin and Bethune. Fairly quiet front I think. The Major who took over command of the 82nd Field Company after Gorringe was killed, was himself killed by a shell on the Chocques–Bethune road yesterday. There was a good deal of bombing all round at night and one night a couple of bombs dropped about 15 yards off the CRE's billet and blew most of the roof off.

On 8 August, British and Canadian troops launched a hugely successful and surprise attack on the German lines around Amiens. The Canadian divisions had not been involved in the fighting of the spring and summer and so were fresh and at full strength. Under a powerful barrage and with clear air superiority, they crashed through the German defences and pushed forward several miles. The

Canadians managed to advance eight miles. Over 12,000 prisoners and over 300 guns were captured along with countless other stores and equipment. Ludendorf, the German commander, called it the 'black day of the German Army in the history of the war'.

The Germans began a long retirement. But they were still capable of putting up very heavy resistance. Casualties on both sides were to remain high right to the very end of the fighting.

14th August. I was posted to the 9th Royal Welsh Fusiliers. At noon I went up to their battalion HQ at Hinges (in support). Colonel Sole, who used to hunt with the Dunstan Harriers and the staghounds at home, commanded the battalion. In the evening we relieved the 9th Welch in the front line across the canal. HQ and regimental Aid Post in fortified houses behind the canal in the outskirts of Hinges – steel shelters and concrete placed inside the rooms. He shelled round about Hinges to a certain extent usually with graze fuse 4.2s but the front was fairly quiet and we didn't have many casualties. The two front Companies held a line of posts and the two support Companies were in trenches a little way over the canal.

On 21 August the IV and VI corps of the Third Army launched a powerful attack along a nine-mile front north of the Ancre from Hamel to Moyennville and made significant gains. The next day the III Corps attacked south of Albert and regained the town. Later in August the Canadian Corps attacked at Arras and pushed the defenders back here as well. The pressure on the Germans was by now constant and relentless.

23rd August. We are taking over the line from the 4th Division on our left. The canal about 2 miles east of Robecq. I lived and had my Aid Post in the cellar of an old farm house. In the night we were shelled with a big 11.2" high velocity gun. They didn't wake me up but next morning there were some enormous craters around the place. One just missed our farm. Lots of people, chiefly girls and women, are working in the harvest fields up here all among the shell holes and trenches. We are lending men and horses to assist. People are coming back to look at the ruins of their homes that they were driven out of last April. They seem to take it all very much as a matter of course. The weather is wet and cool.

27th August. The Battalion moved up into the front line. HQ moved up beyond the Bois de Pacault and we lived in some enlarged shell holes near

Paradis. Took over from the 9th Welch. I had a long chat with Colonel Jones who came out with the 4th Dragoon Guards at the beginning of the war. Fires are burning all along the horizon. The Boche is retiring again. He is evidently going to withdraw to his old positions on the Aubers Ridge for the winter. A good deal of shelling round about in the night.

28th August. Harris and Roberts [*junior officers in the battalion*] went out patrolling this afternoon and never came back. They must have been captured or killed. They are said to have had some maps on them on which were marked the position of the Company HQs and also battalion HQ so they will probably shell us tomorrow. There was a good deal of shelling last night on our support Companies posts. The various platoons are dug in in slit trenches.

The Boche must have had an uncomfortable time here as all this country is overlooked by the high ground across the canal at Hinges and it is well peppered with big shell holes. We had been doing some very good shooting along the roads and seemed to have been using a lot of heavy stuff. All the houses about here are completely wrecked. We came across a good many dead bodies of our men who must have been lying out there since last April. The Boche had left a lot of ammunition and shells behind and an extraordinary number of his stick bombs. We were throwing the bombs about and they were bursting all over the place. The Germans had been living chiefly in slits and little shallow shelters a couple of feet deep.

29th August. Walked round the support Companies. In the morning the Boche put a lot of shells very close to our HQs. He had evidently spotted it so we moved to the other side of the road about half a mile away and dug ourselves some holes to live in.

31st August. The Companies have gone right on again so Battalion HQ were moved up about 2 miles to some big shell holes just west of Zelobes. All this was country we used to be billeted in well behind the line in 1915. Very quiet here; hardly any shelling. Relieved tonight by the Wiltshire Regiment and went back to Hinges.

2nd September. Our front is now east of Vielle Chapelle about a spot called 'les huits maisons'. The corps is to advance tomorrow morning behind a barrage. About 2.30am we moved up in Brigade reserve near to Vielle Chapelle just behind the guns.

3rd September. Cold night. We stood in a field behind the village and watched the show. At 5.30am a light barrage started. It was just getting light and we could see the tracer bullets very plainly from the machine gun barrage. The Boche put a few crumps into the village and put up some SOS lights. We got all our objectives and had light casualties. We captured about 180 prisoners. We moved up another half a mile and sat in some shell holes. Jones, our Lewis gun officer told us funny policeman stories. He had been in the Force. In the afternoon HQs moved again to an orchard about a mile north of Vielle Chapelle and we slept in some old elephant shelters. Harris and Robert's bodies were found a few hundred yards in front of our posts.

5th September. Brigade relieved and the battalion went back to billets at Essars near Bethune. I rode back with Colonel Sole. Vielle Chapelle was all smashed up and our old billet the brasserie was only a pile of bricks. We billeted in a dilapidated farmhouse. Got rather a nasty headache and a temperature of over 100 degrees. Suppose it's a touch of the flu.

6th September. Still have a headache and a temperature. Stopped in bed. Colonel Sole has a temperature of 104 degrees. He's got it too.

8th September. Walked into Bethune to look at the place. The whole of the centre of the town is absolutely destroyed. Nothing but piles of bricks. The stump of the belfry tower is still standing but the church has disappeared entirely.

10th September. To relive the Warwick's in the front line at Neuve Chapelle tonight. HQs in elephant shelters about half a mile east of St Vaast Post where Smalley and I lived at our Advanced Dressing Station in 1916. I saw our old dugouts, rather knocked and tumbled about, but still there.

11th September. Rained like blazes all day. A good many rather random shells flying about.

12th September. Shifted my Aid Post up to Curzon Post, an old strongpoint with dugouts and steel shelters just across the Estaires–La Bassee road. C Company were in support here and I lived in their mess. The Germans put a good many shells on to the La Bassee road close by.

13th September. Heavy gas shelling (mustard gas) all round us today from 9 to 11am and again from 11pm to 1am. He must have sent over about 8000 shells in the 24 hours, many fell about Curzon Post and one went into a dugout and wounded some men. I sent down about 10 gas cases. The area shelled was chiefly between Curzon Post and the Pont Logy corner on the La Bassee road and a little beyond.

14th September. Another spell of gas shelling again in the morning. I had to send down about another 20 gassed men. They weren't very bad but their eyes were very much inflamed and painful and they couldn't see. In the evening there was a lot of heavy shelling over behind us about the battery position. About 8pm I got a message to go down with some stretchers to St Vaast as the Wiltshire's HQ had got knocked out by a shell and their MO was wounded. I found Campaign, the MO, in the Advanced Battalion HQ dugout at St Vaast Post, rather bad with a compound fracture of his left arm. I sent him down to the car post and went on with some stretcher bearers and found a wounded man and bodies of the Colonel, Lord Thynne, and another officer all lying in a ditch about half a mile further back.

When I got back to my Aid Post the effects of the gas began to come on. I thought I was alright as I had worn my respirator all the time it was at all strong. My eyes got frightfully sore and painful. I couldn't keep them open and they went into spasms when I closed them. I spent a very uncomfortable night.

15th September. I had moved the Aid Post to some shelters about 200 yards to the left where the Boche didn't seem to shell. It was pretty quiet and there was nothing special to do so I sat about in a semi blind condition with weeping eyes. My Aid Post corporal was in very much the same state.

We stopped in the line here another three days. My eyes got gradually better but I had a bad cold and a cough as a result of the gassing and felt rather rotten.

19th September. Got unexpected orders to return to the 57th Field Ambulance for duty and Adams came up to relieve me. The 57th are running the Main Dressing Station at Annazin, about a mile behind Bethune. It was a very peaceful spot. The place had been only very slightly damaged by shell fire.

After two or three days I was sent down by car for a week at the XIII Corps Officers Rest House at Paris Plage, near Etaples. It was a nice house with room for 20 officers. A MO from one of the Field Ambulances in the Corps was there in charge. Smalley was down there and I relieved him.

Since the Allied offensive began at Amiens on 8 August, the Germans had been forced to give up most of the ground they had captured in the spring and early summer. German reserves of both men and material were beginning to dwindle. Foch was determined to maintain the maximum pressure on the retreating German armies, whose troops were showing signs of rapidly declining morale, on as many fronts as possible.

By the time Henry would rejoin the 57th Field Ambulance in early October, the British had successfully launched a massive attack on the St Quentin front and were across the Canal du Nord, creating a twelve-mile-wide breach in the Hindenberg position. Important attacks were also commenced by the French and the Americans in the Argonne and by the British and Belgians on the Flanders front. Both attacks were highly successful. Just how successful can be gauged by the fact that in the evening of 28 September, Ludendorf went to Hindenberg to persuade him of the necessity for Germany to make a peace offer and seek an armistice if it was to avoid complete and total defeat on the battlefield.

1st October. Rejoined the Field Ambulance at Annazin.

2nd October. The Division was relieved by the 74th Division [*a yeomanry formation*] and we marched back to billets at Auchelle. The Boche is withdrawing on our front and our outposts were right over the Aubers Ridge.

4th October. We entrained at Calonnes at 4pm and arrived at Saulty, near Doullens about 10pm and went into billets there. The transport coming on by road under the charge of Kidd. [*The 19th Division was transferred to the XVII Corps, part of the Third Army on this day.*]

7th October. The Division is moving up to the Cambrai area by bus. We started about 2.30pm and arrived at our camping area about half a mile south of the famous Bourlon Wood about 9pm. It was a long, chilly journey. We had about 5 bell tents and slept in one. The men slept under 'bivvy' sheets. A few high velocity shells were coming over in the night, but not very close to us.

On 8 October, the Fourth and Third armies mounted a combined attack on the Cambrai front. The task allotted to the XVII Corps was to advance to the north east and encircle Cambrai on the south and compel its evacuation. The main attack would be carried out by the 63rd Division with the 57th Division protecting its left flank as it went forward. The 19th Division would be in reserve, ready to go into the attack if necessary. All of the objectives were taken. The line had been pushed forward several thousand yards.

The speed of the advance posed some difficult logistical issues for the army medical services – in particular, they were finding it hard to keep the casualty clearing stations as close as possible to the action. For example, the most advanced CCS in the Third Army on 7 October was based at Ytres, twelve miles behind the front line. Seven days later it was twenty-four miles behind the front line, placing extra strain on the motor ambulance convoys and their personnel.

8th October. The Division still in reserve. We are attacking today. We hope to envelop Cambrai. Heavy firing and smoke barrages in the direction of Cambrai. Was sent down with Simbo (Simpson, our American MO) to help with the Corps Main Dressing Station in tents 2 miles away. We passed a whole Boche field gun battery still in position.

We dressed cases there all the afternoon and while there I was suddenly given a warrant for a fortnight's leave.

9th October. Up at about 5am. A cold frosty morning. Heavy firing in front. Went down in a motor ambulance to Bapaume and arrived in London on the afternoon of the 10th.

Pop was at home after doing an adjutant's course at Cambridge. We got a couple of days with the Harriers. Great excitement at home. The Boche was withdrawing rapidly or being driven back all along the line and was offering peace terms of a much more humble nature than ever before. His reserve divisions had dwindled down to 9 and everybody was discussing freely the chances of peace in the immediate future.

25th October. Returning from leave, our train arrived at Achiet le Grand about 10pm. 19th Division railhead at Cambrai. No means of getting on until tomorrow so went to the YMCA Officers Club, a marquee, got a supper of sorts and slept in a tent with the others on the ground with a couple of damp blankets.

The XVII Corps front was now being held by the 61st Division. The 19th had just come out of the front line and was in reserve. For the next few days a period of stationary warfare ensued with both sides dug in. The British were preparing for another move forward.

26th October. Our train was supposed to come in at 8am but there was no sign of it. We 'lorry jumped' as far as Bapaume and from there got a lift in a car on to Cambrai. By now we had left the devastated area behind us. Cambrai itself was pretty badly knocked about. Hardly a house had not had a shell into it somewhere but most were easily reparable. All the houses and buildings around the Place d'Armees, the square in the centre of the town had been burnt by the Huns and nothing was left but piles of bricks and stones. The three church steeples were still standing – not much damaged. There were no civilians in the place and hardly any troops. Almost every house was marked 'out of bounds'.

Found the 57th Field Ambulance who were running the Divisional Rest Station about a mile outside the town. I then went on by lorry to Avesnes where DHQ were billeted. The 19th Division was out of the line. They had been in action for a few days while I was away and had done very well at the crossing of the river Selle which was successfully bridged by the RE Field Companies. The Divisions were leap-frogging past each other. We expect to go into the line again in 4 or 5 days.

All the villages here were fought through very rapidly and are hardly damaged at all by shell fire. A good many of the civilians are still living here. The country is all being farmed as usual. I had tea in the CRE's mess and then heard all the news. After tea went back in the CRE's boxcar to the 57th Field Ambulance who were at Cagnoncles.

Smalley is away on leave and Cochrane is going tomorrow morning. Everyone else very fit and very optimistic about the war, I don't think much will come of the peace talk about an armistice but I don't think the Boche will last out next summer. Our casualties in the show last week were slight – not more than a few hundred in the Division.

On 27 October Ludendorf resigned, following a disagreement with the German government over the conduct of the armistice negotiations. Ludendorf, having earlier insisted on negotiations commencing, now wanted to take a much harder line over what terms might be acceptable to Germany.

31 October. Still at Cognoncles. News came in today that an armistice on very favourable terms has been arranged with both Turkey and Austria-Hungary. The Division is to move up to the line tomorrow. Smalley returned from leave this afternoon.

The XVII Corps began a fresh advance on 1 November, crossing the Rhonelle to take the villages of Maresches and St Hubert. Once again, the 61st Division made the attack and would be relieved by the 19th on the evening of 2 November.

1st November. Fine day. Moved up to Vendegies. Smalley and I marched up with the personnel. We camped in a field just behind the village. The men were in holes in a bank with waterproof sheets over and we had a bell tent for a mess and a couple to sleep in. There is a funny sort of rumour going about that Marshal Foche is supposed to have said to somebody that the coming battle is the last one the British Army will be called upon to fight. I don't understand this at all unless the whole British Army is going to be relieved by the Americans.

A good many high velocity shells, mostly duds, seemed to be coming over during the night somewhere in the neighbourhood of the village.

2nd November. Cold drizzly day. There was a small attack this morning on this front. We advanced 5 kilometres with light casualties. About 1000 prisoners were taken. A lot of Boche wounded came through. The Division goes into the line tonight. HQ of our Field Ambulance remains in a house on Vendegies. The 59th are running the MDS in a marquee camp about a mile and a half back. Smalley and I went up with the bearers to our ADS at the Chateau at Artres 3 or 4 miles south of Valenciennes. We arrived about dusk. The village and round about the Chateau had been heavily shelled in the morning. There were some very good roomy cellars in the Chateau. We got some of these cleared out for a dressing room. The 56th Brigade HQ were also in the cellars.

3rd November. The Division is attacking tomorrow morning from the west of Jenlain. Only one Brigade in the line, two battalions in the front and one in support. The whole Divisional front is only about 1,500 yards.

In the morning I walked round the 56th Brigade battalion aid posts at Mareclus. They were using houses and especially the cellars of the houses in the village. There was some shelling here, particularly along the road to Sepeneries. The 18 pounders were all in action right in the open. I picked up a lot of peace propaganda papers that the Boche had been dropping out of aeroplanes. The Boche kept withdrawing all day and by evening the 56th Brigade moved up to tomorrow's first objective. The attack is to start tomorrow with the 56th and 57th Brigades in the front line.

4th November. The attack started with a barrage this morning. Robertson was helping us at the ADS. We got a good many wounded in. Smalley went up to keep in touch with the Regimental Aid Posts as they moved up, to reconnoitre the roads for the cars. 58th Field Ambulance opened up an ADS on the Preseau–Jenlain road and in the afternoon the ADMS came in and told Roberston and me to close our place as soon as we could, clear our cases and open up a walking wounded post in Preseau. Roberston stopped behind to see the cases off in motor ambulances as soon as they turned up and in about an hour I moved off with the equipment and ADS personnel in three cars to Preseau. It was a beautiful clear afternoon with bright sunshine. Already the road up to Preseau was crammed full of all kinds of transport moving up and we could only go at walking pace. Observation balloons were already up in front of us.

We cleared a large cellar at Preseau as a walking wounded post and got tea going. We also cleared some rooms in a house for putting stretcher cases in as this was a loading post for the motor ambulances. Evacuation back to the MDS at Vendegies was frightfully slow as the roads were chock full of transport and heavy guns moving up and were in a very bad condition. Also it was a very dark night. We soon had the cellar and a couple of rooms full of slightly wounded. It was a quiet night. I didn't hear any shells back this way.

About 10pm, Colonel Edmunds, our CO came in. He had been up in Jenlain which was being heavily shelled in the afternoon. He wanted to move up and open an ADS in Jenlain as soon as the roads were clear for cars. Soon after Tom Armitage, our quarter master, arrived with the whole of the transport and before long we were having a good supper in the cellar of the house. Slept in the cellar and had a quiet night.

The attack of the Third Army was going exceptionally well. Nearly 20,000 prisoners had been taken and the enemy began retiring along the whole length of the front.

5th November. In the morning, moved up by car with the Colonel to Jenlain. Went by a roundabout route as the direct road was still impassable. Saw one or two dead Boche lying about. All along the roads were scoops dug into the bank occupied a couple of days ago by the Boche. A good many of their machine guns were lying about and a lot of turnips that they had evidently pulled out of the fields to eat. All the country was peppered over freely with shell holes. Jenlain itself was quiet when we arrived. I remember passing through this village over four years ago, just after the battle of Mons. DHQ were moving into the village and by the time we got opened up we were too far back for an ADS. Smalley was already fixing one up at Bry about a couple of miles further on. The village was not damaged very much. Our house had been hit once in the top storey and we were quite comfortable.

Our casualties yesterday were pretty heavy. The Boche put up a pretty good fight. Awful day today – raining steadily and the roads in an awful state. All the crossroads have mine craters in them and all the bridges are blown up. Cars can't get over the bridges into Bry yet.

In the afternoon the ADMS sent me to Warquies le Grand, the next village, to investigate some cases of sickness among the civilians. There were several cases of measles among the children and a good many of them were suffering from gas. Several of them were very pale and weak from want of proper food as the Huns would not allow them milk even when they were ill. Several had been wounded by shell fire and there were dead bodies in two or three of the houses. The Germans put one or two shells into the place while I was there. There were several dead Boche lying about in the fields.

The ADS was now running at Bry and the transport had gone on there. They say the place is being shelled hard. We still had a good many cases to clear here at Jenlain. We had to wait for some motor ambulances came to clear them, so decided to stop there for the night.

The CO, Roberston and I got some stretchers put down on the floor and lay down but very soon after the Boche began shooting just over the village with a high velocity gun. They were going well over the village – they were gas shells – but they seemed to skim over uncomfortably close to our roof. They kept coming with annoying regularity and kept us awake. The CO and I sat up stoking the fire until about 3am when the gun shut up and we went to sleep.

On 6 November, General Groner, Ludendorf's successor, gave the German Cabinet a very bleak assessment of the military situation on the western front: 'I have come to the conclusion that, painful as it is, we must take the step of asking Foche for terms and meanwhile retreat behind the Rhine.' The German Army High Command were in no doubt whatsoever that the war could not be continued for very much longer without running the risk of an overwhelming defeat at the hands of the Allies. It was now a race against time for the Germans to salvage as much dignity as possible through a negotiated armistice.

6th November. Just before dawn some motor ambulances arrived and took away all our cases. They had to go right away round by Valenciennes on account of road trouble. We immediately packed up to go. Just before we got off, 10 high velocity shells suddenly arrived alarmingly close – one just behind in the garden and two or three just over. Half a mile down the road one of the cars stuck in a big hole in the road but we got her out and arrived soon after in Bry.

The whole Field Ambulance including transport was here, very comfortable in a big farmhouse. There was no shelling about here now. A good many civilians here who were delighted to see the British and to know they had seen the last of the Boche. They were anxious to do anything they could to help the wounded even to do washing up for us after meals etc.

During the morning, Smalley came back from the advanced dressing posts and I went up to relieve him. Parties from the South Wales Borderers were working on the road filling up mine craters just north of Bry. We had a car post about a mile along the road to La Flamengrie. The Mark IV horse drawn wagons had to work in front of this as the road was quite impossible for the cars. The wagons worked as far up as our bearer relay post in a house in La Flamengrie. Soon after I got there I sent off a load of wounded civilians, women and children. Several civilians had been killed in this village.

There was a certain amount of scattered shelling in the village and round about. I walked round the battalion aid posts with Staff Sergeant Blount and Sergeant Dooley. Fry was in the cellar of a house at the other end of the village together with some old women and a lot of poultry. The civilians were living here very much as if nothing unusual was going on. They were all in the kitchen when I was there, making coffee for the Tommies and giving them apples. They didn't seem at all worried by the shells bursting round about. It seemed a quaint kind of aid post after the dugouts we used to have in the old trench days. The Boche were driven out of here only yesterday.

When I got back to the relay post the Boche were dropping a lot of 5.9s a hundred yards behind us, trying for a 4.2 howitzer battery. I saw a terrified old woman covered with mud run up the street and go into a house close by. She said a shell had just burst in her house and killed everybody, seven people and she was the only person left alive. It was an awful day – raining hard. The troops have been soaked to the skin for 48 hours now.

It was rather chilly in this house so I went to see Walker (MO to the Cheshire's), who was in a little cottage just across the road. They all looked very cosy. They were sitting around the fire and a woman was making coffee and gave me a cupful as soon as I came in. The civilians didn't in the least mind having a battle fought over their village. Some shells began coming unpleasantly close so we all retired to the cellar and the story telling went on.

The people all told the same story. The Boche had taken all their milk, butter, eggs, chickens etc. They never paid for them. At first they gave them requisition papers in return but they soon gave this up. The number of cows each man had was noted down and he had to hand over the requisite amount of milk each day or be fined. They weren't allowed milk for their children or invalids. They were very strictly rationed and allowed no meat. A Boche gendarme used to come round during their meals and see exactly what they had and if they had anything in excess of the ration they were heavily fined or sent to prison. Most of the able bodied men and boys were taken away to dig reserve trenches or to work in Germany. Girls and boys were forced to work every day in the woods cutting up timber. Boche officers had to be rigorously saluted by everybody or else the offenders were roughly dealt with. When they finally withdrew they drove away all the horses, cows, sheep and pigs and took away all the poultry, and food and everything they could lay their hands on.

They said that latterly the Boche had become more and more demoralised and depressed. The men were all sick of fighting and the officers were very despondent and had lost control of the men. They said that recently several large parties of German soldiers had been marched back through this village under escort as prisoners for refusing to fight. The Hun soldiers were particularly terrified of the British bombing planes.

They had managed to save plenty of coffee and at least one bottle of cognac in honour of the great day and never seemed tired of handing out cups of the mixture to everybody in khaki they could see. One thing I thought was particularly gratifying was that although they had been under occupation for four years, none of their children could talk a word of German.

About 6.30pm I returned to Bry on foot. They were shelling around La Flamengrie pretty hard when I left. The Boche is slinging a tremendous lot of shells over into this village and the other villages round about tonight. The Shropshire's who are back in Bry resting had several casualties. He is evidently getting rid of his surplus ammunition before moving back his guns. The walls of the farmhouse were thick and nothing seemed to come close to us. We slept on beds and some on the floor and had a very good night.

7th November. Weather foggy but no rain. At 8am walked up through La Flamengrie to the car post now about a mile short of St Waast. A lot of big shells bursting away to the left. The battalions have pushed on considerably. At the cross roads a hundred yards further on the Huns had blown a big mine crater. By the afternoon the road was good enough for guns and gun limbers to go over.

In the afternoon we used the house where the car post was as a temporary ADS intending to open one up as soon as possible in St Waast, a mile or so further on. During the afternoon a shell dropped bang in the middle of the road just outside the house just as a Company of the Cheshire's were passing. Two men were killed outright, two died a few minutes later and there were several bad stretcher cases. Fortunately Smalley, Dunbar, the CO and myself were all there. The CO had been dashing about, mostly on a horse, almost incessantly for the last few days, reconnoitring roads and sites for possible ADSs.

Before dark we got one of the cars over the mended crater and I went down to the Ferme de la Tour and picked up some cases of the Warwick's who had been left behind there. The battalion aid post had moved on right over the stream to Brangies. The new ADS is to open at St Waast at midnight.

We had some tea at 6.30. I started off to find the Warwick's and Worcester's aid posts and to take them some more bearers. We went through St Waast. There was a terrific crush of traffic in the street mixed up with infantry and guns. The bridge over the stream had been destroyed of course but a rough temporary bridge had been put up. It looked as if we might get the light Ford cars over it. Fortunately the Boche was not shelling the place. We went on up the road to Brangies. Here we found 57th Brigade HQ but the battalion HQs had gone on to the next village – Houdain.

It was quiet at Houdain when we arrived. I found Simbo who was temporarily with the Warwick's and Meyer with the Worcester's both in a pretty good cellar. They had a few cases to clear but none were serious. They were to advance next morning and their next aid post would be at Taisnieres. While I was there the Boche started a spell of shelling and strafed the place pretty briskly for a quarter of an hour or so. When it was quiet I went back to Brangies and looked in at Brigade HQ. House (the Brigade Major) was there.

The news was rather exciting. [The Germans, under] a white flag, were to come through the French lines tonight to ask for peace terms. It certainly sounds cheerful. They would hardly go to all that trouble about asking for terms unless they had at least some intention of taking them. The French have taken Mezieres and have thus cut the main Hun lateral railway on this front. The battalions are to advance tomorrow at 6am without any barrage. Practically all our casualties yesterday were from our own barrage. The orders for tomorrow are to push on 'regardless of fatigue and of exposed flanks'. The infantry are certainly well tired out as it is after 4 or 5 days continuous fighting and marching.

Got back to the car post and found Smalley packing up to move off. We brought the whole party with cars and wagons down to St Waast to a house where the 58th Field Ambulance were running the ADS. Arrived there about 3am. The Huns only left this place about 7am yesterday.

8th November. I lay on the floor by the fire and dozed for about an hour. Then we had some tea and bread and jam. Smalley and I started off about 6am in a couple of Ford cars up to Houdain. The place was quite quiet; civilians were standing about in the street. Simbo and Meyer were still there. Smalley stopped up at Houdain and I went back to St Waast. I saw one or two shells burst in the fields on the way back.

During the morning the ADMS came round. The Hun peace delegates had been received through the French lines. The general idea at DHQ seemed to be that the war would be over in a couple of days. The General was keeping the troops in the line although they were very tired as he wanted the Division to be 'in at the death'. The 20th Division were behind us waiting to relieve us and anxious to get into action before the war stopped. All this peace talk seems extraordinary. It is too good to be true.

Came up to Houdain again about 11am on foot with Sergeant Evans and some more bearer squads. The Germans were shooting at the Brangies crossroads as we came up from right away on the left. Three of them skimmed over our heads and burst 50 or 60 yards over in the fields. All our transport is now coming past here and the Germans are still doing some nasty shelling along the roads. He has just got a direct hit on a lorry – the A mess lorry again. The two men on the front were killed and several people wounded. The lorry is blazing and blocking the road.

Great excitement! The 57th Brigade have advanced already to the middle of the Bois de la Laniere – five and half miles from where they started this morning and more than half way to the Mons–Maubeuge line. The Division on our right are pushing on towards Maubeuge but the Division on our left are hanging right back and so our left flank is exposed to attack. As far as I can make out the Germans are only about one and a half miles from here due north.

The 58th Brigade are forming a defensive flank, so I suppose it's alright.

The weather is still overcast and drizzly. About 2pm it cleared a bit and I saw a lot of our planes going over – the first time I have seen a plane for three days. If the weather was only fine we could get planes over to observe and bomb and the Boche would be in an awful state of confusion.

All the bridges in front are down as usual and all the roads mined but we managed to open an ADS at Taisnieres, three miles in front of here by 6pm. I and Sergeant Evans remained where we were at Houdain to act as a sort of rear or flank ADS for local casualties or from the 58th Brigade. We got several casualties in. About 4 or 5 he began shelling again pretty close with some big high velocity shells and we retired to the cellar for ten minutes. These shells were still coming from due north. By dark all was quiet. The glow of big fires burning in the distance. Dossed down with a blanket on some straw and slept until morning.

9th November. Up about 7. Beautiful morning. Clear blue sky and bright sunshine. Crowds of aeroplanes going over. I saw a big crowd of sick and then went in to the Royal Welsh Fusiliers HQ who were close by.

The Guards Division have taken Maubeuge. Further north we are close to Mons. The French are in the outskirts of Mezieres, the Americans have taken Sedan and the Germans are retreating in confusion. The 11th Division on our left have now pushed up level and our Division are about 5000 yards in front of the Bois de la Laniere and up to the Mons–Maubeuge road. Foche had given the Boche 72 hours in which to accept the terms of the armistice.

Very quiet here. DHQ are in the Chateau here and the Divisional band is playing. No sound of guns. Observation balloons are up a good way in front.

58th Field Ambulance took over the place about midday. Took my small party by road to join up with the Field Ambulance who were at a big farm on the main road about half a mile from Malplaquet. Beautiful afternoon.

Arrived about 3.30pm. The general opinion in the mess is that the war is practically over! The Division has now been squeezed out of the line by the 24th and the 11th and are no longer in action. Apparently the Corps cannot feed the troops beyond this present front and for the present they are not to advance any further, ie until railheads can move up closer and the roads are mended. Some cavalry are said to have gone on to hunt the Boche.

The great question is – will the Hun accept the terms which means peace, or will the war continue? I suppose it will be decided by Monday. Nice civilised dinner again, a bath and a bed.

10th November. Up at 8. Started off at 8.30 back to Wargnies le Grand with the staff captain to arrange billets. White frost and a clear sunny morning. Roads very bad. Arrived to find the usual boxup. The whole village occupied by the XVII Corps and DHQ and our Field Ambulance have to come in with nowhere to put them. Managed to find a big warm warehouse in a factory for the men. Got a little house at the edge of the village for officer's mess and quarters.

The Kaiser has abdicated and renounced all claim to the throne. Revolutionary riots in Kiel, Hamburg, Hanover. Bavaria had proclaimed a republican government. The Hun has up until 11am tomorrow to take our terms.

The rest of the unit arrived in the afternoon; Colonel Edmunds, Kidd, Smalley and Armitage. I believe in the last ten days we had only one casualty in the unit – a bearer who was killed on the 4th.

11th November. Immediately after breakfast went round to Corps to hear the news and was shown a copy of the following wire:

Following received from XVII Corps, Nov 11th No GB 575 timed 06.55.
'Hostilities will cease 11.00 hours today November 11th aaa Troops will stand fast on line reached at that hour which will be reported by wire to Corps HQ aaa Defensive precautions will be maintained aaa There will be no intercourse of any description with the enemy aaa.'

The Canadians entered Mons this morning so we have ended the war on the same ground where we began it. It is rather interesting that I am only a few miles from Maubeuge which is where we detrained before marching up to Mons in 1914.

Yesterday was a day of great excitement. Everybody expected that the Huns would accept the armistice terms and the war would be over next day. Today, when we had heard the news, after the first relief of knowing it was all over, a kind of reaction set in and most of us feel rather depressed. We sat in the mess and began discussing how long it would be before we got home again. Colonel Hartigan, the ADMS, came in and congratulated us all in having reached the end of the war. Like us he seemed to think there was something missing. Somebody suggested that perhaps it was a jolly good champagne dinner. Perhaps that is what was wanted.

At present I can not properly realise that the war is over. Only three months ago we were discussing whether we should take back Kemmel Hill before settling down for the winter.

The morning of the 8th when we walked up the road to Houdain was the last time in the war that I was under fire and those shells that skimmed over our heads were the last I saw burst.

I remember someone saying before the war that he imagined that when troops were in action under fire, each man thought to himself that whoever else might be hit, he himself would be alright. Well I don't think this is correct – at any rate not in this war. I think men fully expect to be hit or killed but carry on just the same. Personally, I was always thinking I was going to get hit or killed and was often surprised when I found I wasn't.

The last few months of the war had been particularly bloody and violent. From the start of the Battle of Amiens on 8 August to the ending of hostilities on 11 November, the British Army sustained almost 300,000 battlefield casualties, a higher rate of losses than at any time during the entire duration of the war.

Après la Guerre.

We remained in billets in the area just east of Cambrai until the end of November. One day Colonel Edmunds, Smalley and I motored over through Valenciennes to Jemappes near Mons. Colonel Edmunds was badly wounded at the Battle of Le Cateau in 1914 and taken prisoner and he showed us the identical spot in the yard of a school where he had laid on the ground for a fortnight with other wounded British soldiers and a great many wounded Germans.

The roads were full of civilians going in all directions and pushing along handcarts of furniture and various household goods. They were sorting themselves out and shifting back to their proper homes and villages.

On December 1st we began a three day march right across the old Cambrai–Bapaume–Albert battlefield back to billets in the Beauquesnes area, north of Amiens.

A few days later Kidd and I went on 10 days' leave to Paris. We saw President Wilson and saw the whole of the Place be la Concorde and the whole length of the Champs Elysees right up to the Arc de Triumph lined with hundreds of captured German guns.

When we got back our Brigade had shifted to equally poor billets at Noeux and round about. It was very dull here. We spent Christmas here and also got a couple of days' wild boar hunting.

Early in January I unexpectedly got my demobilization papers and on the afternoon of January 7th I boarded the leave boat for the last time and saw the town and harbour and the dome of the cathedral of Boulogne fade out of sight in a blue haze.

On Friday, 17th January 1919 about twenty of us waited at the bottom of one of the Gressenhall coverts in West Norfolk. Frank Crossley was out. I had last seen him just before he was wounded and captured at Messines in 1914. A moment later a fox whisked out with a fine white tag to his brush. Somebody hollered 'Gone away'. Hounds came rattling out of covert and settled to his line. We shortened up our reins ready for a gallop and I thought to myself – at last I realise that we really have reached the end of the war.

Index